The

The Most Important Rap Song

RAP

From Every Year Since 1979

Year Book

Discussed, Debated, and Deconstructed

BY
SHEA SERRANO

FOREWORD BY
ICE-T

ILLUSTRATED BY
ARTURO TORRES

ABRAMS IMAGE, NEW YORK

1979
—
2014

Foreword

Ice-T

I did this interview with a twenty-year-old girl. She asked me, "Ice, when did you sell a lot of records?" I said, "When people went to the record stores." She said, "What's a record store?" I said, "Well, like, Tower . . . but it's gone . . . Wherehouse . . . ?" I couldn't name any record stores that were still open. She said, "Like Best Buy?" I said, "Really, they'd rather sell you a refrigerator than a record."

♦

A lot of people, when they rap, they say they wanna be the best. They want to be rich. They want to be famous. My only objective was to get out of the street. My objective was to change my occupation, to just become a rapper. I knew my days were numbered to low digits in the streets. I wanted out, but I didn't know how to get out. When I saw rapping—honestly, when I was in the streets hustling, I thought it was silly. I liked it, but nobody was getting money. And me being a hustler, you gotta get some money for me to really respect you. I was on some street shit. Right now, if you go to a real-life drug dealer in the streets, he might be like, "Fuck rap." The brain is in another place. It's kind of corny to you. People who are breaking the law, they look down on everything else. So, I was listening to rap, but it wasn't triggering me to do it yet. Then I heard Schoolly D's "P.S.K."

Melle Mel was the first one I'd heard who put any real thoughts or ideas into a song. He did it on "The Message" in 1982. That was what kind of pulled me in at first. Then I was in this spot hustling, I had a gun on me, and I heard "P.S.K." come over the mic and I was like, "This shit sounds like how I feel." The way Schoolly D was spitting it—he was talking about being in the streets; he wasn't real explicit with like what would come later, but it was the seed. When I heard it I immediately was like, "Whoa, that connects to my life."

So now I saw this lane where I could have the things, the money and the cars—see, because hustlers and players, they want flashy shit. That's all a hustler'll think about. He wants girls, he wants jewelry, he wants cars. I did, too. And I was getting it on the street. But when I saw a lane where I could have all that and not go to jail, it was like, "Aw, yeah, that's what I wanna do." But I knew I had to get better at rapping. Even by then, by the mid-'80s, there was a hierarchy of talent. But again, people wanted to be the best. I didn't. I just wanted to be named among the rappers because that meant I was a rapper and not a street hustler anymore. That was my goal. I just wanted to be named. If someone said, "Kool Moe Dee," then I wanted someone else to say, "Ice-T." That's all I wanted. I wanted to be included. I couldn't give a fuck about being the best. If someone said, "EPMD," I just wanted someone else to go, "What about Ice-T?" That was all that mattered.

The most important moment of my rap career is different from my biggest moment personally, even though one kind of led to the other. My most important moment was when the "Colors" video hit. *Colors* was a movie starring Sean Penn and Robert Duvall. They were cops in it and it was set in L.A. when L.A. really had a bad gang problem. I'd been rapping for a while, I had an album out. But I hadn't popped yet. When *Colors* came, Dennis Hopper—he directed it—he asked me to do the song for it. I knew there was going to be a lot of controversy around it so I did it. When I did the song and the video, it took off, that's when I got that national attention. "Colors" woke the country up to me. That was 1988. It wasn't long after that that I spoke for the Congressional Black Caucus in Washington, D.C., and then later was on Oprah. "Colors" was why. And right after "Colors" was The Dope Jam Tour, my *biggest* moment.

The Dope Jam Tour was *just* . . . I was out there with Doug E. Fresh and Kool Moe Dee and Eric B. and Rakim and Biz Markie and Boogie Down Productions; all these greats. It meant so much because that was the first time I got to get across the country and really see with my own eyes that I had fans. It's one thing to think you have fans or hear you have fans. It's another thing to actually see them. That tour was the first time I saw that they knew me. That's such a big thing. You could have fans in London but until you go there you don't really know it.

My first show on the tour was San Antonio, Texas. I was the opening act and they went fucking bananas. I was just blown away that they were excited to see me. I was coming from playing small clubs, playing garage parties and small bullshit shows, and then to be able to play an arena and have the whole crowd go off, that's when it really sinks into you like, "This shit is real. I got real fans out here." I knew after that I was always going to be mentioned with the rappers. I knew I was becoming important.

♦

A song that's "important" is a song that changes the route of the music or introduces a new element to the music. Like "Fight the Power," that was Public Enemy in 1989. The video showed people marching in the street. That was the first time, to me, a rap group looked like a political movement. That was a huge change. That turned Chuck D into a spokesman instead of just a rapper. If somebody does that, it changes the course of music. When I came out and I was cursing and talking about drugs and the cops, no one had done that. It changed the course again. Important songs birth new things: new rappers, new groups, eventually new movements altogether. If a song comes out and it's a new style and it flops, nobody'll take that route. When it comes out and it hits, it becomes a subgenre. It's not restricted to violence, either. The Native Tongues movement—De La Soul, A Tribe Called Quest, people like Queen Latifah, all that—that was a lane. That was important. It was on the other side of what we were doing. It was necessary. Picture it like branches on a tree. Rap started out in this straight line going up like a tree and then spread out into all these different things. The songs that caused those changes, they're important.

If I'm picking important songs, songs that are going to last forever, that changed rap, I'll say "It's Like That"/"Sucker M.C.'s" by Run-DMC in 1983. I'll say "Rapper's Delight," of course. There was rap before then that wasn't recorded—Spoonie Gee, Cold Crush Brothers, the Treacherous Three. But "Rapper's Delight" was the first commercially successful record. That was 1979. I'll say "Eric B. Is President" by Eric B. and Rakim because when I was making my first album I was in New York and that record

was *everyfuckingwhere*. Rakim—to me, he invented the flow. Kool Moe Dee and T La Rock had introduced rhyme patterns that were a little more difficult than the Sugarhill Gang or Busy Bee Starski. But Rakim took this technicality and made it cool. Schoolly D's "P.S.K." in 1985 was what inspired me to make "6 in the Mornin'," and that was a big song that caused a lot of changes. Toddy Tee was an inspiration of mine for that song, too. I can't leave him out. And "Fight the Power," that one always should be included.

Rap will always evolve. This stage we're in now, there's all this singing. It'll turn into something new and then that'll turn into something new, too. Rap's gonna be around forever. I don't know where it's headed, though. They probably didn't know in 1979 what we were gonna be doing in 1986.

Introduction

It would seem to me that the best way to begin this book would be to explain exactly what is going to happen in it, so that's what I'll do: The whole entire point of this book is to identify which rap song was the most important rap song each year from 1979 to 2014, so that's what's going to happen.

Now, to be clear, there are two very critical points in that sentence that need to be fleshed out. The first is the thing about it being one song per year and the second is about picking the "most important" song.

One song per year. Even though it seems like a small distinction, picking one song per year from 1979–2014 as the most important is a lot different than, say, just picking the thirty-six most important rap songs of all time. Here's an easy example: There's no way ever that "Grindin'" by the Clipse could ever be considered more important to rap than Nas's "N.Y. State of Mind." It just couldn't. That's a thing that's easy to understand and an easy concession to make. So if the book was just about the thirty-six most important songs in rap of ever, then "N.Y. State of Mind" would get in and "Grindin'" wouldn't. However, in this particular setting of this particular book, "Grindin'" doesn't have to compete with "N.Y. State of Mind" because "Grindin'" was released in 2002 and "N.Y. State of Mind" was released in 1994. So "Grindin'" slides in while "N.Y. State of Mind" doesn't because 1994's spot was gobbled up by Biggie's "Juicy." So it's new conversations, really. All of a sudden you have these decisions you have to make where you have these very transcendent years where rap was just obscenely good and doing obviously important work and it's a true firefight picking one above all the rest, but that's what has to happen. Grandmaster Flash and the Furious Five's "The Message" and Afrika Bambaataa's "Planet Rock" are both divinely significant, but you can only pick one because they both arrived in 1982. N.W.A's "Straight Outta Compton" and Public Enemy's "Rebel Without a Pause" and you can only pick one. Wu-Tang Clan's "C.R.E.A.M." and Snoop's "Who Am I (What's My Name)?" and you can only pick one. On and on and on.

The "most important" song. "Most important" does not always mean "best" and "best" does not always mean "most important." There are for sure instances where those two things overlap—"Mind Playing Tricks on Me" by the Geto Boys was the most important song *and* the best song of 1991; Dr. Dre's "Nuthin' but a 'G' Thang" was the most important song *and* the best song of 1992—but there are also instances where this doesn't occur. Kanye West's "Jesus Walks" was the best song of 2004 but it wasn't the most important, because it didn't (really) accomplish anything outside of its own success. Puffy's "Can't

Hold Me Down" wasn't better than Biggie's "Hypnotize" in 1997, but it was more important. The difference might seem semantic, and maybe it is, but an easy way to think of it is: What sort of impact did the song have on rap, or on the surroundings of rap? That's usually how you determine the difference between what's important and what's just fun to move your body and arms and legs to.

The question that follows, then, is natural: What was the criterion? How did a song make itself eligible to be chosen?

For a song to be eligible to be picked for a year, either its release date as a single was used, or, in the event that it differed, the song could also be picked for the year the album it was on was released. For example, Tupac's "California Love" was officially released as a single on December 28, 1995. So it was eligible for 1995. However, it was on his *All Eyez on Me* album, and that album was released on February 13, 1996, so "California Love" was also eligible for 1996 (which, incidentally, was the year it ended up being chosen for). Beyond that, no other considerations were taken into account. It didn't matter if it was a stand-alone song that never made it onto an actual album, and it didn't matter if it was the B side of a record, like what was going on with early rap.

There are other things in the book. There is a lot of art because I like art. There are charts and graphs and other things like that, because I like those too. There are footnotes and sometimes those footnotes have important ancillary information and sometimes they talk about Arsenio Hall. You'll see a fair number of these things called "Style Maps" or "Style Grids," which are explained in the next section. Each chapter also has an argument in it where a very good writer or editor who is not me lobbies against the song I chose as the most important for a year and offers up an alternative choice. The writers and editors are from places like *Rolling Stone* and the *New York Times* and MTV and *Vice* and *Pitchfork* and Grantland, and so that's just a different way of saying that they're all smart.

So that's the book. I am certain there will be choices in here that you agree with and choices in here that you do not agree with. That's generally how these types of things go.

Style Maps, Explained

There are seventeen different "Style Maps" that work as accompanying art for chapters in this book. A Style Map is a visualization of the way a person is rapping at a particular time during a particular song. That might seem like a complicated thing, or maybe even an annoying thing, and I suppose maybe it *is* an annoying thing, but it's definitely *not* a complicated thing.[1] The main function of a Style Map is always to look cool, but sometimes their other main function is to act as a reinforcement of the main point of a chapter.

Here's how they work: OK, let's say with the 1979 chapter, that chapter's about the Sugarhill Gang's "Rapper's Delight." There's a Style Map there. Over the course of that song, the guys are on there rapping rap in a number of different styles and tones because they're expressing a number of different ideas and thoughts. Key moments get taken from the song, placed on a timeline map, and then given a symbol to represent the style.

Regarding the symbols: There are more than twenty-five different ones in total (each Style Map has no more than seven, though). Most of the styles are paired with symbols that make sense; The symbol for "Introspective" is a brain, the symbol for being "Observational" is an eyeball, the symbol for being "Declarative" is a fist, etc. Some of them are paired with a style that only kind of makes sense but maybe not really: The symbol for "Lifestyle" is a car, the symbol for "Name Brand" is a tennis shoe, the symbol for "Considerate" is a teddy bear, etc. And a few are paired with a style that would seem to not be connected at all, and in those instances mostly it's just because I thought they'd look fun: The symbol for "Descriptive" is a turtle, the symbol for "Comparative" is two hands making the "whatever" W, the symbol for "Thrilling" is a lightning bolt shooting out of a cloud, etc.

Regarding the styles: It's easiest to explain those with an example, so let's do that, and let's stick with "Rapper's Delight" since that's where we started. At the 9:14 mark[2] of that song,

Wonder Mike raps, "Like Dracula without his fangs . . . " It's part of this whole bit he's doing where he's laying simile on top of simile ("Like a rainy day that is not wet / Like a gambling fiend that does not bet"). Right there, he's being Comparative. It's important to note that part because, as you'll read, "Rapper's Delight" was the first commercially successfully rap song, which means that it was the first rap song a lot of people heard, which means that it was an instantly influential thing. Comparative rapping has always been an especially popular form of rapping. It's a thing that still happens very often today, and it will be a thing that happens until forever. So that line gets pulled out, highlighted, and then assigned the aforementioned symbol that represents that style. There's another part in the song where Big Bank Hank raps, "Now there's a time to laugh and a time to cry," and that's him being (or at least *trying* to be) Insightful, and so that part gets pulled out and highlighted with a different symbol (an owl). Half a minute later, Hank raps, "I didn't even bite a goddamn word," and that's him being Confrontational,[3] so it gets pulled out and highlighted with another symbol (a bulletproof vest, in this case). They all follow that same template. In the instances where a chapter was slightly longer than another one and there wasn't enough space to accommodate an entire Style Map, you'll find a *"Style Grid,"* which is a modified version that acts in the exact same way. Really, it's all very intuitive. I suspect you'd have been able to figure it out very easily without this explanation.

You'll notice that several of the Style Maps have symbols that repeat over and over again. That's because those are songs that have a very clear and obvious intention. The 1983 chapter is all about Run-DMC's "Sucker M.C.'s," the first rap song that actively aimed to be provocative, so the Style Map represents that. There are multiple timestamps for Inflammatory rapping and for Boastful rapping, as well as spots for Descriptive ("I'm light-skinned") and Comparative ("Fly like a dove") and Lifestyle ("Champagne, caviar, and bubble bath") and more. The

DECLARATIVE　　DEADLY　　THRILLING　　AGGRESSIVE　　CONSIDERATE　　BOASTFUL　　POWERFUL

1985 chapter is about Doug E. Fresh and Slick Rick's "La Di Da Di," a song that set the template for raps that were either based around telling a story or advocating primping or both, so that Style Map represents that (multiple timestamps for Name Brand rapping and for Self-Reflective rapping). The 1995 chapter is about Tupac's "Dear Mama," and so that Style Map looks how you'd expect it to look (multiple timestamps for Powerful rapping and for Insightful rapping and for Considerate rapping and for Introspective rapping). I suspect you'd have been able to put this together, too.

A neat thing that happened while I was working on these was it became easier to watch the trends and varieties in rap unfurl themselves. There would be little to no instances of a certain style of rapping before a date, then someone would do it, and then after that it'd begin to vibrate all through the rest of rap. It was easy to see in early rap—Ice-T on "6 in the Mornin'," Rakim on "Paid in Full," moments like that—and that made sense because there was still so much unexplored space for rap to balloon outward into. But it also happened later, too (Tupac on "California Love," 50 Cent on "In Da Club"), and even later after that (Kendrick Lamar on Big Sean's "Control," Young Thug on "Lifestyle"). I didn't create any of the Style Maps until I'd already written all of the book, so I had a very clear image in my head of what the trajectory of rap looked like in history as it moved from 1979 to now, so I will admit that maybe there was some sort of confirmation bias involved. But maybe not. Hopefully not.

1. This sentence, incidentally, is both annoying and complicated.
2. "Rapper's Delight" is a very long song.
3. It's also him being a very big liar. Hank stole a considerable amount of his part in "Rapper's Delight" from Grandmaster Caz.

1979

RAPPER'S DELIGHT

THE

SUGARHILL GANG

WHAT THIS SONG IS ABOUT

So much stuff. It's goddamn fifteen minutes long.

• •

WHY IT'S IMPORTANT

While it's not the first rap song ever, it's the first commercially successful rap song, and it's nearly universally recognized as the moment modern hip-hop became an official genre.

Let me start this book with a fact, because while much of the information in it from here forward will be up for debate, this will not: Establishing a "first-ever rap song" is always only ever telling a half-truth.

There's no definitive answer. There's no inarguable pick. It's very likely it was "King Tim III," a song recorded and released by a funk and disco band called the Fatback Band in 1979. This song contains the traditional cadence and feel of rap, though that's questionable, because it assumes you're (1) only considering officially recorded and released music, and (2) talking about the version of rap that we all know and understand and recognize. If you wanted to be really obtuse you could argue that rap traces back beyond that, back before the house and block parties of the Bronx in the early '70s, back before Gil Scott-Heron poetry, back even before the Delta blues artists of the '20s and before the vaudeville shows, back all the way to the nineteenth-century griots in West Africa. That seems unnecessarily complicated and planted in the most unlikable kind of semantics, but some people are unnecessarily complicated and enjoy the most unlikable kind of semantics, so that's a conversation that occasionally happens.

So, in the interest of brevity and unilaterality, we will assume that the general account of the creation of rap given by DJ Kool Herc, regularly considered the father of hip-hop, and Afrika Bambaataa, its first revolutionary, is true. If you are not interested in the history, I recommend skipping through this section, as it is rather perfunctory and contains exactly zero jokes that reference genitals or old action movies, which I know some of you are here for.

In the '70s, the predominant (or at least the most successful) black music was disco. But disco, very light and airy and toothless, was not an appropriate representation of the lifestyle blacks were experiencing at the time. It was too soft.[1] Black living was hard. In that gap between the two, in that empty space, that's where the beginning of rap formed, and it was DJ Kool Herc who filled it in.

Herc, a Jamaican immigrant, was a DJ, and he played parties and gatherings mostly in the South Bronx. Herc is important because he was the first to take the break of a song—the moment when the singer stopped singing and just the instruments would be playing, typically the drums—and blend it together with a similar break in another song. The "B" in the phrase "B-boy" or "B-girl" stood for "Break," and it was used because during the break of a record was usually when the B-boys and B-girls would dance. Originally, it only lasted for a moment, but when Herc figured out how to transition from one break to the next by using two turntables, the break got extended, and he stretched it out so long that it wasn't a break anymore; it was this continuous rhythm, this new, living thing.

Up through 1975, the style grew and grew and grew, which led to advancements. DJs, in an attempt to one-up other DJs, began incorporating rarer and rarer break beats into their mixes, then figured out scratching,[2] then back spinning,[3] then emceeing, where a person would talk to the crowd while the DJ played. The talking led to boasting, then the boasting led to rhyming. In the late '70s, it picked up the name hip-hop,[4] and emceeing became a more and more integral part.[5]

Still, through 1978, it only ever existed as a live medium. There were roughshod cassette tape recordings of parties that got passed around, but nobody was properly recording anything, and certainly nobody was properly releasing anything.

Then, in 1979, as pieces of rap began to peek out of disco musicians' styles, the Sugarhill Gang—Wonder Mike, Big Bank Hank, and Master Gee—recorded and released "Rapper's Delight." It feels like that sentence needs to be written in sixty-point font, or maybe someone needs to run up and punch you in the chest as hard as they can as soon as you read it, or maybe someone can drop a nuclear bomb on your forehead, because "Rapper's Delight" was that big of a moment.

♦

"I've got these kids who are going to talk real fast over it; that's the best way I can describe it." —Sylvia Robinson, who assembled the Sugarhill Gang, explaining what she was planning on doing with an instrumental she was putting together

That "Rapper's Delight" would be the first rap that most of America would hear is so great and wonderful because it's so appropriate and almost unbelievably prophetic. Through the first three verses (THERE ARE TEN VERSES) the group creates what would eventually become nearly the entire rap narrative, both directly and indirectly. A look:

First Verse: It's delivered by Wonder Mike, and he raps, "Now, what you hear is not a test, I'm rappin' to the beat," and that's super-smart, because rap had never really been played on the radio before this song, so it's kind of a "Hey, here's this new thing, and here's what I'm doing" announcement. The second line is equally foretelling: "And me, the groove, and my friends are gonna try to move your feet." To be thorough, moving people's feet, that wasn't the whole entire point of rap when it started, but it was a large share of it, and still is today. So over those first two lines, Wonder Mike's already expressed the kind of defiance that rap has always possessed and also established the argument for its existence, at least as far as he was concerned.

1. "It was something that seemed very far away from what a ghetto kid on the street could realistically hope to attain or be a part of. That whole idea of the flashy, gaudy, the costume, all that stuff was something hip-hop reacted against." —Fab Five Freddy
2. Mixing a record as it played.
3. Playing the same record on both turntables so you could jump back and forth and repeat moments in the song.
4. There are contrasting stories about how it picked up the name, but the general premise for all of them is that phrases like "hippity-hop" were often used to describe the music, and eventually that just got shortened to "hip-hop," and thank goodness for that, because can you even imagine someone saying, "And here's the new hippity-hop song from DMX . . ."?
5. Hip-hop as a culture is most often identified as having four parts: DJing, break dancing, graffiti art, and rapping.
6. A third criticism came from Nile Rodgers and Bernard Edwards, from the group Chic, which made the song "Good Times" that "Rapper's Delight" borrowed heavily from. "Rapper's Delight" was also the first rap song to illegally use a sample.
7. The best is that he brags about having "a color TV so I can see the Knicks play basketball."
8. "Hear me talking 'bout checkbooks, credit cards, more money than a sucker could ever spend / But I wouldn't give a sucker or a bum from the Rucker not a dime 'til I made it again."
9. "You see, if your girl starts actin' up, then you take her friend."

After that, he introduces himself ("See, I am Wonder Mike and I'd like to say hello . . ."), then indirectly asserts that rap is for everyone ("To the black, to the white, the red and the brown, the purple and yellow"). Rap lingo and abstractions follow ("But first, I gotta bang bang the boogie to the boogie"), and lastly, an introduction of the next person ("And next on the mic is my man Hank"). And that's all stuff—saying who you are, attaching yourself to listeners by encouraging them to listen to you, creating vernacular, cosigning your friends—that is important and necessary in rap. The second verse does the same thing, except this time it begins to mold an early ideology.

Second Verse: There are a handful of criticisms of "Rapper's Delight," one of them being that Big Bank Hank wholesale lifted lyrics from a rapper named Grandmaster Caz. The story Caz tells is that Hank asked him to help him write his verse, and Caz offered him a notebook full of stuff he'd written out already, and Hank grabbed the pieces he wanted and used them verbatim. The very first line of Hank's verse confirmed Caz's accusations, because Hank raps, "I'm the C-A-S-A-N, the O-V-A, and the rest is F-L-Y," and earlier in his career Caz had briefly gone by the name Casanova Fly, and that seems like a very large coincidence. Rhyme thievery in rap is a part of rap's history, too.

Another criticism here is that the Sugarhill Gang wasn't authentic, and really, it's not an untrue thing. The group, three guys from New Jersey, was piecemealed together by a woman named Sylvia Robinson, who was running Sugar Hill Records, a then-flailing record label. She had been exposed to rap almost by accident and decided she wanted to record a rap record. She found the guys she wanted, had them record it, and there you go. When the song popped, the guys who had been nurturing rap up from a pup were very confounded and even more offended. When Melle Mel, one of the first rappers and song-writers, was asked the temperature of the grassroots musicians when it was three outsiders who'd become the genre's first breakout stars, he said, "Every traditional rapper was fucking mortified. What the fuck are they doing with our art form? It's like they ax-murdered the shit. We didn't think that was credible." Credibility has always been a part of rap, too.[6]

Beyond the criticisms: Hank then goes through a series of brags,[7] establishes rap's relationship with money[8] and women,[9] then alley-oops it up to Master Gee, who delivers the third verse, which is basic enough, save for his curious implication that height is indicative of rapping ability ("Now, I'm not as tall as the rest of the gang / But I rap to the beat just the same").

RAPPER'S *Delight*

"You see I got more clothes than Muhammad Ali" (1:31)

"Now, what you hear is not a test, I'm rapping to the beat" (0:43)

"The beat don't stop until the break of dawn" (2:26)

"The women fight for my delight" (5:32)

"But we like hot butter on a breakfast toast" (4:26)

"But I can bust you out with my super sperm" (6:45)

"Rest a little while so you don't get weak" (5:19)

"Like Dracula without his fangs . . ." (9:14)

"If your girl starts actin' up, then you take her friend" (7:17)

"I didn't even bite and not a goddamn word" (11:42)

"Now there's a time to laugh, and a time to cry" (11:10)

"Like Farrah Fawcett without her face . . ." (12:43)

OBSERVATIONAL BOASTFUL THRILLING INSIGHTFUL **CONSIDERATE** CONFRONTATIONAL COMPARATIVE

After that is where it kind of starts to wander into the ridiculous, which somehow makes it even more iconic.

Fourth Through Tenth Verses: Wonder Mike expresses love of country, then transitions into an explanation of the way the group prefers their breakfast toast (with hot butter, FYI). Later he says he knows a man named Hank who "has more rhymes than a serious bank," and I guess really I just want to know what bank that is because that's a bank I need to be involved with.

Big Bank Hank follows behind Mike, calling himself "Imp the Dimp," and at first I was like, "What the fuck is an Imp the Dimp?" but then he continues his story and says he was walking home one day and a reporter asked him some questions and he responded by rapping some rhymes that were so devastating she fell in love with him and then I was like, "Oh, *that's* an Imp the Dimp." More: Turns out, the reporter was Lois Lane, and so she has to call Superman to break up with him. Hank says not very nice things about Superman's clothes and also about Superman's penis, and I think still to this day it's the only reference to a superhero's genitals in all of rap.

Mike spends a sizable portion of the eighth verse telling a story about going to a friend's house for dinner and being served food that possessed a bizarre ability to decompose at an accelerated pace. In the ninth verse, Big Bank Hank talks all about how nobody should ever steal his rhymes, and I figure Grandmaster Caz's eyes aren't even halfway through with the eye roll he started when he heard that. In verse ten, Master Gee talks about: Johnny Carson; Big Bank Hank's semen; Perry Mason; Farrah Fawcett, if she didn't have a face; rapping for

freaks when he was only four years old; having to pick up sticks for money when he was six (the freaks were not altogether impressed with his rapping, I suppose); how he died at seven and performed in heaven; and he reinforces the Sugarhill Gang's advocacy for dairy products.

◆

"Rapper's Delight" has big accolades: *Rolling Stone* placed it at number 251 on their list of the 500 Greatest Songs of All Time and number two on their list of the 50 Greatest Hip-Hop Songs of All Time. It was number two on VH1's list of the 100 Greatest Hip-Hop Songs,[10] and is usually somewhere close to that same position on any other list of the greatest rap songs. The Library of Congress preserved it in the National Recording Registry.

It was the first true rap song, which is to say it was recorded by a group that billed itself as a rap group and sold as a song that presented itself as a rap song rather than a song that had some elements of rap in it. It coined the term "rapper." It turned Sugar Hill Records into the premier record label for rappers. It sold more than two million copies.

In short: It changed everything forever.

---

10. *Rolling Stone* had Grandmaster Flash and the Furious Five's "The Message" at number one (see page 28). VH1 had Public Enemy's "Fight the Power" in their number-one spot (see page 70).

REBUTTAL: "RHYMIN' AND RAPPIN'" PAULETTE AND TANYA WINLEY

"Rapper's Delight" is undoubtedly a cute, fun, cheeky piece of early hip-hop history, but the most important song of 1979 was actually made by two sisters, Tanya "Sweet Tee" and Paulette Winley, whose single "Rhymin' and Rappin'" proved both prescient and influential. Backed by the Harlem Underground Band—house band for their dad Paul Winley's Winley Records—the teens recite braggadocio rhymes over a propulsive, soulful groove that is far less disco fever than uptown park jam. Absent the polished, commercial sheen of other popular early rap recordings, "Rhymin' and Rappin'" says more about hip-hop's break beat–driven origins than it does the pop charts. The Winley sisters were undoubtedly the First Ladies of hip-hop.

—PAUL CANTOR

1980

The
Breaks

—

Kurtis
Blow

WHAT THIS SONG IS ABOUT

Different types of breaks, and also even different types of brakes.

....

WHY IT'S IMPORTANT

"The Breaks" did several big things, and those will all be discussed on the following pages, but the biggest thing was that it helped take rap from the free-wheel rambling that it was and gave it structure by instituting a chorus.

In 1997, an R&B group from the midwestern United States got famous for singing a song about getting erections while slow dancing with girls, and that would maybe seem like a weird way to start an essay about Kurtis Blow, and it probably is, but it's not the wrong way, at least not in this particular setting.

The group was a mostly unlikable trio called Next, and the song was a mostly unlikable track called "Too Close." One way to talk about "Too Close" is to go over all of the lyrics, but an easier way to talk about it is to just say that its first line is "I wonder if she could tell I'm hard right now. Hmmm," and things don't get any better from there. Now, I will concede that describing the group and the song as "mostly unlikable" is a personal preference. By quantitative measurements, it was actually quite liked; it was number one on *Billboard*'s Hot 100 chart in 1998 for four weeks straight and helped the album it was on eventually go double platinum. Still, I have to assume Minnesotans find it disappointing that the second most popular thing tied to their state is a song about predatory boners.[1]

At any rate, I mention Next because they are connected to Kurtis Blow because "Too Close" heavily samples 1979's "Christmas Rappin'," Blow's first single and the moment when it became obvious he was going to change rap irreversibly.

And on his next single, "The Breaks," that's exactly what he did.

◆

A short, personal aside: The first time I heard of Kurtis Blow was when I watched *CB4*, a 1993 movie where Chris Rock, the second main bad guy from *New Jack City*, and a guy I'd never heard of or seen before pretended to be hardcore rappers. It was really a parody, but really it was a satire.[2] At the end of the movie, Rock's character, MC Gusto, is being interviewed alongside his groupmates right before going onstage for a reunion show. The interviewer asks what they have planned for the future. Gusto says he's going to get a search squad together and go down to South America and find Kurtis Blow. It was a reference to how Blow, having been part of a faction that dominated early rap, was basically invisible in the years that followed. I wasn't concerned with any of that, though. I was concerned with the scene that occurred right before it.

In that scene, Chris Rock dresses up in lingerie to help catch a criminal. I didn't see *CB4* until 1996, and that was a year after Rock had appeared in an episode of *The Fresh Prince of Bel-Air*, where he also dressed up like a woman. Rock is a moderately handsome man, but he's an uncomfortably unattractive woman.

◆

It's easy to calibrate Kurtis Blow's importance because all of the important things Kurtis Blow did are easy to identify.

He was the first rapper to sign a deal with a major record label (Mercury Records). Sugar Hill Records had become the preeminent indie rap label behind "Rapper's Delight" and then also the signings of Grandmaster Flash and the Furious Five, Funky 4 + 1, Treacherous Three, and others, but even still they didn't carry the sway that Mercury did. He was the first rapper to release an actual rap album (*Kurtis Blow*, 1980). He was the first prominent solo rapper.[3] He was the first rapper managed by Russell Simmons. He was the first rapper to say the phrase "alley-oop" in a song[4] and also the first to have a rap video where a basketball game turned into a karate fight,[5] and also the

first to indirectly advocate growing a mustache.[6] Kurtis Blow did that. Kurtis Blow did all of those things. And still, "The Breaks," his magnum opus, was more meaningful to rap than he was, if that even makes sense.

"The Breaks" did many things as a song, and some of those are tiny factoids that are more fun to remember than they are actually significant, but three are truly vital.

SOME TINY FACTOIDS

It was the first rap single to win the *Village Voice*'s Pazz & Jop music critics poll; writer/author/producer/filmmaker Nelson George is one of the voices chanting in the background of the song; it didn't sample any funk songs like most of the other rap songs had before it.

THE THREE TRULY VITAL THINGS

First, it was the first rap single to go gold and only the second 12-inch in all of music up to that point to have done that.[7] This was very much when there were still doubts about whether or not rap was going to be able to stand as a genre of its own long-term or if it was going to fade off into nothingness like disco was beginning to do. In 1981, *20/20* ran a mini-documentary on rap. Hugh Downs opened it by describing what rap was, saying it was "A music that is all beat—*strong* beat—and talk," and that it was becoming "a new phenomenon." It's weird to watch now because rap is the most popular form of music in the world, and Downs talks about it with the same disengaged and curiously unfamiliar tone I imagine he'd have used if he was telling people the army had found aliens in the desert. But it was representative of the way rap was seen then, which is to say new and with an uncertainty. "The Breaks" followed behind the Sugarhill Gang's "Rapper's Delight" and Blow's own "Christmas Rappin'," which sold more than four hundred thousand copies and showed that rap could be profitable.

---

1. The first thing is Kevin Garnett, the Hall of Fame–worthy power forward on the Timberwolves. I would very much like to know Garnett's opinion of "Too Close," though. I assume he'd probably only be concerned with whether or not one's defensive coverage of the pick and roll would be hampered or helped by being aroused.

2. The three guys are an N.W.A rip-off.

3. Russell Simmons tells a story in his 2001 book, *Life and Def: Sex, Drugs, Money, and God*, about how Kurtis Blow performed as part of three separate shows of fifteen thousand–plus people in three separate states on the same day (with Graham Central Station and the Bar-Kays in Alabama; then in North Carolina with the Commodores, Patti LaBelle, and Stephanie Mills; then in Georgia with Con Funk Shun and Cameo).

4. "Basketball."

5. Also "Basketball." I really love the song "Basketball."

6. He literally still has a mustache to this day. I wouldn't be surprised to learn he was born with one, and even less surprised if archaeologists excavated his corpse in 2252 and the only things there were bones and a mustache.

7. The first was "No More Tears (Enough Is Enough)" by Donna Summer and Barbra Streisand. They were not rappers.

Second, it was the first rap song to incorporate a stayed theme and wordplay. In "The Breaks," the term "breaks" is said eighty-four times and is used to reference good things that can happen to you, bad things that can happen to you, things that actually break, things that only break metaphorically, and actual brakes on vehicles.[8] Most of the good things mentioned are spatial and broad-spectrum (breaks to win, breaks to make you a superstar, breaks that are hot, breaks that are cold, etc.), but the bad things are hyper-specific. For example:

- Your significant other leaves you for another person and then they move to Japan. (I'm not sure how their moving to Japan makes it worse, but I guess it does.)
- You get audited by the IRS because you tried to claim your cat as a dependent. (This one would seem to be your own fault, really.)
- You get a big phone bill because you called Brazil eighteen times. (Again: your fault.) (Also, eighteen calls feels like a suspiciously large amount. Was this you trying to track down another ex-girlfriend? And if so, really, you have to start looking at yourself if every time someone leaves you they move to another continent.)
- You borrowed money from the mob because you lost your job.
- You met a guy you thought was perfect. Turned out, he was poor and also married.

The point is this: Kurtis Blow tied all of these different things and ideas together into a cogent and coherent idea on "The Breaks." Rap large-scale adopted the idea almost immediately after he did it.

Third, "The Breaks" was the first rap song that had a hook, which is to say it was broken up into easily digestible sections rather than the long-form and borderless structure rap had up until then. It's hard to state how crucial a move this was. Here's what Kool Moe Dee said about Kurtis Blow in his 2003 book, *There's a God on the Mic: The True 50 Greatest MCs*:

> If you listen to all of the records that came before Kurtis Blow's "The Breaks," you would notice that there was a very important element missing. The hook! Kurtis Blow is the inventor of the hook for rap songs. All of the significant records at the time had emcees rhyming continuously with a music break to break the monotony. So in a sense, Kurtis Blow showed us how to write songs, because if there's no hook, there's no song.

"The Breaks" took rap music and turned it into rap songs, which is a wholly different, wholly more influential thing.

---

8. A bus, a car, a plane, a train.

REBUTTAL: "ZULU NATION THROWDOWN" AFRIKA BAMBAATAA

First thing to understand is that "Zulu Nation Throwdown" wasn't just one record—there was a Volume #1 and a Volume #2, credited on their orange and black labels to "Afrika Bambaataa Zulu Nation Cosmic Force," and "Bambaataa Zulu Nation Soul Sonic Force," respectively.

That first volume—maybe partly because of the line that says, "Punk rock to the left, and Patty Duke to the right"—is what first got Bambaataa into downtown Manhattan new wave clubs. It's an exciting, endlessly charming performance in rap's super-old-school, amateurs-from-the-street roll-call mode, all nonstop energy and bubbling spirit from Cosmic Force (Lisa Lee, Chubby Chubb, Ice-Ice, Little Ikey C). It's important to note on this version Lisa Lee comes off like the group's leader, or at the very least a member on equal footing with all the guys, in a way that'd pretty much disappear from increasingly machismo-minded hip-hop as the '80s progressed.

On Volume #2, Soul Sonic Force—Mr. Biggs, Pow Wow, the G.L.O.B.E.—feel a bit more professional, and at least marginally less propulsive, but still awesome; each gets his own sharp verse, but their throwdown really picks up steam when they all come back chanting together, showing off teamwork "with all due respect to the Zulu Nation." Bambaataa told David Toop on *Rap Attack* the single "never went nowhere." But three and a half decades on, it hasn't stopped going.

—CHUCK EDDY

RAPPERS IN MOVIES

Game, *Waist Deep* + DMX, *Romeo Must Die* + Ice Cube, *Are We There Yet?* +

Young Jeezy, *The Janky Promoters* + Xzibit, *xXx: State of the Union* + RZA, *The*

Man with the Iron Fists + Rah Digga, *Thirteen Ghosts* + Nas, *Belly* + Andre 3000,

Semi-Pro + Snoop Dogg, *Bones* + Fat Joe, *Thicker Than Water* + Ludacris, *Fred*

Claus + Ja Rule, *The Fast and the Furious* + Busta Rhymes, *Halloween:*

Resurrection + Lil Wayne, *Who's Your Caddy?* + Big Boi, *ATL* + Wiz Khalifa, *Mac*

& Devin Go to High School + Dr. Dre, *The Wash* + Eminem, *8 Mile* + 50 Cent,

Before I Self Destruct + Beanie Sigel, *State Property* + Ice-T, *Leprechaun: In the*

Hood + Sticky Fingaz, *Leprechaun: Back 2 tha Hood* + N̶ ̶ ̶ ̶ ̶ ̶ Plane

+ Cam'ron, *Killa Season* + Vanilla Ice, *Cool as Ice* + Ma̶ ̶ ̶ ̶ ̶k Up +

Will Smith, *Men in Black* + T.I., *American Gangster* + LL̶ ̶ ̶ ̶unday

+ Eve, *Barbershop* + Lil' Kim, *You Got Served* + Kid 'N' ̶ ̶

Def, *The Hitchhiker's Guide to the Galaxy* + Queen La̶ ̶

Blow, *Krush Groove* + N.O.R.E., *Paper Soldiers* + Fred̶ ̶

Lover, *Who's the Man?* + Ghostface Killah, *Black and W̶ ̶*

Best Actor:
Tupac, *Juice* (1992)

1981

Jazzy Sensation

—

Afrika Bambaataa
AND THE Jazzy Five

WHAT THIS SONG IS ABOUT

How jazzy the Jazzy Five were.
(The best alive, to be thorough.)

• •

WHY IT'S IMPORTANT

It's the opening call from Afrika
Bambaataa, a DJ and rapper who
revolutionized rap by taking it
away from the funk band arena
that the Sugarhill Gang had made
famous and pushing it toward the
electro version he perfected in
1982 with "Planet Rock." It was
also the first big record to come
from Tommy Boy, which became
a vital record label.

The key figure on "Jazzy Sensation" is Afrika Bambaataa, a former gang member turned glam outfit enthusiast and civic activist. The most visible figures on "Jazzy Sensation," though, are the people who rap on it. There are five of them—Master Ice, Master Dee, Master Bee, A. J. Les, and Mr. Freeze—even though it sounds like there are six[1] (and occasionally seven[2]). And each one spends a fair amount of time saying nice things about himself, because that's how rap was in the early '80s. I suppose a lot of contemporary rap is still like that, it's just like that in a different, less charming way.

There's a part here, for example, where Master Ice raps that he has "sweet brown eyes." That's a very likable thing, and a part of the body not nearly enough rappers rap about when they talk about themselves anymore. Mostly the thing they describe as "sweet" in rap songs since 1990 is their penis. Nas did it on a song called "Live Now": "Admit I did live a little bit, sweet pickle dick." Freddie Gibbs did it on a song called "Thuggin'": "Swiftly 'bout to stick a sweet dick in your sweetheart." The most uncomfortable time was when the Game did it on Too $hort's "I'm Wit It," because he gave an explanation for it. He said, "Bitches call me Sweet Dick Willie 'cause my cum tastes like Now or Laters," and I wonder if anyone mentioned to him afterward that they're actually called Now and Later, and I also wonder if the executives at the Now and Later corporation rap the line around the office as a joke.

To extend the point, there's also a whole history of rappers saying their dicks taste like things. Without being too complicated: Danny Brown said his tastes like "tropical

fruit Skittles." Gucci Mane didn't cite a specific candy when he talked about his, only that it tastes "like candy," so I guess he gets blow jobs from girls who aren't as good at identifying types of candy as the ones Danny Brown keeps company with. Soulja Boy said his tastes "like ribs," which is either very fortunate or very unfortunate, depending on your opinion of barbecue. There's more and more and more and more still, and I want you to know that when I agreed to write this book I did not consider the possibility that I would be required to research rapper dicks for more than two hours.

But, so on "Jazzy Sensation," each rapper says nice things about himself. History has mostly scrubbed away mentions of the members of the Jazzy Five from rap's story. This, it would appear, hints at their having never really done anything beyond being on an Afrika Bambaataa song, and that's true: This is the only song they recorded with Bambaataa, and the only part of any of their work that's remained vital. So a majority of what's known about them is what they say in the song. A list:

MASTER ICE SAYS . . .

- He's nice. (Twice as nice as everyone else, as it were.)
- He's the dedicated Prince of the Disco Slice, and he says it with a very clear hubris in his voice, so I suspect this is a high honor.
- His formal name is Rodeo Rock of the Microphone.
- He's 5'8" and he has the aforementioned sweet brown eyes.

MASTER DEE SAYS . . .

- He believes in astrology, or at least is familiar with it. ("An Aquarius man.")
- That "rappin' on the microphone is my pet peeve," so he either does not enjoy rapping or he does not understand what a pet peeve is. Either way, he kind of sounds like the least jazzy person in the Jazzy Five.
- He's the "ladies' grand rocker," so I guess that means he's good at sex, which probably makes him feel better about not understanding idioms.

MASTER BEE SAYS . . .

- He's the Microphone Chief of the Jazzy Five. I'm not sure if that's a higher rank or lower rank than Prince of the Disco

Slice. It sounds lower, but I can't say for certain.
- He has a key to the door to society. I don't know what this means.

A. J. LES SAYS . . .

- He's very unique.
- He's very good at speaking, so much so, in fact, that he asserts that hearing him doing so is a very real blessing for you.
- He also believes in astrology. ("I'm a Leo man.")
- He's presidential.
- He has many women. (Likely on account of his being so good at speaking and appearing presidential, which I hear women like. Sadly, I do not look presidential. At my best, I maybe look like the comptroller for a small city.)

MR. FREEZE SAYS . . .

- He is real and true, though not in those exact words.
- He is interested in confronting people he says are copying his style. (I think this makes Mr. Freeze the Tough One, inasmuch as someone in a group called the Jazzy Five can be described as tough.)

The origination of the Jazzy Five is similar to the origination of a lot of early rap groups: It started out as one group of people, parts were moved around, then eventually it became another group of people, and that's that.

♦

Of all of the songs in this book, I suspect "Jazzy Sensation" is the least well-known, though that makes sense because it sits in the shadow of "Planet Rock," Afrika Bambaataa's 1982 megahit. There are four points I'd like to go over here, so let's do that.

1. Afrika Bambaataa and the Zulu Nation: Bambaataa is one of three DJs often cited as having helped hip-hop—the other two being DJ Kool Herc, discussed in the 1979 chapter (see page 10), and Grandmaster Flash, discussed in the 1982 chapter (see page 28). And while it's easy to mush them all together, each of the three influenced the music separately. To be short about it: Herc's the one who first figured out to take the break beats from records and stitch them together. Flash is the one who turned DJing into a complex and intricate art form. And Bam-

---

1. There's a guy who identifies himself as "Chuck Chuck." It's Mr. Freeze. It's a thing he used to say at the beginning of a bunch of his rhymes, possibly because he was reciting Charlie Choo's party raps, but also possibly not.

2. There's a part where Master Dee says his name and it sounds a lot like he's saying "Master Gee," who is a guy from the Sugarhill Gang.

baataa took what was acceptable to use as reference material in rap and extended it outward in each direction about a hundred thousand miles. The most obvious example is his fondness for Kraftwerk, an electronic music group from West Germany mildly popular in the '70s and '80s.

But Bambaataa's influence is even larger than that. When Nelson George wrote about Bambaataa in *Hip Hop America*,[3] he said, "Bambaataa's most important contribution to developing hip hop may have been sociological," and when he said that, he was referencing the Zulu Nation and the ideology it spread.

In 1974, Bambaataa founded the Zulu Nation, a cooperative of DJs, break-dancers, graffiti artists, and (eventually) rappers. The history of the Zulu Nation is a long and curvy story, but the essentials are: Bambaataa was a member of a very strong gang in New York called the Black Spades.[4] Following either a trip to Africa or the death of a friend of his, depending on the article you happen to be reading, he opted to dedicate his life to providing an alternative to the gangs in the city. That's the Zulu Nation. It's still around today.

2. The Song's Sound: "Jazzy Sensation" steals its musical base from a song called "Funky Sensation," which had come out earlier that same year and was a hit on black radio. It was by singer Gwen McCrae, a woman most famous for a song where she asks a guy if she can be his rocking chair. It was the first time Bambaataa worked with producer Arthur Baker, who was already experimenting with drum machines, synths, and samplers. So what you hear are the first whispers of rap moving away from the disco or funk and toward the energetic electro-funk that Bambaataa would become most famous for, a sound that eventually morphed into a hundred different things.

3. The Song's Philosophy, Part I: There are two versions of "Jazzy Sensation." There was the A side, most regularly known as the "Bronx Version," and then there was the B side, a gentler, less funky iteration featuring singer Tina B. The B side was called the "Manhattan Version," and so right here is one of the first examples of rap marketing itself to two different audiences. And this grays into . . .

4. The Song's Philosophy, Part II: When the Sugarhill Gang made "Rapper's Delight," they used the spellbinding bass line from "Good Times," a massive disco hit by Chic, to draw a familiarity to this new thing they were doing. By Bambaataa co-opting McCrae's "Funky Sensation," he followed that same template, except "Jazzy Sensation" was more rugged, more raw than what the Sugarhill Gang presented. It was, on the surface, a very mainstream sound, but it was also an underground song, this mash-up of sounds and voices and call-and-responses and brags and low-key mayhem.

That's a large part of what makes "Jazzy Sensation" so remarkable: Only two years into having rap on the radio, and we already see this tug and pull between what is obviously acceptable and what will eventually become acceptable, which is essentially the core characteristic of rap. It's that duality, and whether Bambaataa aimed for it to be that way or it accidentally turned into that later isn't what matters. What matters is that it happened. It's what ties "Jazzy Sensation" to the earliest days of hip-hop and also how it predicted what the genre's future became. You take parts of what's already being done, what's already been agreed upon as okay, and then you tweak them and twist them just enough that they become new thoughts and new actions and new ideas that are exciting and a little intimidating.

The biggest example, the most obvious example of it happening was when DJ Screw did it in Houston in the '90s. He took songs that were hits, cut them up, and slowed them down a ton until it felt like they weren't doing anything except drooping out of your speakers, and so all of a sudden there's this thing that's new and exhilarating (the Chopped and Screwed sound) but also recognizable enough that it would eventually be adopted by basically all of rap.

"Jazzy Sensation" was the same way. It's a fun song, a happy song. But it's also quietly the design for rap as a countercultural movement.

---

3. This is my favorite book about the history of rap.
4. Nearly every article on Bambaataa that mentions this also mentions that he rose to the position of warlord in the gang, though no one seems to know what a warlord's role was, or is, outside of expanding the territory of the gang. I can't imagine it was anything nice.

JAZZY SENSATION

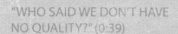

 "WHO SAID WE DON'T HAVE NO QUALITY?" (0:39)

"I'M FIVE FEET EIGHT, WITH SWEET BROWN EYES" (3:01)

"NOW I'M THE MASTER ICE AND I'M TWICE AS NICE" (1:07)

"SO TELL ME YOUNG LADIES, WHAT YOU WANNA DO?" (3:12)

"AND I'M THE DEDICATED PRINCE OF THE DISCO SLICE" (1:10)

"I HOLD THE KEY TO THE DOOR OF SOCIETY" (3:17)

"LET'S PARTY 'TIL YOU CAN'T NO MORE" (2:20)

"A PRESIDENTIAL RAPPER WITH A LOT OF FINESSE" (3:27)

 THRILLING   DESCRIPTIVE   BOASTFUL   CONFRONTATIONAL   COOL ON PURPOSE   PSYCHOLOGICAL   CONSIDERATE

REBUTTAL: "THAT'S THE JOINT" FUNKY 4 + 1

"That's the Joint" was a giddy explosion of group harmonies, ball-passing team exercises, chattering cowbells, and the fearless Sha-Rock, the first female rapper in history. All told, the most ecstatic nine-minutes-and-change released during Sugar Hill Records' historic first half decade. Technically released in 1980, "Joint" became a historic mile marker on February 14, 1981, when the Funky 4 + 1 performed it on *Saturday Night Live*, the first national television performance from a hip-hop group, at the behest of hosts Blondie.

"The people on the show were so nervous about them doing it, I remember trying to explain to them how scratching worked," guitarist Chris Stein told *Wax Poetics*. "Trying to verbalize what that is for someone who has no idea, it's really difficult." It's unclear if America fully understood it in '81. The group performed live but DJ Breakout pantomimed his record manipulation; plus their mics got cut, since rap songs in the early '80s could go on like hot butter on popcorn. But even in truncated form, hip-hop was now something that could be seen in any suburban home before MTV launched their first transmission. Also, nearly thirty-five years later, how many great rap collectives don't have a show-stealing alpha woman—word to the Juice Crew, the Native Tongues, Three 6 Mafia, Junior M.A.F.I.A., the Click, No Limit, Roc-A-Fella, Flipmode Squad, Ruff Ryders, Murder Inc., Terror Squad, and Young Money.

—CHRIS WEINGARTEN

1982

THE

Message

—

GRANDMASTER
FLASH
AND THE
FURIOUS FIVE

WHAT THIS SONG IS ABOUT

How hard it is to be alive when you're poor and also when you're black and especially when you're poor and black at the same time.

. . . .

WHY IT'S IMPORTANT

It was the moment that rap gained a conscience; the moment that broadened what rap was (and would eventually become); the moment that rap hinted at the sort of social significance it could (and would) carry.

Three things need to be in place before we get to the following interview transcript, because if they are not in place then it will only carry a portion of the weight it should. Additionally, without these two notes the information in the interview will seem unnecessary and unrelated to "The Message," as there are no specific references to it anywhere in the copy, and that could not be further from the truth, for reasons that will be made obvious soon, if they are not already. The three things are:

1. Chuck D is the half-god frontman for Public Enemy, and Public Enemy is, by all measures, the greatest, most impactful political rap group to ever have existed.
2. To describe a rap group as having been "political" is to assert that it spent a great deal of its energy discussing/critiquing the sociology of America.
3. Without "The Message," there is a likelihood that Chuck D and Public Enemy would have never become what they became, meaning the weight of "The Message" is one that bends the line of history that connects 1982 to today.

The following is an excerpt from a big interview that ran in *Spin* magazine in 1988, the year Public Enemy released *It Takes a Nation of Millions to Hold Us Back*, among the most potent rap albums ever recorded. The title of the article is "Armageddon in Effect," and that should tell you the sort of tone the interview carried.

SPIN: Do you consider yourselves prophets?

CHUCK D: I guess so. We're bringing a message that's the same shit that all the other guys that I mentioned in the song have either been killed for or deported: Marcus Garvey, Nat Turner, all the way up to Farrakhan and Malcolm X.

What is a prophet? One that comes with a message from God to try to free people. My people are enslaved within their own minds.

Rap serves as the communication that they don't get for themselves to make them feel good about themselves. Rap is black America's TV station. It gives a whole perspective of what exists and what black life is about. And black life doesn't get the total spectrum of information through anything else. They don't get it through print because kids won't pick up no magazines or no books, really, unless it got pictures of rap stars. They don't see themselves on TV. Number two, black radio stations have neglected giving out information.

SPIN: On what?

CHUCK D: On anything. They give out information that white America gives out. Black radio does not challenge information coming from the structure into the black community, does not interpret what's happening around the world in the benefit of us. It interprets it the same way that Channel 7 would. Where it should be, the black station interprets information from Channel 7 and says, "This is what Channel 7 was talking about. Now as far as we're concerned . . ." We don't have that. The only thing that gives the straight-up facts on how the black youth feels is a rap record. It's the number one communicator, force, and source, in America right now. Black kids are listening to rap records right now more than anything, and they're taking it word for word.

By 1988, it had become clear that the most threatening and intimidating iteration of rap was the one focused on social commentary, on reflecting what was happening in black America back out to the rest of the country. Culture reporting was really the first true stance rap took (minus the act of rap existing as rap, which was for sure a defiant stance already). N.W.A did it most aggressively; their apoplectic and unapologetic examination of the country's racial dynamic all but set fire to the White House. And Chuck D and Flavor Flav turned the angst into action, perfecting rap as protest and political music.

And when that shift was made, when it was fully vetted, when it was given the opportunity to mutate into a hundred million different things, that's what it did. Rap changed irrevocably. Rap changed with "The Message."

♦

"The Message" was not the first rap song to be politically slanted.

A large percentage of the early rap music was party-based, that's for sure, but not all of it. It even came in gradations. A handful of songs secretly high-fived social uprising by including a variation of the line "You gotta dip-dip-dip dive, so-so-socialize / Clean out your ears and then open your eyes," which was only a slight deviation from a Black Panthers chant. Kurtis Blow hinted at creating a song with gravity on 1980's "The Breaks," (see page 16), which sounded very much like a happy song but was quietly about some unhappy things, and then he got closer still to the idea with "Hard Times." And Brother D and the Collective Effort made "How We Gonna Make the Black Nation Rise?" that same year, which was about exactly what it sounds like it was about. But where Kurtis dulled the edge of his knife with humor (one of the things he was upset about was that he couldn't claim his cat as a dependent when he filed his taxes) and mostly only spoke in generalities, Brother D and the Collective Effort were so militant that the profoundness of their overall message (America's not that great of a place to be right now if you aren't white and wealthy) was muted by the conspiracy theories they also spoke on (cancer was being pumped into the water; America was cooking people in ovens in secret concentration camps). "The Message," though—"The Message" was pitch-perfect.

It was poppy but slowed down just enough that it was nearly impossible to hear the song without *really* listening to it, and Melle Mel emoted out this beautifully colored picture of an austere and bleak New York that nobody had presented before. He talked about being frustrated by all the noise. He talked about homeless people eating garbage. He talked about receiving a subpar public education. He talked about always being surrounded by either rats or roaches or junkies, and let me tell you, a roach crawled across my calf one time and I gave very real consideration to cutting my leg off.

It was insightful without being preachy. He talked about the inevitability of poverty begetting poverty and TV being unhealthy and said the phrase "Neon King Kong standing on my back," and that is an unbelievably powerful statement when you pull it out into the open space all by itself.

It was magnetic and captivating and immediately satisfying. Its first lines, "It's like a jungle sometimes / It makes me wonder how I keep from going under," are still all-world even thirty-some-odd years later, and the first bar of his actual verse, "Broken glass everywhere / People pissing on the stairs, you know they just don't care," is even more transformative. And then all

NOT PICKED

THERE'S A REASONABLE (ALBEIT WRONG) ARGUMENT TO BE HAD THAT AFRIKA BAMBAATAA'S "PLANET ROCK" SHOULD'VE RECEIVED THE 1982 CHAPTER. OTHER SONGS THAT WEREN'T PICKED:

Fatback Band, "King Tim III (Personality Jock)" (1979) + Blondie, "Rapture" (1980) + Grandmaster Flash and the Furious Five, "The Adventures of Grandmaster Flash on the Wheels of Steel" (1981) + Afrika Bambaataa & the Soulsonic Force, "Planet Rock" (1982) + Too $hort, "Don't Stop Rappin'" (1983) + Kurtis Blow, "Basketball" (1984) + Schoolly D, "P.S.K. What Does it Mean?" (1985) + Eric B. & Rakim, "Eric B. Is President" (1986) + The Beastie Boys, "No Sleep Till Brooklyn," (1987) + Public Enemy, "Don't Believe the Hype" (1988) + 2 Live Crew, "Me So Horny" (1989) + Digital Underground, "The Humpty Dance" (1990) + Cypress Hill, "How I Could Just Kill a Man" (1991) + House of Pain, "Jump Around" (1992) + Ice Cube, "It Was a Good Day" (1993) + Snoop Doggy Dogg, "Gin and Juice" (1994) + The Notorious B.I.G., "Big Poppa" (1995) + Outkast, "Elevators (Me & You)" (1996) + Missy Elliott, "The Rain (Supa Dupa Fly)" (1997) + Master P, "Make 'Em Say Uhh!" (1998) + Nas, "Hate Me Now" (1999) + Mystikal, "Shake Ya Ass" (2000) + Jay-Z, "Takeover/Life" (2001) + Nelly, "Hot in Herre" (2002) + T.I., "Rubber Band Man" (2003) + Kanye West, "Jesus Walks" (2004) + Three 6 Mafia, "Stay Fly" (2005) + Lupe Fiasco, "Kick, Push" (2006) + Soulja Boy Tell 'Em, "Crank Dat (Soulja Boy)" (2007) + Wale, "The Kramer" (2008) + Gucci Mane, "Lemonade" (2009) + Wiz Khalifa, "Black and Yellow" (2010) + A$AP Rocky, "Purple Swag" (2011) + Killer Mike, "Reagan" (2012) + YG, "My Nigga" (2013) + Run The Jewels, "Lie, Cheat, Steal" (2014)

of that bundled up together, presented in this video that reinforced everything Mel was talking about, in this video that was such an aberration from the videos rap had known, with shots of homeless people smoking and tow trucks and broken bottles. The reverb it caused is still felt today.

◆

There are for sure some things that need to be mentioned when talking about "The Message," because it was not a record that came together perfectly:

- Grandmaster Flash isn't anywhere on the song. He has zero parts. It's the group's most famous record, and its most ego-driven member is absent from it.[1] While neither Flash nor any members of the group have ascribed their breakup to this fact, it seems to be at least partly attributable to it. They never recorded another song together after "The Message." (I imagine Flash would respond to that with something like, "We barely even recorded this one together.")
- Nobody in the group wanted to record the song. It was too much of a bummer, they told people in interviews later. Melle Mel was the only one who could be convinced to record it, which is why he's the only member of the group on it. After it took off, that's when they accepted it, and even then Grandmaster Flash did so grudgingly.
- It was written by one of the staff songwriters, Ed "Duke Bootee" Fletcher, at Sugar Hill Records, the label Grandmaster Flash and the Furious Five signed to after the success of the Sugarhill Gang's "Rapper's Delight" (see page 10). He com-

posed it in the basement of his mother's house. There's no small amount of irony in the fact that the first truly popular radical rap song came from a record label that had been derided for not being authentically hip-hop.

And yet none of that matters. None of it muddles the luster of "The Message." None of it siphons away any of its historical significance.

Here's an easy way to see how important "The Message" was: It was the first rap song added to the National Recording Registry by the Library of Congress, and the National Recording Registry is a collection of "sound recordings that are culturally, historically, or aesthetically important, and/or inform or reflect life in the United States." Another good way to see its reach is that *Rolling Stone* picked it as the best rap song of all time. Another good way is to listen to Melle Mel talk about it. Here's what he said about it during an interview in 2005:

> That was the one that separated us from everybody else, you know what I mean? If it wasn't for, you know, that record, we would still be a good group but we'd be kind of jumbled in with everybody else. That record kind of made the separation because of what it meant to society and what it meant to the record industry.

"The Message" turned Grandmaster Flash and the Furious Five into insta-legends. And rap into an art form with the power of a colossus.

---

1. This is also a good indicator of how, only three years after "Rapper's Delight" had exploded into popularity, rap had firmly and irreversibly shifted away from the DJ and toward the rapper.

REBUTTAL: "MAKING CASH MONEY" BUSY BEE

It's hard to argue that "The Message" is not the most important rap song released in 1982. Having introduced social-conscience protest music to rap, it's very high on the list of most important songs of any kind, from any year. But what's more hip-hop (and more fun) than arguing? So for the sake of argument: In lots of ways, Busy Bee's slick, funky, stream-of-consciousness how-to guide "Making Cash Money" is the polar opposite of "The Message." Largely frivolous, dedicated to nothing but the almighty dollar and the acquisition thereof, it's about as pure a piece of capitalism as you

can find. But that's what's so important: Rap music, more than any other art form before it, stepped itself up and over the boring old art-vs.-commerce argument that has plagued makers of things for so long. Think of how many of rap's milestones—from *Paid in Full*, to *Get Rich or Die Tryin'*, to *Watch the Throne*—blur the line between paper chasing and art creation to the point where it's basically erased. Rap music is a form of expression so powerfully modern as to render such old-world distinctions meaningless. "Making Cash Money," from way back in 1982, stands as a seminal example. —DAVE BRY

SUCKER M.C.'S
RUN-DMC

WHAT THIS SONG IS ABOUT
It's about Run-DMC getting discovered, and also about how cool
and good they are at rapping and
how uncool and not good sucker
M.C.'s are.

••••••••••••••••••••••••••••••

WHY IT'S IMPORTANT
"Sucker M.C.'s" marks dual points
in rap's evolution, and the two
things coalesce, as they often do
in situations like these. It's when
rap parted itself between old and
new (or uncool and cool, really)
for the first time, and it's also
the first time a rap song could be
described as a "battle rap" song,
even if the antagonist was a general idea and not a specific foe.

When Run-DMC became a thing, a trio, that's when rap aggressively separated into classes. That's a big thing, and it all started with "It's Like That" and "Sucker M.C.'s." There's a fair amount to unravel here, so the rest of the chapter is broken up into a Q&A format.

When did Run-DMC release "Sucker M.C.'s"?
"Sucker M.C.'s" was the B side to Run-DMC's first single, "It's Like That," which was released by Profile Records.[1] So, picture—you've got a vinyl record. There are two songs on that record, because you can fit two songs on it. "It's Like That" was to be the mar-quee song on the record; the group's first official song that was recorded and properly released. "Sucker M.C.'s" was basically the filler on the backside of the record, except it ended up being way more than that.

How is "Sucker M.C.'s" more important than "It's Like That" if "It's Like That" was Run-DMC's first true song?
I think it might actually make more sense to talk a little about why Run-DMC was so important before we get to why "Sucker M.C.'s" was so important, because even though the two ideas are kind of similar, they're not the same.

Most all of the key figures in the early chapters of this book were the first to do things, none more so than Run-DMC. They were the first rap group to be nominated for a Grammy, the first to have a gold album (and then platinum album and then multi-

How?

Much of the early rap—actually, basically ALL of the early rap—was strongly influenced by the R&B rhythms and disco atmospherics that had preceded it. It was all very lush and rhythmic and sometimes ornate and usually big. Run-DMC, when they showed up, they went the opposite direction. It was easy to *see* the difference—Afrika Bambaataa used to dress like he was some bizarro future space alien; Run-DMC settled on all-black outfits that proffered much more aggressive imagery[2]—and it was even easier to hear the difference.

Run-DMC stripped away all of the instrumentation and replaced it with drum machines (and then later they pushed it even further and melded it together with hard rock guitars and histrionics), which made it feel more real, more visceral.[3] They were shout-rapping their rhymes, alternating words during lines, sneering and being very confrontational. All of a sudden, the party rap records that had been operating as the spine of rap sounded foolish and childish and all-the-way outdated. And there you have the separation. On the one side, you had the people who were still for party rap. On the other side, you had the people who were for this new thing, this more aggressive thing, this thing that wasn't acquiescing, that wasn't compromising any of its jaggedness. That's where rap went after Run-DMC.[4]

Kurtis Blow was cool when he started rapping, sure, but he was cool the way that people who are nice and handsome are cool, which is to say nonthreatening cool. LL Cool J, a direct-line descendent of Run-DMC, he was cool when he started rapping, too, but he was cool the way people who are truculent and handsome are cool, which is to say the most overwhelming and intoxicating version of cool.

Rick Rubin did a lot of that early production you're talking about, right? He did a lot of that rap-rock-style stuff at Def Jam.

platinum album). They were the first to perform on *American Bandstand*. The first to have a video on MTV. The first to be on the cover of *Rolling Stone*. They were—

You're telling me a lot of important *accomplishments* but not anything about how they were important.
I'm getting there. Chill.

They were the first to do a whole bunch of things, but really they were the first to establish a distinction between the first group of rappers that preceded them, and then the group that came after them. In effect, they marked the beginning of rap's second generation.

No. I mean, yes, he did stuff like that at Def Jam Records, but he didn't work on anything for Run-DMC until 1986's transcendent *Raising Hell*.[5] Russell Simmons helped work on Run-DMC's earliest music, and he and Larry Smith produced "Sucker M.C.'s," but it wasn't as part of Def Jam.

How many albums did Run-DMC release when they were with Def Jam?
None, actually.

Wait, but so then why does it seem like they're always connected?
Because they were, and because they are. Russell Simmons, who helped cofound Def Jam Records,[6] is the older brother of Joseph Simmons. Joseph Simmons is the Run in Run-DMC. Russell is why Joseph felt compelled to wiggle his way into rap. Joseph actually served as a DJ for Kurtis Blow for a short while (Russell managed Kurtis), which maybe you know because you read it in one of the (many) books about Russell or Def Jam or Joseph or Run-DMC, or maybe you know it because you watched *Krush Groove*[7] and remember the scene near the end where Kurtis confronts Joseph about ditching out on Russell to sign with another label and reminds Joseph of how he got his start.

Isn't *Krush Groove* the best?
It really is. The third best thing about *Krush Groove* is Kurtis Blow in it. He's probably the all-time most likable rapper. He's like a human hug. I want to marry his smile, and if his smile is already married to someone else, then I want to marry his eyebrows and eyes. They're remarkable. Nobody's ever made better use of his or her eyes and eyebrows as a rapper than Kurtis Blow.[8]

The second best thing about *Krush Groove* is that Run, one of the movie's main characters, is still a (semi-) hard-charging rapper in it. Run has been varying shades of famous since the early '80s, but he's been definitely famous since 2005 as a reverend, attributed mostly to his role in the MTV reality show *Run's House*. I mostly only knew Run from the show, which means I mostly only knew him as a reverend. And watching a reverend cuss and try to have sex with Sheila E. is a fun thing.

The first best thing about *Krush Groove* is that Blair Underwood was cast as Russell Simmons in it. Russell Simmons casting Blair Underwood to play Russell Simmons has to be the most bold catfish move that's ever been pulled off.

Since we're here, what's a fun Russell Simmons story?
Before Russell Simmons helped turn Def Jam Records into a company he'd eventually sell his portion of for nearly $100 million, he sold fake cocaine to make money. What's smart about that is, if he got picked up by the police, he was generally okay because he was only selling fake cocaine to people and not real cocaine to people. What's dumb about that, though, is I can't imagine people who like real cocaine are very happy when they're given fake cocaine.

Can you get back to Run-DMC now, because you still haven't answered my first question: How is "Sucker M.C.'s" more important than "It's Like That" if "It's Like That" was Run-DMC's first true song?
"It's Like That" and "Sucker M.C.'s" were the first anyone really heard of Run-DMC, so they're both important for that, because it all led to what we just talked about a little earlier. I don't want it to sound like "It's Like That" wasn't a big moment, because it was. But "Sucker M.C.'s" did a thing that "It's Like That" didn't.

---

1. Here's a crazy thing to think about: Run-DMC was paid $2,000 for "It's Like That"/"Sucker M.C.'s." The record sold more than 250,000 copies.
2. Another thing it did was make them much more relatable, and another-*another* thing it did was make it seem like they weren't trying, which is always cool.
3. Run makes mention of this on the first verse, saying they "cut the record down to the bone."
4. Another thing to mention here is that Run-DMC was also the first prominent rap group to come from the suburbs, and you can tie that to the way they connected with their white fan base any way you want. To be thorough, Jam Master Jay, the group's DJ—he was a street tough. Run and DMC, though, they were not. The best example on "Sucker M.C.'s" is when DMC shouts, "I'm DMC in the place to be / I go to St. John's University," and a fun thing to mention is, in 2004, Wu-Tang released *Legend of the Wu-Tang* that had a cover of "Sucker M.C.'s," and Ol' Dirty Bastard raps, "I'm ODB in the place to be / Didn't go to St. John's University."
5. Rick Rubin's version of this was for sure the best version, even if it wasn't the first. Another thing that ended up happening with Rubin and Russell pushing their artists in this direction was that rappers started making albums that existed as projects instead of just songs plus songs.
6. This is actually only sort of true. Technically, Rick Rubin started Def Jam while he was still a student at New York University. He'd released one song before Russell Simmons showed up.
7. *Krush Groove* is a 60-percent-true musical based on the beginning of Def Jam.
8. Ice Cube is a close second, though he used his very differently.

What thing?

The first true rap battle is generally understood to be Kool Moe Dee vs. Busy Bee Starski. It happened in 1981 at the Harlem World's Christmas Rappers Convention. Now, there had been rap battles before then, but the way it (generally) worked was you'd have two rappers and they would take turns working to see who could get the crowd the loudest, the most fired up. Busy Bee, he was probably the top dude of all at this. Nobody could beat him. He was king. And so when Kool Moe Dee was matched up against him, in a brilliant tactical switch, rather than focus all his energies on the crowd, he turned it toward Busy Bee. He called him names, said his rhymes were "bullshit," made fun of him endlessly. The crowd was uproarious, laughing and shouting with each punch line. You can listen to it now and it's still electric. In the background, you can hear poor Busy Bee shouting over and over again for Kool Moe Dee to shut up. It's super sad. I can't even imagine how hurt Busy was watching it all happen, knowing he was going to be remembered forever for a terribly embarrassing reason. Do you even understand how big of a thing that was? Rap had been a competitive sport up through then. Kool Moe Dee's surprise bombing turned it into a blood sport. Rap absorbed all of that fury. It was perfect for the genre.

And the first time anyone bothered to put it on an actual, real record: "Sucker M.C.'s."

Ah. Okay. I get it.

Good.

What sort of things were Run-DMC saying?

Mostly they were just arguing against, and at, people who they thought weren't good rappers, which was turned into the phrase "sucker M.C.'s." They'd tell sucker M.C.'s they should "catch a heart attack" and that they were copycats and everyone knew they were fake, and called them "sad-face clown" and also "bad-face clown" and things like that. My favorite insult was when Run rapped, "You're cheatin' on your wife," because cheating on your wife or girlfriend became, like, one of the most important parts of being a rapper within the next five years.

Did you ever consider the idea that the confrontational nature of "Sucker M.C.'s" is also a good indicator that it was a new, youthful thing? Like, maybe it wasn't just a thing that possibly happened by accident like you mentioned in that Why It's Important blurb at the beginning of the chapter. Maybe it was actually a buck back *against* the old school?

That's a good point. There's a line in there where Run raps, "Everybody know what you been through," and it kind of feels like it's directed at Grandmaster Flash and the Furious Five's "The Message." And if that's the case, then it's even more important, and accidentally prophetic and ironic.

How's that?

Well, at the time that Run-DMC was doing what they were doing, they could never have imagined rap as it is today. Similarly, their predecessors, and even some of their contemporaries, couldn't imagine what Run-DMC would bring to the genre. That's a beautiful thing: the aliveness of the music. How it steals and guts the things around it in other genres, and things from its own past, and then for a brief moment whoever coins that style rises to the top, only to be surpassed by someone who learned and stole from it. And on and on and on.

REBUTTAL: "WHITE LINES (DON'T DON'T DO IT)" GRANDMASTER FLASH AND MELLE MEL

"White Lines (Don't Don't Do It)" isn't actually antidrug, the argument goes, because the people who made it snorted. That doesn't matter and it's way off base—BASS!—anyway, because if it isn't antidrug, it's anti the institutions that keep drugs illegal just to arrest the people they want to arrest. And *that* Melle Mel addresses cogently, birthing street rap's tradition of stoic resignation along the way, when he contrasts what happens to a "street kid" holding (three years) with what happens to "a businessman" (he is quickly "out on bail and out of jail"). Great moral art always flirts with the devil's party appeal of the thing it tells you not to do, and the power of powder hides inside "White Lines"'s stuttering, coke-drip percussion and hypnotic, heart-racing bassline—all cribbed from white post-punkers Liquid Liquid's "Cavern." So yes, Melle Mel was supposedly doing coke in the studio while recording, but there's nothing more hip-hop than attempting and not entirely succeeding at reconciling impossible-to-reconcile opposites. Like all the best hip-hop, "White Lines" is both full of it and honest to a fault.

—BRANDON SODERBERG

SUCKER M.C.'s

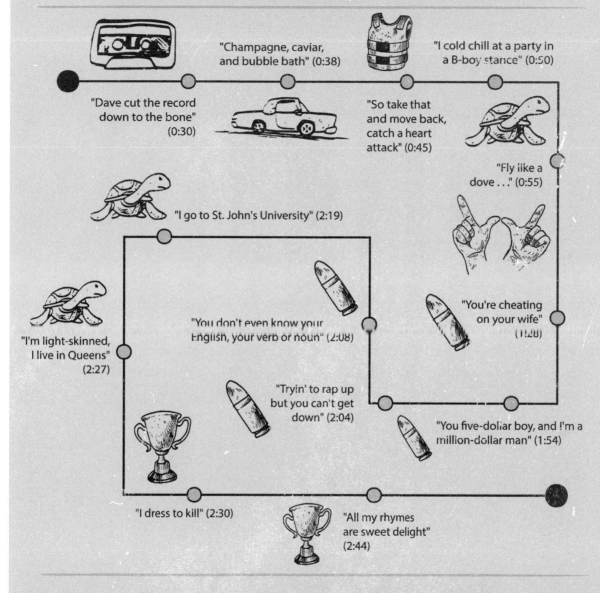

"Dave cut the record down to the bone" (0:30)

"Champagne, caviar, and bubble bath" (0:38)

"So take that and move back, catch a heart attack" (0:45)

"I cold chill at a party in a B-boy stance" (0:50)

"Fly like a dove . . ." (0:55)

"You're cheating on your wife" (1:18)

"You five-dollar boy, and I'm a million-dollar man" (1:54)

"Tryin' to rap up but you can't get down" (2:04)

"You don't even know your English, your verb or noun" (2:08)

"I go to St. John's University" (2:19)

"I'm light-skinned, I live in Queens" (2:27)

"I dress to kill" (2:30)

"All my rhymes are sweet delight" (2:44)

COMPARATIVE   BOASTFUL   DESCRIPTIVE   INFLAMMATORY   LIFESTYLE   CONFRONTATIONAL   SONIC

FRIENDS

—

Whodini

WHAT THIS SONG IS ABOUT

Friends.

. . . .

WHY IT'S IMPORTANT

By this point, there had been some rap songs that had gotten popular enough that they'd become seen as pop songs. When Whodini made "Friends," it was the first time a rapper or rap group tried to make a pop song on purpose.

It's very likely that you know Whodini's music—"Friends," "Freaks Come Out at Night," possibly "One Love," and, depending on the kind of company you keep, even "Five Minutes of Funk"—but do not know Whodini, and that makes sense because that's how it went for all but the most iconic figures from 1980s rap. And while the group Whodini—two rappers, Jalil Hutchins and John Fletcher, and DJ Drew Carter—was fun enough,[1] it's what they did that's had a lasting impact.

There was a short article in the December 1984 issue of *Billboard* called "Whodini Makes 'Friends' at Radio, Retail." It was about Whodini and the success that "Friends" was experiencing,[2] but really it was about how in the little more than five years since "Rapper's Delight" had wandered its way onto the radio, rap music had gone *from* something to aspiring *toward* something. There were two quotes in the story that I'm going to use right now that, reading them today, seem especially profound, though I suppose that shouldn't be all that surprising given that two especially profound people gave them.

This first one is from Larry Smith, who, by then, had coproduced Run-DMC's radical first album and all of Whodini's *Escape*.[3] He was talking about Whodini's record company trying to steer them toward sounding a certain way. He said, "They wanted the whole thing to be more like Run-D.M.C., but I didn't want to do exactly that. Whodini's a bit more adult, I think, and rap's not just for kids anymore." I suspect he meant this literally, as stems of rap music had already begun to grow a bit salacious (Whodini had a song called "I'm a Ho," and on it they admitted to playing a game called Tag Team Sex[4]), but I also suspect he meant this figuratively. Rap album sales were increasing at a tremendous rate. *Escape* was actually the first rap album ever to go platinum, an easy indicator that the stakes were getting higherHigherHIGHER

from merging fully with mainstream R&B and more than a full decade away from the most perfect version of it.[6] "Friends" helped introduce the idea of a more conventional sense of melody to rap, de-emphasizing rhythm as an end in itself. It directly predicted the rap and R&B trend. It probably started it.

The two have commingled ever since.

◆

To expand on the point made by Larry Smith about rap growing to become a demonstrable genre:

FOUR KEY MOMENTS FROM 1984 THAT WERE DIRECT EVIDENCE THAT RAP MUSIC WAS BIGGER THAN A FAD (AND TWO MOMENTS THAT WERE TANGENTIALLY RELATED)

DIRECT: Rap began being shown on TV. There were two shows that debuted on local TV in 1984 that focused on rap. Both were in New York. The first was called *Video Music Box*, which ran all the way through 1996. It played rap videos, though at the time that usually just meant footage of a group or person performing somewhere. The two guys who ran it/hosted it—Ralph McDaniels and Lionel C. Martin—eventually started producing the videos themselves, putting proper money behind them. The other show, *Graffiti Rock*, presented a rounder view of hip-hop, highlighting not just the music but also break dancing, graffiti, and DJing. Also, it was around this time that MTV started to occasionally play rap videos, too, owed largely to Run-DMC's distinctly rock-inspired version of rap. It's strange to think about now, but there was for sure a period where MTV was not all that interested in music by black musicians.

DIRECT: Rap got movies. There were two. There was *Beat Street*, which was praised immediately and is now fondly remembered for its authenticity. And there was *Breakin'*, which was pooped on immediately and is now fondly remembered for its accidental silliness. I remember watching both of them when I was a

This second one is from Barry Weiss. At the time, he was the manager of artist development at Jive Records. However, if you know his name it's likely because he was one of the key figures behind the careers of Britney Spears, 'N Sync, and the Backstreet Boys, and if your brain is telling you, *But those are all pop acts, not rap acts,* that's sort of exactly the point, my dude. He told *Billboard,* "The rap market's moving from novelty to mainstream R&B, and with 'Friends' there is a very concerted effort to capture the older, sophisticated demographic[5] and to open them up to rap." This would seem like commonplace thinking, but that's only because we know that this is exactly what ended up happening. In 1984, rap was still years away

kid, probably somewhere between eight and ten years old. *Beat Street*, most famous for the scene where two guys get electrocuted to death while fighting on a subway track, was way too heavy for me. Conversely, the most serious part of *Breakin'* was when a guy who was very good at break dancing swept the sidewalk outside of a convenience store with a magic broom. That was something I could get behind.[7]

DIRECT: Rap got a radio station. Los Angeles beat New York to it. They premiered KDAY that year, the first station in the country that played mostly rap music. Dr. Dre worked there, if you can even believe that (which you should be able to because it makes total sense).

DIRECT: The Fresh Fest tour was booked. It was the first rap tour to play the big arenas and coliseums and it was a resounding success. Kurtis Blow, Run-DMC, Whodini, the Fat Boys, Newcleus, some separate break-dance crews—they toured twenty-seven different cities, introducing rap's swaggering bravado and aesthetics to large-scale audiences. The tour grossed more than $3.5 million dollars.

TANGENTIALLY RELATED: Oprah debuted as the cohost of a local TV show in Chicago. This wasn't important to rap at the time, but it would be later. There's a bit more information about this in the 2003 chapter (see page 156).

TANGENTIALLY RELATED: The NBA introduced the slam dunk contest to the All-Star festivities. The slam dunk is connected to rap, if not for the philosophical connection then at least for the visual representation, because as far as sports moves are concerned, it is the closest to a physical manifestation of rap as it gets. If we continue the line of thought: A well-executed crossover likely comes in a very close second. A no-look pass, third. On the other end, the sports move second-furthest away from rap would be an underhand serve in volleyball. First-furthest away would be anything that Scott Skiles ever did during his career.[8]

♦

TOP 1,000 RAP SONGS ABOUT FRIENDSHIP, RANKED

1. **"I Ain't Mad at Cha," Tupac (1996).** It's perfect. I would very much like to meet the person Tupac wrote this song for. I'm sure he's quite something.

3. **"Just a Friend," Biz Markie (1989).** Did you know that Biz Markie was in *Sharknado 2*?[9] He was.

4. **"I Miss My Homies," Master P featuring Pimp C and Silkk the Shocker (1997).** This was like when Puff Daddy made "I'll Be Missing You" with 112 and Faith Evans, except Sting was not involved. Master P rapped about a dead friend, Pimp C rapped about a dead friend, and Silkk the Shocker rapped about three dead friends and one incarcerated friend. Stacey Dash played a flying angel in the video, making her the second-most popular angel in a rap video in the '90s (the death angel from Bone Thugs-N-Harmony's 1995 "Tha Crossroads" video is the first).

7. **"Talk to 'Em," Young Jeezy (2005).** Young Jeezy raps to a frined of his who got locked up. It's very good. I wish I was Young Jeezy's friend. I saw him one time. It was right before a concert Jeezy had in Houston. I was walking around in the corridor area before the show started and he walked right by me. We literally brushed shoulders. When I realized who it was, I was like, "Oh snap! Jeezy! Hey, man. Wow. I'm such

1. Fletcher used to wear a hat like Zorro and call himself Ecstasy.
2. The song made its way all the way up to number four on the Black Singles chart and number eighty-seven on the Hot 100.
3. Smith would go on to coproduce Run-DMC's second album, *King of Rock*, and also Whodini's follow-up to *Escape*, *Back in Black*, as well as other things.
4. This is either a very great game or a very not great game, depending on how you feel about certain things.
5. A fun thing to note here is that Whodini was, if not the very first, then among the very first rap groups to have their own dancers perform while they rapped. It was very sophisticated at the time.
6. Blackstreet's "No Diggity."
7. The sequel, *Breakin' 2: Electric Boogaloo* is actually a decidedly better—or at least more fun—movie. It leaned all the way into its goofiness, opting for an easy-to-follow plot (noble neighborhood break-dancers vs. greedy government officials) and accelerated hyperbole (in one scene, one of the main stars break-danced upside down on the ceiling of his apartment).
8. On the surface, it would seem the premise for this statement is "Scott Skiles is white." That's incorrect, though. Scott Skiles is white, yes, but the two aren't related (at least not in this particular instance). Proof: Allen Iverson is universally agreed to be the most hip-hop basketball player that's ever been. But do you know who the second person is? Chris motherfucking Mullin, that's who. Chris Mullin is the illest white person.
9. *Sharknado 2* is the sequel to *Sharknado*, a movie about a water tornado filled with sharks.

a big fan of yours." He stopped for a moment, looked at me, then said, and I'll never forget this, he said, "I'm not Young Jeezy." It wasn't Young Jeezy.

24. **"A'Yo Kato," DMX (2003).** This one's DMX rapping to a friend of his who'd died. Being a rapper's friend is very hazardous, it would appear.

1,000. "Best Friend," 50 Cent featuring Olivia (2005). Nope.

"Friends" goes tenth on this list. It's enjoyable to listen to still, but generally only when you want to be nostalgic or ironic. In terms of consequence, though, it's first place—at worst, second.

"Friends" was an advice record where the group talked about paying attention to the type of friends you had, and that was kind of weird, because there just aren't a bunch of times where a rapper tells you that you should try to be friends with a woman before you sleep with her. It was also very smart because they were vague enough in it that it was kind of a pop platitude ("Friends / How many of us have them?") but also left enough gray area that it was able to remain a rap song. That's really where Whodini excelled, and why their music remains vital, why "Friends" is the most important song of 1984. It smoothed out rap enough that it could be pop while still remaining a rap song. It suggested what would eventually become the entire premise behind mainstream rap.

REBUTTAL: "ROXANNE'S REVENGE" ROXANNE SHANTÉ

U.T.F.O.'s "Roxanne, Roxanne" was a cautionary, catcalling tale for the ages in which three dweebs rapped about being rejected by the same woman. So even though the Brooklyn trio's balls were already blue by the end of the song, fourteen-year-old Lolita Shanté Gooden still gave them a swift kick with her answer track, "Roxanne's Revenge." The Queensbridge high schooler offered Roxanne—along with countless other ladies fed up with smooth-talking dudes in Kangols—a no-nonsense, gum-smacking voice. Not only was "Roxanne's Revenge" an early example of female empower-ment in the dick-swinging world of rap (a baton that Lil' Kim and Nicki Minaj would pick up in the ensuing decades), it was a classic case of hip-hop as expletive-filled cultural dialogue, too; the track spurred on a brief cottage industry of Roxanne-based songs from the perspective of the imaginary femme fatale's equally imaginary brother, sister, and parents, not to mention a conspiracy-theory twist titled "Roxanne's a Man (The Untold Story)." But there was only one real revenge.

—**RYAN DOMBAL**

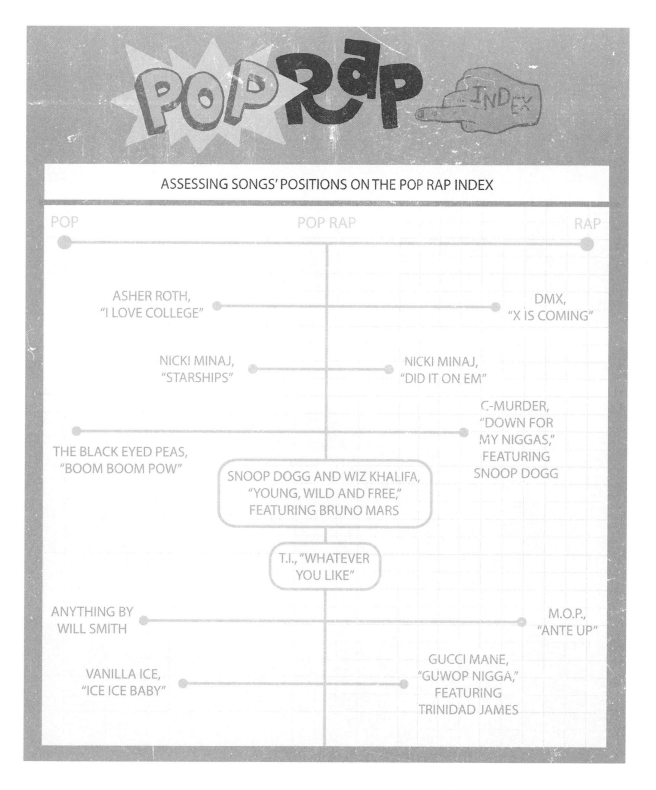

POP RAP INDEX

ASSESSING SONGS' POSITIONS ON THE POP RAP INDEX

POP   POP RAP   RAP

ASHER ROTH,
"I LOVE COLLEGE"

DMX,
"X IS COMING"

NICKI MINAJ,
"STARSHIPS"

NICKI MINAJ,
"DID IT ON EM"

C-MURDER,
"DOWN FOR
MY NIGGAS,"
FEATURING
SNOOP DOGG

THE BLACK EYED PEAS,
"BOOM BOOM POW"

SNOOP DOGG AND WIZ KHALIFA,
"YOUNG, WILD AND FREE,"
FEATURING BRUNO MARS

T.I., "WHATEVER
YOU LIKE"

ANYTHING BY
WILL SMITH

M.O.P.,
"ANTE UP"

GUCCI MANE,
"GUWOP NIGGA,"
FEATURING
TRINIDAD JAMES

VANILLA ICE,
"ICE ICE BABY"

LA DI DA DI

DOUG E. FRESH
AND SLICK RICK

WHAT THIS SONG IS ABOUT

Slick Rick being romantically pursued by a woman and also the woman's ultra-aggressive mother.

....

WHY IT'S IMPORTANT

It's the archetypal storytelling rap song. It also made clear what would be rap's eventual relationship with casual misogyny. It *also* hinted at the lavish pimp-lifestyle version that would fully form itself in the next decade.

By now, I figure you're comfortable (or at least familiar) with the pacing and general structure of this book. In each chapter, there's straight-arrow information about the song chosen for that year, there's secondary color stuff that supports or buttresses the main idea of the chapter, and then, sometimes tucked away inside all of that and sometimes stated flat out in the open, there is the argument for why that song was chosen as the most important of the year.

This chapter will have all of that, too (as will the rest of the book), but I'm going to front-load this one because the last 70 percent of it will be taken up by a story.

INFORMATION

- Slick Rick was rap's first great storyteller, and also its most influential. A large part of that was his actual rapping, which was fluid and effortless, and I'll point you to the opening of "La Di Da Di" as proof. He owls his way through the first few lines before Doug E. Fresh begins beatboxing, saying he and Doug are going to show you something you've never seen before because he knows "You're all sick of all these crap rappers / Biting their rhymes because, um, they're backstabbers / But, uh, when it comes to me and my friend Doug Fresh here / There is no competition 'cause we are the best, yeah," and he gets all that way and you don't even realize that he's already started rapping. Nobody who had come before him had flexed that sort of preternatural smoothness, that silkiness, that languidness. His words just strolled out of his mouth in silk pajamas. It was mesmerizing. Snoop Dogg remains the only other rapper to pull off a similar feat.
- Snoop Dogg covered "La Di Da Di" on his album *Doggystyle* in 1993. He called it "Lodi Dodi." It was the first time a rapper had covered another rapper's song on an album, and so "La Di Da Di" was important indirectly as well as directly.

- "La Di Da Di" was the first rap song to use up all of its time telling a cohesive story, which makes it an evolutionary step. To stay within just the bounds of this book, a fast comparison to make to "La Di Da Di" is the part in "Rapper's Delight" (see page 10) where Wonder Mike raps about going to a dinner at a friend's house. "La Di Da Di" was like that, except laser-focused. There's a very distinct beginning, middle, and end, and more important than that, there's a very clear point to his telling you a story, which hadn't happened before he did it. Basically every storytelling rap song that's come after 1985 has used "La Di Da Di" as its template.

- "La Di Da Di" was the second rap song ever where the rapper referred to a woman as a "bitch,"[1] and it was the first rap song ever to discuss the general appearance of an elderly woman's vagina. ("And with your wrinkled pussy, I can't be your lover.") Rick's low-volume British[2] coo managed to make casual misogyny seem cool. That's not a good thing, but it was a thing that had a tremendous effect on rap.

- Another thing "La Di Da Di" did was pioneer high-toned brand narcissism. Things Slick Rick mentions: Polo cologne, Oil of Olay, his Kangol hat, Gucci underwear, Bally shoes, Johnson's Baby Powder, a bubble bath, and filing his nails.

- "La Di Da Di" was the B side of a record. The A side was "The Show," also an iconic track, and so a fun thing to consider is that "The Show"/"La Di Da Di" is maybe the best combo record in all of rap.

- There aren't any instruments on "La Di Da Di," which was also peculiar and incredible. It's all voice. Slick Rick raps the song, and Fresh makes the beats and buttresses Rick's words with punch-ins. Doug has long argued that he invented beatboxing even though the Fat Boys had a song called "Human Beat Box" in 1984 and also even though Michael Winslow was on *Police Academy* making robot noises in 1984, too. Doug said that the Fat Boys stole the idea from him. He's never said anything about Winslow though. *Police Academy* is beyond reproach.

◆

STORY

This is a story that I think about almost every time I hear either Doug E. Fresh and Slick Rick on "La Di Da Di" or just Slick Rick by himself on "Children's Story." The story is about a date I went on, but really I think it's about how sometimes the bigness of the universe is overwhelming even when it's not trying to be. The reason I think about it is because, as I was driving the girl home that evening, "La Di Da Di" came on and then "Children's Story" came on two songs after that. This was slightly weird, I suppose, because it was 1998, so Slick Rick had not been popular for a while, but it's less weird when you remember that I was on a date and so I'm (almost) certain I purposely put those two songs on the tape we were listening to in an effort to appear interesting.

The story: When I was in the eleventh grade, I took a girl on a date to the beach. I'd like to say that we went there because I was very romantic when I was seventeen, but mostly I took her there because it was free and I didn't like her all that much so I didn't want to spend any of the tiny amount of money I had on her.

When we got to the beach, we laid out a blanket on the sand to put all of our stuff on, walked up and down the beach talking for a bit, then got in the water. Maybe twenty or so minutes into being out there, I noticed this thing floating out a ways from us. It was a brown leather wallet. It was very clearly a brown leather wallet. I said something close to "Is that a wallet?" and I'm not sure why I said that because I knew for sure it was, but I said it. I swam out, got it, then swam back. "Yep. Wallet," I said, and I don't know what I expected her to do, but what she did was nothing. I opened it and saw an ID. The wallet belonged to a man named Orlando something-or-other. I remember his first name because after I glanced around at the people in the water near us and realized I couldn't tell if anyone was Orlando or not, I shouted, "Orlando! Ay, Orlando!" to see if anybody would look up. Nobody did. And so I took the nonresponse as proof that the wallet had become my property.

As I waded my way back to the shore, I thumbed through it. There was a $20 bill and four $1 bills, and so I was excited, but then I noticed there was more tucked off in the side, and I got even more excited. I pulled the edge of the money out and ohhhhh fuuuuuuuck. It was a $100 bill that Orlando had folded in half and tucked into the corner (for safer keeping, I'm assuming). Have you ever found a $100 bill before? It's for real the best feeling. I lost one of my sons in a grocery store once for, like, forty-five seconds when he was three. I felt as good about finding him as I did about finding that $100. It felt life-changing, and I can tell you I liked that girl a whole lot more with a sudden extra $124 in my possession.

---

1. Duke Bootee said it first on "New York, New York" in 1983.
2. Slick Rick was born in England and moved to New York with his family when he was eleven years old.

But so here's what happened: The girl and me, we decided to walk over to this little pier gift shop place that was down the beach a ways that we'd walked under earlier. The plan was to go in there, buy some stuff, maybe get some food, and then, hooray. Great date. But as we were standing in line, the guy in front of us, when he got to the register, we could overhear him asking if anyone had turned in a wallet. IT WAS GOD-DAMN ORLANDO. He described the wallet, gave her his name, everything. He was literally standing three feet in front of us. I was frozen. I looked at the girl. She looked at me. I looked back at her. She looked back at me. And I don't know what she expected me to do, but what I did was nothing. I just stared straight through him. It was terrible. I know that now and I knew that then. But being amoral with $124 seemed like a way better thing than being moral with $0. So: nothing.

I told her, "Let's go," and so we left. We walked back to our blanket in the sand. I said, "I have a good idea. Let's stop at a gift shop and we can use this money to buy stuff for our people." I had three sisters and a mom and a dad and a grandma I lived with and she had an older sister and a mom and a nephew who she lived with. "Okay," she said, and she actually seemed kind of happy about it, and I actually thought every-

thing was going to work out. So the new plan was to stop on the way home at a beach store and buy our way out of the abyss we'd jumped into. And we did that. We spotted a store, we stopped, and in we went. We walked around for however long it was (it could've been ten minutes but it also could've been ten hours; time is weird in those sorts of situations), gathered some items—earrings, a T-shirt, things like that. And I won't say that we felt all the way good about what we were doing, but we definitely felt better.

So after we picked out all of the stuff, we walked to the register. I took out the wallet, grabbed the $24, stuffed it into my pocket, then grabbed the folded-up $100 bill and put it in my pocket, too. I looked around for a second, saw no one was looking at me, then tossed the wallet at one of those circular racks retailers hang T-shirts on, figuring someone more ethical than me would find it and mail it back to Orlando, bless him. And I was for real feeling righteous at that point. *I could've thrown the wallet in the trash and he'd have never gotten it back*, I silently reasoned with myself. *Wow, you're very decent, Serrano*, I continued. It was really something. It really was.

The man at the register, he smiled, not knowing he was looking at criminals. "You find everything okay?" he asked. "Yes, sir," I said, and I glanced at the girl and smiled, but I'd not yet gotten braces so I'm sure my smile did not have the effect on her I'd intended it to. The cashier tapped the register's buttons and placed the items in two plastic bags and gave us the total. It was just under $100, and I felt really happy because robbing Orlando was more work than I'd realized and I figured we'd use that last bit of money to buy some food. When he told us how much it was I said, "Sure," and reached into my pocket and pulled out the $24 and set it on the counter. Then I reached into my pocket again and found the $100. Then I unfolded it. And that's when I died.

It wasn't a real $100 bill. Ben Franklin was not looking back at me. Do you know who was looking back at me? JESUS CHRIST WAS LOOKING BACK AT ME. It was some church promotional thing. When it was folded up, it looked exactly real. But when you unfolded it, it was a half-size $100 bill with Jesus on the front and some scripture about accepting the Lord into your life underneath his picture. I couldn't even believe it. I just stood there holding it. I showed it to the girl. She didn't say a word. The cashier? Who even knows what he was thinking because I walked right TF out the store without saying anything at all.

The ride home was super weird. What I should've done was talk about what had happened, because, really, it was a kind of amazing thing. I should've tried to have some sort of conversation, maybe about God or reverse serendipity or something, anything. But I was wearing a T-shirt that had flowers on it so I was in no position to pretend that I knew anything about anything. So we just sat there as the tape I'd made played itself through. "La Di Da Di" came on. Then right after that the version Snoop Dogg made in 1993 came on. Then some other song I don't remember. Then "Children's Story." She asked, "Is this the same guy as 'La Di Da Di'?" I said, "Yeah. His name is Slick Rick." She said, "You must really like him." I said, "He talks like that because he's from England. He has this other song called 'Teenage Love,' but I didn't put it on here." And she really didn't say anything else the rest of the trip home.

REBUTTAL: "KING OF ROCK" RUN-DMC

From a pure rapping standpoint, "La Di Da Di" is the Song of 1985. But rap has never really been pure. Since its dawn on earth, the genre has sampled and repurposed other bits of culture. There's nothing more hip-hop than music venturing outside of its comfort zone. Enter "King of Rock." Run-DMC could rap their asses off, albeit not with the same dexterity or nuance as Slick Rick. Don't think of "King of Rock" as a guitar-driven crossover, or pandering to white listeners, or a welcome mat for Aerosmith. This was the invention of the hard-as-fuck mentality that's preoccupied the genre ever since. Thirty years later, "King of Rock" still knocks.

It's more streamlined than what came before but also liberating. The half-shouted bars and Rik Rubin's stripped-down production are all about tension and suspense. If "King of Rock" sometimes sounds like two competing hype men, it's because "King of Rock" is the feeling of next. Instead of living in the moment, Run-DMC were spokesmen for the future. They weren't amped off of what was happening in that moment but for what was ahead. This wasn't good-times music or skills on display; it was "You have no fucking idea what's about to go down." In a lot of ways, we still don't.

—BETHLEHEM SHOALS

LA-DI-DA-DI

 "You're about to witness something you've never witnessed before" (0:04)

"There is no competition 'cause we are the best, yeah" (0:33)

 "We don't cause trouble, we don't bother nobody" (1:13)

"Who is the top choice of them all?" (1:49)

 "So listen close, to what we say" (1:31)

 "I threw on my brand new Gucci underwear" (2:18)

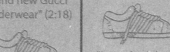 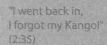 "I got the Johnson's Baby Powder and Polo cologne" (2:23)

 "I said, 'Um, don't cry, dry your eye'" (3:13)

"Threw on the Bally shoes" (2:28)

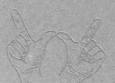 "I went back in, I forgot my Kangol" (2:35)

"The bitch was strong" (3:30)

"And with your wrinkled pussy, I can't be your lover" (4:30)

"So I broke the hell out like I had the chicken pox" (3:42)

 CONSIDERATE   BOASTFUL   NAME BRAND   SELF-REFLECTIVE   OBSERVATIONAL   INFLAMMATORY COMPARATIVE

1986

6

in the

MORNIN'

ICE-T

WHAT THIS SONG IS ABOUT

It's a first-person account of a story that includes, but is not limited to, physical confrontations (perpetrated against both male and female), the drug trade, police chases, and murder.

• •

WHY IT'S IMPORTANT

Because nobody had ever been as criminally explicit in a rap song before. "6 in the Mornin'" is, in the estimation of many, ground zero for true gangsta rap.

In 1988, Robert Duvall told a joke. More accurately: In 1988, a character Robert Duvall was playing in a movie called *Colors*[1] told a joke. The joke was short and only mildly funny, but it was also powerful and complex, which is probably the way a lot of people have described Robert Duvall as an actor during his career.[2] He told the joke to Sean Penn. More accurately: He told the joke to a character Sean Penn was playing. He said:

"These two bulls are sitting on a grassy knoll overlooking a herd of Guernseys, and the baby bull says, 'Hey, Pop. Let's run down and, uh, fuck one of those cows.' But the papa bull says, 'No, son. Let's *walk* down . . . and fuck 'em all.'"

In the movie, Duvall and Penn played partnered police officers in it. Duvall was the older, smarter, well-respected one. Penn was faster, meaner, and had hair that looked like it was spring-loaded. Duvall told the joke to Penn as a way to explain that Penn's very aggressive policing style[3] was only conducive to short-term gains, if even that. Duvall laughed when he finished telling the joke because Penn didn't laugh. Penn just smirked a little, because mostly he was (probably) just daydreaming about sleeping with a Hispanic woman he was staring at.[4] Come the end of the movie, Duvall is dead (he was shot during an assassination attempt on a gang member), and Penn and his hair are telling the same joke to his new partner, a black officer who is even more belligerent.

Ice-T, the first rapper signed to Warner Bros. Records, wrote and performed the theme song for *Colors*. He[5] was chosen to do so because *Colors* was obviously about Los Angeles gangs and gang culture but also less obviously about other things (like honor and diplomacy in places you wouldn't expect), which is probably the way a lot of people have described Ice-T as a rapper during his career.

◆

"People often say I created the gangsta rap genre with that record, but let me give proper credit. It was Schoolly D who inspired me to write the rhyme." —Ice-T, talking about "6 in the Mornin'" in his autobiography, *Ice: A Memoir of Gangster Life and Redemption—from South Central to Hollywood*

though. Instead, he offers up a different assignment for the letters.[6] Ice-T was not interested in allusions.[7]

Three comparisons: (1) In the last verse of "P.S.K.," Schoolly pulls a gun on a man but decides against shooting him because he doesn't want to go to jail. In the last verse of "6," nine people are killed in a shootout Ice-T is involved in. (2) In "P.S.K.," Schoolly's first encounter with a girl ends with him having sex with her and then underpaying her (turns out, she's a prostitute—Schoolly D offers her $10 after they have sex, and so this girl is either not that great of a prostitute or Schoolly D is a ruthless negotiator). In "6," Ice-T's first encounter with a woman ends with her getting beaten up in the street for calling him and his friends "punk pussies." (3) In "P.S.K.," Schoolly goes to a fancy bar. In "6," Ice-T goes to jail for seven years for being caught with an Uzi, a .44, and a hand grenade in his car. A HAND GRENADE, like he's goddamn *Commando* Arnold Schwarzenegger.

"P.S.K." *inspired* the first gangsta rap song. That's not the same as being the first gangsta rap song itself. It's close, but it's not the same.

◆

A fast note about Ice-T's autobiography: There's a section where he tells a story about hanging out with Flavor Flav that involves going to Red Lobster in a Ferrari. I suspect the phrase "going to Red Lobster in a Ferrari" is the most accurate description of Flavor Flav anyone will ever come up with.

◆

SOME OTHER GENERAL KNOWLEDGE ABOUT ICE-T

Ice-T was asked to star in the film *New Jack City* by Mario Van Peebles after Van Peebles heard him talking shit in a bathroom in a nightclub. Ice-T was paid $28,000. The movie grossed over $60 million. Ice-T was also in a movie about a leprechaun who murdered people for gold coins, which is a real, actual thing. The guy who signed Ice-T to Sire Records, an arm of WB, had

Schoolly D is a rapper from Philadelphia. In 1985, he recorded and released a song called "P.S.K. What Does It Mean?" It's the song Ice-T is referencing in the preceding quote and has referenced before in other interviews.

In "P.S.K.," Schoolly talks about drugs and having sex, which hadn't really happened before in a rap song, so that was large, and those are definitely two pieces of what gangsta rap eventually grew to be. But when it came to criminality, another major branch, he either only alluded to it or stopped just short of being properly offensive. The easiest example: The acronym "P.S.K." means "Park Side Killers," a gang Schoolly was affiliated with in the early '80s. In the song, he never actually says that, also signed the Ramones, the Pretenders, Madonna, Depeche Mode, the Smiths, the Cure, and more. Ice-T went to a Tupperware party once because he thought Denzel Washington was going to be there. Denzel Washington was not there. Ice-T is interesting.

◆

"6 IN THE MORNIN'" IS A MONSTROUS TEN VERSES LONG

- **Verse One:** This one is about running away from the police. Ice-T hears them knocking at his door at six A.M. He escapes out a window, bringing with him his pistol and his money. He does not grab his cassette tape, which he regrets.
- **Verse Two:** This one is about playing dice (he doesn't say if he won or lost, though I suspect he won because nobody dies afterward) and then beating up a woman who becomes a tad too mouthy—though this is evidence he possibly lost at dice.
- **Verse Three:** This one is about getting arrested for having weapons in the car and then getting into a fight in jail.
- **Verse Four:** This one is about getting out of jail. (The ease with which the third verse is delivered might lead you to believe that his weapons charge was a small infraction. It was not. He reveals here he was locked up for seven years.) He finds out that everyone he knew before going in is now in the drug trade. He joins up.
- **Verse Five:** This one is about becoming a pimp and then getting into a gunfight in a strip club because that's what pimps do, probably. Six people are wounded, two of whom are fatally injured.
- **Verse Six:** This one is about running away from the police again, this time in a stolen car.

- **Verse Seven:** This one is about how he successfully evaded the police, and so then he goes to a girl's house and takes a bath. I imagine this is also a pimp activity, though I suppose it could be he just chose a bath over a shower so he wouldn't get his hair wet.[8]
- **Verse Eight:** This one is about having sex with a skilled lover.
- **Verse Nine:** This one is about helping his friend jump bail.
- **Verse Ten:** This one is about going to a party in New York, then getting into a shootout. Nine people die this time.

It's like a season of *Sons of Anarchy*, basically.

◆

Ice-T testified before the Congressional Black Caucus in 1988. This was a year after *Rhyme Pays* had established him as a star.[9] And it was the same year he'd done the song for *Colors*, which was a hit and of course in the news as a controversy, so his reach extended beyond music. More to that point: It was also after L.A. had been christened the face of the crack epidemic in America by national media, so he appeared the most appropriate, qualified counsel.[10] He was asked a very complicated simple question: Why are there gangs and drugs? His response: "I said, 'All you fools sitting in here and you're gonna ask me and you know exactly why there's gangs and drugs. Because you don't care about it,' you know what I'm saying? And the gang situation in Los Angeles has been here twenty years. And then a lady got killed in Westwood, you know, a non-black somebody out of the neighborhood, and all of a sudden there were 387 murders that year and seventy thousand gang members. And I said, 'They didn't join that night.'"

---

1. There was also a scene in *Colors* where Damon Wayans danced with a large plush rabbit in a pawnshop while wearing only boxers and a shower cap because he was high on PCP. It was less central to the plot, but it's something a lot of people remember.
2. The thing I'm not sure of is whether or not his best role was Tom Hagen in the first two *Godfather* movies, Lieutenant Colonel Bill Kilgore in *Apocalypse Now*, or Otto Halliwell in *Gone in 60 Seconds*. I kind of want to say *Godfather*, but I don't remember Marlon Brando pulling off a sixty-car heist in a single night.
3. My favorite example: He catches a kid spray-painting a wall. He holds the kid up and spray-paints his face. Sean Penn is not that great at graffiti.
4. He later slept with her, FYI. You have to appreciate his focus.
5. Rick James was originally tapped to do the song. His contribution, which is actually on the *Colors* soundtrack, is as ill-fitting for the movie as you'd expect.
6. P = people who don't understand how one homebody became a man; S = the way we scream and shout; K = the way his DJ was cutting.
7. "I wasn't alluding to *shit*. I harped on the criminal exploits." —Ice T, *Ice: A Memoir of Gangster Life and Redemption—from South Central to Hollywood*
8. That's why my wife takes baths sometimes. Best I can tell, she is not a pimp.
9. *RP* was actually the first hip-hop album to have a parental advisory sticker on it. It sold over 500,000 copies, and nobody seems to be sure if the sticker helped album sales or hurt them.
10. "I have the ability to break things down so a ghetto kid can understand what rich white people see and rich white people can see what ghetto kids see. That's what I do. That's my job." —Ice-T, on his *Behind the Music* special

Ice-T is very charming + very smart + very insightful, particularly when it comes to discussions of race as it relates to the economics and mechanics of gang culture and its net force. That's why he became such an influential rapper, same as Ice Cube and Tupac Shakur, two other captivating speakers. He's also very self-aware.

He spoke about the moment he realized the world was broader than the ghetto in 1989 on *The Arsenio Hall Show*. This is the exchange. It took place after he talked about how he'd been offered a bit part in a movie called *Breakin'* and initially turned it down:

Ice-T: My homeboys came at me and they were like, "Ice, man. You need to cool out, man. You need to cool out, man. You need to go on and get that money, man. White people like you, man."

Arsenio: Someone came and told me that same thing years ago.

[audience laughs]

Ice-T: It's sad, though. It's sad, though, you know. So they told me, they said that I could make it. And I'm, like, looking at them like, "Man, I thought I got it made, man." And they're like, "Nah, you got a chance." And right then, that's when my whole life kind of flipped 'cause I realized what we were doing really wasn't what the guys I looked up to [gangsters] wanted to be doing.

◆

The Notorious B.I.G., Tupac, the lot of them, those guys figured out how to be the most financially successful with gangsta rap music. N.W.A, the guys in that group, they figured out how to make gangsta music the most popular (basically, just let Dr. Dre produce for you and Ice Cube write for you, as it were). And Schoolly D leaned toward becoming the first gangsta rapper.

But Ice-T fully figured out what it was supposed to represent: frontline reporting from a figurative (and sometimes literal) war being fought by communities America didn't seem all that interested in protecting, and presented in a way that advanced the idea of bucking authority.

REBUTTAL: "WALK THIS WAY" RUN-DMC

Ice-T doesn't get enough credit for pioneering West Coast hip-hop and gangsta rap, but while "6 in the Mornin'" was an important record, it wasn't the most important one from 1986. I'd argue that Run-DMC's cover of Aerosmith's "Walk This Way" (which was produced by Rick Rubin) was hip-hop's first real crossover record and showed the world the genre's limitless potential. Really, from there you could draw any number of lines, because it's the song that first fused rock and rap, a thing that's happened countless times since. Incidentally, Run-DMC's 1986 version of "Walk This Way" also helped revitalize Aerosmith's career as they were getting set to release their now seven-times-platinum 1987 album *Permanent Vacation*. So the next time you listen to Kanye West and Paul McCartney's "Only One" or watch Eminem and Elton John perform "Stan" together on YouTube, put one in the air for Run-DMC.

—ROB MARKMAN

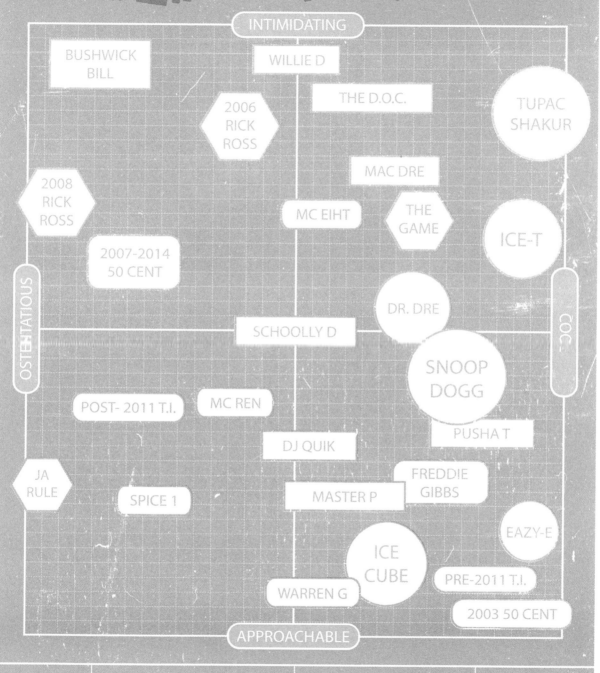

GANGSTA RAPPERS, CHARTED

INTIMIDATING

BUSHWICK BILL

WILLIE D

2006 RICK ROSS

THE D.O.C.

TUPAC SHAKUR

2008 RICK ROSS

MAC DRE

MC EIHT

THE GAME

2007-2014 50 CENT

ICE-T

OSTENTATIOUS

DR. DRE

SCHOOLLY D

COOL

SNOOP DOGG

POST- 2011 T.I.

MC REN

PUSHA T

DJ QUIK

JA RULE

FREDDIE GIBBS

SPICE 1

MASTER P

EAZY-E

ICE CUBE

WARREN G

PRE-2011 T.I.

2003 50 CENT

APPROACHABLE

○ ICONIC   ▭ UNDERAPPRECIATED   ⬭ OVERAPPRECIATED   ⬡ PERFECTLY APPRECIATED

1987

PAID
IN
FULL

ERIC B. AND RAKIM

WHAT THIS SONG IS ABOUT

It's about figuring out a way to make some money, but also figuring out a way to make yourself complete without money. It's also about a plate of fish.

. . . .

WHY IT'S IMPORTANT

Rakim perfected rapping on it.

The most popular rap song in 1987 was LL Cool J's "I Need Love." It was the second single from his second album, *Bigger and Deffer*, and it came out while his first album, 1985's *Radio*, was already firmly on its way to eventually selling a million-plus copies, so it had a fair amount of kinetic energy behind it. It became his first-ever Top 40 hit (number 14) and was the only rap single to make it to number one on *Billboard*'s Hot R&B/Hip-Hop Songs chart in 1987, though back then the chart was called Hot Black Singles, and nineteen-year-old LL Cool J on a chart called Hot Black Singles is the most accidentally appropriate thing I can think of.

But, so "I Need Love" was a big song. And it has sat in history as a big song since, because up until then there'd been rap love songs but no rap love ballads, and "I Need Love" was definitely that.[1] And let me be clear when I say that Early Career LL Cool J was something truly special and occasionally transcendent, so "I Need Love" worked, and "worked" is the important word, because it worked, but it didn't fit what we'd been told about LL *by* LL.

LL had aggressively marketed himself as cool over his first six singles, most perfectly with "Rock the Bells" and most intentionally with "I'm Bad," which came with a video that was about LL taking down a gang of kidnapper bad guys by taking off his jacket and then pretending to squish a jelly bean. And right after "I'm Bad" is when "I Need Love" came out. It was a foot sweep. All of his uncontainable bravado, his alpha-male arrogance, his unstoppable hubris—he traded it in to talk about the temperature of his loveless soul (cold, as it were). LL was simpin'. It was like the end of *Napoleon Dynamite* where Napoleon does that dance scene, except the reverse.

"People are just like, 'Oh, rap music now? It sucks. It's so bad. Rap music now sucks. Back in the day, that was the *good* rap music. That was where the *good* rap music was at.' . . . No, it's not. Have you ever listened to rap from back in the day? It's always some dude being like, 'Well, I went to the hat store today / And I bought myself a hat / Huh-ha ha-huh.' Nigga, I don't wanna hear your hat stories." —Donald Glover, *Weirdo*, 2011

Rakim revolutionized rap by revolutionizing rapping, and so let's talk about that, and a good comparison to draw here is to Michael Jordan, because both are regularly considered the greatest of all time, so let's do that:

Henry Abbott is a senior writer and an editor at ESPN. He knows a lot about basketball—more than I could ever hope to know, really. So I emailed him and asked him to send me a list of some of the ways that Michael Jordan changed the game. I had an idea of the way Jordan had affected the literal style of basketball (the bald head, the longer shorts, the tongue as expressionism, etc.), but I wanted actual ways the actual game actually changed after him. Abbott sent back four things, and those four things are all how Rakim changed rap, too, because being great at something is universal:

But that's sort of when it became clear, if it wasn't clear already: LL, rap hero, was cool, but he was a version of cool that required upkeep. He was cool the way Tom Cruise was cool, or the way Samuel L. Jackson[2] was cool. Not the way Paul Newman was cool or Philip Seymour Hoffman was cool or John Coltrane was cool, which is to say effortlessly cool, quietly cool, cosmically cool.

Rakim was all of those things. Rakim was more. And he injected all of it into rap. 1987 belongs to him. 1987 belongs to the God MC.

◆

Before MJ, there was no building around a shooting guard to win a title. Without a killer center you were pretty much not winning titles, which is why two centers were drafted before him.[3]

The line to connect here is that the earliest kinds of rap were often DJ-centered and DJ-driven. The DJ was the central figure, and that's easy to see by just looking at the names of the first batches of rap stars, because lots of times the DJ was listed first: Grandmaster Flash and the Furious Five, Afrika Bambaataa & Soulsonic Force, then Eric B.[4] and Rakim, DJ Jazzy Jeff and the Fresh Prince, and so on. That's why in so much of the first kinds of rap the rapper is bouncing around doing the call-and-response. His job was mostly to keep the crowd engaged. Rakim didn't do that. His voice wasn't cartoonish or overblown. It was this cold, icy, methodical thing that "interjects danger into even harmless phrases,"[5] and he wielded it with forethought and jurisprudence, delivering perfectly metered declarations that moved with the sort of velocity nobody had seen.

Rakim told a story to *Vibe* in 1997, explaining how the first time he recorded with Marley Marl and MC Shan they kept telling him he wasn't energetic enough, imploring him to stand up and be louder while he rapped because otherwise he wasn't going to get anyone's attention over the DJ. Rakim seemed to be the first rapper to realize he was in a recording booth.

Before MJ, there was a lot less money to spread around.
This is true of record contracts and deals, but also true of rap itself. Rakim introduced rap's materialism explicitly on "Paid in Full" (the song is called "Paid in Full"), but also on the album cover (he and Eric B. are both holding stacks of money and wearing large gold chains and medallions, and the background behind them is a screen of money, too, and also the album is called *Paid in Full*,[6] too). All of the complexities of the Five Percenter philosophy[7] hiding inside the song don't negate that it's a rap song about getting money.[8]

After MJ, everybody drafted super-athletes, because that seemed to really matter, but most of them couldn't fly and switch hands or drain a pull-up jumper, so they ended up just being all these physical beasts who didn't make for exciting basketball, but did get really physical on defense, which actually made the game less exciting for a while, with all the grabbing and shoving and in-your-face D that led to rule changes, zone D, and, over time, the three-point revolution that is taking over right now this very second. Everybody wanted to be the next Rakim. Nobody was. However, all of the attempts at replicating him or his style changed rap—but sometimes not in good ways.[9]

Before MJ, nobody really took working out seriously.
In this case, and this is truly how Rakim became a king, what he did was take the very basic rap style that all of the first rappers were doing—that hat-store style—and then placed it in a super-missile and fired it toward irrelevance. The sophisticated terms for what he did are internal rhyming schemes (where words within a sentence rhyme rather than just the words on the ends of sentences) and multisyllabic rhyming schemes (more than one syllable rhymed). He used these instead of the end rhyme style. But another way to describe this that is just as accurate is: He was making shit that could never be considered corny or unartistic.

Example: Run DMC rapped, "You can see a lot in this lifea pan / Like a bum eating out of a garbage can," on a song called "It's Like That" in 1983.

Example: Kurtis Blow rapped, "Basketball is my favorite sport / I like the way they dribble up and down the court," on a song called "Basketball" in 1984.

---

1. "I Need Love" was also well timed, at least as far as expanding the LL Cool J brand was concerned. You could probably even argue that his willingness to make it was the first indicator that he was going to eventually transition out of rap and into Hollywood with little trouble, though I'm not so sure how many people sit around and discuss such things.
2. Nobody has suffered more from being labeled "cool" early in their career than Samuel L. Jackson. The same thing happened to Common, though it's a less extreme case.
3. Hakeem Olajuwon and Sam Bowie.
4. Eric B. was an especially talented DJ. There are parts across *Paid in Full* where he fills in empty space with mixing and scratching, and it lives as its own thing. He also helped popularize sampling multiple records at once, as well as concentrating a song's efforts around drums rather than making them a supplement. All that is to say he did some very impactful things and was still relegated to an existence in this chapter found mostly in the footnotes, because that's just how massive Rakim's presence is in rap.
5. Nelson George, *Village Voice*, 1987.
6. Eric B. speculated that the album, which cumulatively took about a week to record, cost possibly less than $5,000 to put together.
7. Rakim is a member of the Five Percent Nation. They are "an American organization founded in 1964 in the Harlem section of the borough of Manhattan, New York City, by a former member of the Nation of Islam." And "members of the group call themselves Allah's Five Percenters, which reflects the concept that ten percent of the people of the world know the truth of existence, and those elites and agents opt to keep eighty-five percent of the world in ignorance and under the controlling thumb; the remaining five percent are those who know the truth and are determined to enlighten the rest."
8. Sidebar: The first car Eric B. ever owned was a Rolls-Royce. He said he bought it because Rick James told him to.
9. I suppose if we were going to extend this metaphor, Young Thug would be the three-point revolution.

On "Paid in Full," Rakim said, "I used to roll up, this is a holdup, ain't nothin' funny / Stop smiling, be still, don't nothing move but the money," and all of the lithospheric plates on earth shattered into a trillion pieces and everyone died wow you're a ghost right now R.I.P. you.

On "My Melody," he said, "I take seven emcees, put 'em in a line / And add seven more brothers who think they can rhyme / Well, it'll take seven more before I go for mine / Now that's twenty-one emcees ate up at the same time," and oh wow your spirit was just raised from the netherworld you're no longer dead wow welcome back your family is going to be so happy.

Nobody had ever done anything like that, said anything like that, the way that Rakim rhymed. He took it seriously. He rapped seriously.[10] He was an orator, and he was so utterly skilled that he was able to rap in this supreme way without spreading his personality all over the track, which is what people who weren't even talented enough to do what he was doing were unable to avoid when they came along later.[11] This is no hyperbole and no half-truth: All of every style of rapping that has occurred since 1987 and will ever occur can be traced back to when Eric B. and Rakim released *Paid in Full*.

---

10. A good peek into the way Rakim's brain works: While talking to *Vibe* in 1997, he spoke briefly about how his father's passing affected him. He said, "I had on Miles Davis's *Tutu* and Bob James's "Nautilus." I ain't play nothin' else for, like, a month. The textures of those records—that's the state of mind I wanted to be in." I read that quote several times, over and over again, and each time I did, the word "textures" just got bigger and bigger.

11. Jay Z, Nas, Biggie, Wu-Tang, so on.

REBUTTAL: "9MM GOES BANG" BOOGIE DOWN PRODUCTIONS

The author, while deft with his pen, is only partially correct. "Paid in Full" is indeed a noble jam rich with that rolling beat, Rakim's sing-song flow, and the best culinary couplet involving "fish, which is my favorite dish" this side of Three 6 Mafia's "We eat so many shrimp / I got iodine poisoning." But Shea ultimately stumbles when it comes to '87. That year, and much of '88, was all about Boogie Down Productions' "9mm Goes Bang" and the album on which it appeared, *Criminal Minded*. Long before KRS-One's self-righteous teacher-poet pose grew tired, *Criminal Minded* tore through the country one B-Boy cassette at a time. In the St. Louis record store where as a youth I stocked a massive hip-hop tape wall, *Criminal Minded* was everywhere. We sold thousands of copies of that, *Paid in Full, How You Like Me Now,* and *Yo! Bum Rush the Show*. For a lot of us, it was the year that changed hip-hop. BDP's wicked, proto-gangsta, first-person-shooter narrative "9mm," part of the lone album-length collaboration between KRS-One and the late DJ Scott La Rock, is raw and scary. Where producers Eric B. and the Bomb Squad were crafting layered tracks that took full potential of sampling technology, "9mm" is menacingly simple, a bullet of a track. Skeletal snare snaps echo, a basic melody circles, gunshots ring.

—RANDALL ROBERTS

PAID IN FULL

 "THINKING OF A MASTER PLAN" (1:08)

"'CAUSE AIN'T NOTHING BUT SWEAT INSIDE MY HAND" (1:20)

"I USED TO ROLL UP, THIS IS A HOLD UP, AIN'T NOTHING FUNNY" (1:42)

"I NEED MONEY, I USED TO BE A STICK-UP KID" (1:32)

"IF I STRIVE THEN MAYBE I'LL STAY ALIVE" (1:53)

"FEELING OUT OF PLACE 'CAUSE, MAN DO I MISS…" (2:00)

 "BUT NOW I LEARNED TO EARN 'CAUSE I'M RIGHTEOUS" (1:46)

"FISH, WHICH IS MY FAVORITE DISH" (2:07)

"HIT THE STUDIO, 'CAUSE I'M PAID IN FULL" (2:21)

"'CAUSE I DON'T LIKE TO DREAM ABOUT GETTING PAID" (2:11)

 DECLARATIVE

 DESCRIPTIVE

 GET MONEY

 INTROSPECTIVE

 HOPEFUL

 OBSERVATIONAL

EXAMINING

Straight

Outta

Compton

—

N.W.A

WHAT THIS SONG IS ABOUT

It's about where three guys are coming from and how they feel about things and the crimes they either have already committed or will commit if they feel they have adequate reason to do so.

• •

WHY IT'S IMPORTANT

It's the song that introduced America to N.W.A, but more specifically: It's the song that introduced America to gangsta rap.

Widely regarded as the greatest year in rap, 1988 saw albums from Public Enemy, Ice-T, MC Lyte, Big Daddy Kane, Eric B. and Rakim, Biz Markie, DJ Jazzy Jeff and the Fresh Prince,[1] Slick Rick, the Jungle Brothers, Run-DMC, Boogie Down Productions, EPMD, and more, and more, and more. What's more: None of it was empty space. Each of them seemed to be marking something historical.

Public Enemy's *It Takes a Nation of Millions to Hold Us Back* is one of rap's most influential records, and when *Rolling Stone* wrote about it they said Chuck D "didn't invent righteous belligerence, but he certainly got it on MTV," and that's just about the best way to talk about the album, too. DJ Jazzy Jeff and the Fresh Prince's *He's the DJ, I'm the Rapper* helped frame up the walls that "wholesome rap" would eventually live safely inside of. Eric B. and Rakim's *Follow the Leader* set Rakim on the path to become the first (and probably only) person to perfect rapping as a skill. EPMD's *Strictly Business* all but copyrighted building tracks up from funk samples. MC Lyte's *Lyte as a Rock* proved women were as capable as the men (and in a lot of cases more capable than the men). More and more and more.

And there, louder than all of them, more confrontational than all of them, more controversial than all of them—there was N.W.A.

◆

N.W.A was a gangsta rap group from Compton, California. They had a few different line-ups, but the strongest version was the too-brief period when it was Ice Cube, Eazy-E, MC Ren, DJ Yella, and Dr. Dre. That's the core group behind *Straight Outta Compton*, which

has become the most impactful album within the gangsta rap subgenre. N.W.A was substantial for a handful of reasons, but they all wiggle back to the same premise: They were the first rap group that America actively tried to ignore, and then eventually tried to stop.

They were railed on by politicians and members of the media. They were blocked from the radio and TV and banned from performing in certain cities. They were just too crude, too aggressive, too mean; these were the main complaints, at least. Even the cover of *Straight Outta Compton*, which was a photo of the group's members gathered around looking down directly into the camera very much in a manner that seemed to represent that they were either going to shoot you (Eazy-E is aiming a revolver[2]) or had already shot you, was scary. And so they were bottlenecked.

The most famous example: In 1989, Milt Ahlerich, then an assistant director in the FBI, sent a letter to Priority Records, the label that was distributing *Straight Outta Compton*. He admonished them for doing so, saying that "Fuck Tha Police," the album's supercharged second song, was promoting violence against law enforcement officers. These actions, of course, all had the opposite effect of what was intended. The album's popularity only grew [3]

Straight Outta Compton was a rough-cut job—recording took six weeks and it was done on a budget of approximately $8,000—but that only seemed to confirm the rawness of the group. In less than two months, the album sold more than five hundred thousand copies, later topping the three-million-copies-sold mark following the buzz of media talking about how nobody should be talking about the group. It was the first time in history an album had gone platinum without being played on the radio.

In 1990, Ice-T was on *The Oprah Winfrey Show*. That particular episode was about censorship in music, and the panel was Ice-T; music critic Nelson George; Tipper Gore, who cofounded the Parents Music Resource Center, which aimed to put parental advisory stickers on music they deemed objectionable; a

writer from the *Washington Post* named Juan Williams; Rabbi Abraham Cooper of the Simon Wiesenthal Center, who was there to talk about the defamation of Jewish people by musicians and the silence that came from record labels afterward; and Jello Biafra, a former lead singer of the punk rock band the Dead Kennedys, who'd been taken to court because of complaints about the DKs' music by the PMRC. In the closing moments of the show, when things were properly exciting and people were talking over one another, Ice-T raised his voice a little louder than most and declared that he could neatly sum up the entire situation. Everyone went quiet to listen to him.

"The real problem here with the one side versus the other is not that my homeboys are hearing [this music]," he began. "If only my friends were hearing these records, nobody'd care. It's that [affluent] kids are buying more rap records than our kids. And the white kids now from suburbia are listening to N.W.A and the parents don't know what to do about it. If only the brothers in the neighborhood listened to it, nobody'd care. It's rock and roll going into suburbia and it's getting to *his* kid," he said, pointing at a white man in the audience who earlier on had talked about the threat of rap music.

Straight Outta Compton was not the first gangsta rap record. But it was the one that fully bent the trajectory toward reporting the dejection and desolation of the inner cities of the country. And that meant it was no longer just for those populations anymore. *Straight Outta Compton* popularized gangsta rap in America. Ice-T advanced what Schoolly D had done and made gangsta rap a recognizable genre. N.W.A advanced what Ice-T had done and made it a threatening one.

◆

N.W.A was always a very serious group, or at least that's what they purported to be. But there were certainly moments where their villainy contained at least a hint of goofiness to it. Sometimes it was sly, sometimes it was overt.

Example: The song "Fat Girl" is all about an overweight girl falling for Eazy-E. The two best lines: When she meets him and

---

1. The DJ Jazzy Jeff and the Fresh Prince album was called *He's the DJ, I'm the Rapper*. It was amazing. There was a song on it called "A Nightmare on My Street" and it was about Freddy Krueger from *A Nightmare on Elm Street* and that was the first time in my life pop culture had been folded over onto itself for me. Also, there was a song on there called "Parents Just Don't Understand," and I will always care about it deeply because in the second verse Fresh Prince says the word "hell," and when I would rap along my parents would let me say it, and it really made me feel powerful. In that particular case, I suppose parents *did* understand.

2. This is a bigger deal than it seems. The year before, Boogie Down Productions' *Criminal Minded* became the first rap album to show a gun on the cover.

3. Also, both Dr. Dre and Ice Cube poked the FBI with sticks about it in songs afterward. (It might be more appropriate to say they poked them with dicks, as both Dre and Cube told the FBI to get off each one's respective penis.)

he raps, "She gave the grin, I showed the frown / And with a bear hug picked me off the ground." And when he tries to run away from her and she follows, so he raps, "She kept on coming because of addiction / Legs on fire because of friction." The song ends with him shooting her with a harpoon, which is not a thing that I recommend.

Another example: When they appeared on *Arsenio Hall*[4] in 1990 and Eazy-E spent the whole interview wearing a hockey mask and loosened straitjacket and cleaning his fingernails with a knife while whispering things to MC Ren.

Sometimes N.W.A was ultra scary. Sometimes they were ultra not.

◆

Eazy-E was the most compelling figure in N.W.A.[5] He was a short, loud, cartoonishly gangster former drug dealer with a voice that chirped in your ear like a very belligerent small bird. But he was not the best rapper in N.W.A. That was Ice Cube.

Ice Cube raps first on "Straight Outta Compton." He has the best verse of the three (all three are good, his is just the best).

He talks about being crazy. His measurement is, he is as crazy as a "motherfucker," as it were, and I didn't check but that's probably not the term a psychiatrist would use professionally to describe someone, even if that someone was, in fact, as crazy as a motherfucker.

He talks about shooting people, specifically with a sawed-off shotgun, which is somehow more intimidating than shooting

people with basically any other gun. The only real exception would be an AK-47, an assault rifle especially popular with rappers and also members of the militia. Of course, later in his verse on "Straight Outta Compton" he talks about using one of those to shoot people, too, so I mean, I guess Ice Cube's always been good at establishing and advancing his brand.

He talks about beating people up daily, weekly, monthly, yearly, and I very much have to respect his dedication to punching people.

And he talks about cooking his enemies in a pot of gumbo. I'm almost certain he means this metaphorically, but he was one of the most menacing figures in rap for many years, so there's a slight possibility he meant it literally.[6]

In 2014, Ice Cube was on *Sesame Street*. It was a two-minute segment where he did magic tricks while explaining to Elmo what the word "astounding" means. "Astounding is when something is soooo amazing, it catches you by surprise," Cube said, wearing a long-sleeve, nonthreatening aqua-blue button-down shirt, shortly before making a baby dinosaur appear from a top hat.

I wish there was a way that 1988 Ice Cube could be introduced to 2014 Ice Cube. He would be as astounded as a motherfucker.

---

4. The best part of researching for this book was that it gave me a reason to watch about twenty different episodes of *The Arsenio Hall Show*. I can't think of a better argument for becoming a writer.

5. A neat thing: Eazy-E's most iconic song, "Boyz-n-the Hood," was originally made for a New York duo named HBO. Ice Cube had written it and Dr. Dre had produced the instrumental. HBO passed on it, though. Eazy decided to record the song himself because he'd already paid for the studio time where HBO was supposed to record. The whole situation would seem to be a metaphor for his whole existence.

6. I don't want to know what human gumbo tastes like, but I also don't not want to know what human gumbo tastes like, if that makes any sense.

REBUTTAL: "CHILDREN'S STORY" SLICK RICK

This ain't funny so don't ya dare laugh: The most important rap song of 1988 was Slick Rick's "Children's Story." What could be better than a chilling fable about crime and poverty delivered by an eye-patch-wearing Aesop with a British accent over a nursery-rhyme piano beat? Nuffin'—nuffin' is cooler than that. Slick Rick the Ruler is the only one who could possibly put even a mild hurt on N.W.A. "Children's Story" wasn't

the first storytelling rap, but it's the first iconic one, and the one whose skeleton is always the easiest to see in the storytelling songs that have come after. (For obvious examples, see Mos Def's version and Snoop's "G Bedtime Stories.") Don't fight the Ruler—without him, without "Children's Story," none of this would even exist.

—MOLLY LAMBERT

N.W.A

Swear [F...] Words

Number of times each swear word is used on *Straight Outta Compton*

FUCK	134
MOTHERFUCKER	73
BITCH	54
SHIT	5?
ASS	45
NIGGA	12
DICK	9
HO	4
PUSSY	3
GODDAMN	3
BULLSHIT	1
HOOKER	1
PRICK	1
DYKE	1
SLUT	1
BALLS	1
CUM	1
FAG	1

1989

FIGHT
THE
POWER

Public Enemy

WHAT THIS SONG IS ABOUT

It's about fighting the power, and while "the power" is never specifically identified, we all understand it to mean anyone or anything in power who is wielding it unjustly.

WHY IT'S IMPORTANT

It gave a voice to the underrepresented, and positioned Public Enemy as the greatest political rap group of all time.

Public Enemy's first album, *Yo! Bum Rush the Show*, came out in 1987, and almost immediately their thematic presentation of black militancy was invigorating and exciting. By their second album, *It Takes a Nation of Millions to Hold Us Back*, they'd created a new style of song production that was super innovative and mesmerizing. It was this beautiful texture of samples woven together and looped 'round and 'round and 'round, sped up just enough to feel even more frenetic.[1] It was really remarkable, and a thing that, save Bambaataa (see page 22) and maybe a pinch of others, only the production duo the Bomb Squad was doing back then.

But Public Enemy was also philosophically overpowering. They rapped about impeaching the president ("Rebel Without a Pause"), the inevitability of time spent in incarceration for black men ("Bring the Noise"), metaphorically lynching critics ("Don't Believe the Hype"), things like that. These were timely and important discussions—this was near the end of the '80s, so there were of course racial tensions in the country,[2] and there was also a general lack of black civil rights leadership—but Public Enemy was also seen as hyper-threatening, and, more troublesome to their purpose, hyper-exclusive.

"Fight the Power" carried the same fury as the seven singles they'd released before then, but it was also wider, more inclusive, and that made it more impactful. Public Enemy had always been expert hostage takers, particularly as policy and pathology related to

blacks, but "Fight the Power" encouraged active participation from *all* listeners who felt listless, not just all *black* listeners who felt listless. It was the perfect measure of anger and insight, and in 1989, that's exactly what rap music needed to be.

◆

In 1995, my friend Miguel and I had gone to the movies. We hadn't gone with our parents because we were old enough to go alone (I was fourteen, he was fifteen). And we hadn't gone with any girls because we didn't want to pay for any girls' tickets, but also because I'd not grown into my head yet so my body + head looked very much like a Blow Pop, and girls like Blow Pop the candy but not Blow Pop the human. So we were there at the movies on our own (hopefully watching something sophisticated like *Sense and Sensibility* or even something hip like *Kids*, but probably watching *A Goofy Movie* or *Ace Ventura: When Nature Calls*[3]).

After the movie let out, Miguel and I started walking the quarter mile or so back to the mall, which was where our ride was going to pick us up. To get there, you had to cross through the parking lot of this semi-populated business strip. As we walked, these two kids came into view. Miguel, unprovoked, hollered at them, because that's the type of person he was.[4] They turned back toward us, seemed to say something but it was inaudible, then turned back around and kept walking. Miguel became incensed. "Come on," he barked, and then he sprinted off after them. I blindly followed behind him, because that's the type of person I was.

When we got there, when we were close enough that we could see their eyes, Miguel shouted, "What the fuck? You want some shit?" And before anyone could say anything, he punched Guy A in the head. Me and Guy B, we just stood there. Miguel leaned back, punched Guy B, then turned back to Guy A. I was like, *Oh, okay, I guess we're just fighting these strangers now*, and

then tried to pretend like I knew what I was doing.[5] This was a fight, but only in a loose application of the word. Miguel was the only one to get any actual shots in. Guy A just sort of rolled around hoping to avoid catastrophe, and me and Guy B mostly just hugged each other very aggressively for a bit. After, say, somewhere between about twenty-five seconds and two hours, someone came out saying something about the police and so we all separated, them running one way and us the other.

When we got a ways away, I asked, "What the hell, man? What just happened?"

Miguel: "They called us some *maricóns*."[6]

Me: "No they didn't."

Miguel: "I heard 'em."

Me: "Those white guys definitely did not call us *maricóns*."

Miguel: "It doesn't matter. We were gonna fight them anyway."

And then I don't know if he actually paused for a second or if I just began inserting it later when retelling the story, but he paused for a second and then he finished his thought: "They were white."

I don't think the world ever looked quite the same again, even if I didn't realize that for several more years.

I grew up on the southwest side of San Antonio, Texas, which is just a different way of saying that I grew up in an aquarium full of Mexicans. All I'd ever really known was Mexican people and Mexican culture. As far as I knew, the whole world looked like my neighborhood. I mean, I knew there were other races, but I'd never really given them any more thought than a regular young person would, and I'd certainly never had them presented to me as threats before, which is definitely how Miguel saw things at that moment.

I didn't know I wasn't supposed to trust white people or black people or anybody who wasn't Mexican, which was, essentially, what Miguel was fighting for. I'm saying, Miguel stole

---

1. In "Up from the Underground," an episode of the documentary series The History of Rock 'n' Roll, Chuck D explained, "Most rap records at the time had a BPM of 98 BPM. Our stuff was around 109."
2. In a survey conducted in 1987 by the New York Times, 64 percent of the people polled felt race relations between blacks and whites had either not improved or worsened since 1977.
3. Very underrated.
4. "Angry," if you're looking for a term.
5. Watching a lot of karate movies, it turns out, is not the same as actually learning karate.
6. Maricón is the Spanish version of the very first homophobic slur you think of.
7. The saddest thing of my whole life is that my sons will never make or receive a phone call on the house phone. Do you even know how many girls I sang R&B songs to while sitting at the kitchen table on the house phone?
8. Probably: "Um, it's about these black guys, and one of them has some shoes, and this other guy has a radio. The guy from commercials with Michael Jordan is in it. There are some other guys who make pizza. The guy with the radio gets killed. It's crazy."

one of my Sega Genesis games after we'd already been friends for a couple months. By my knowledge, he was likely the least trustworthy person in that fight.

But what he said—or at least the general ideology that was there after you scraped off the ignorance—stuck to my chest. It crawled inside my rib cage and lived there. Race is a real thing, he accidentally explained to me. *You are not the same as everyone.*

About a year or so later was the first time I watched Spike Lee's *Do the Right Thing*. I watched it in my bedroom. Public Enemy's "Fight the Power," which isn't necessarily exclusively about race but is inextricably tied to it, is played prominently throughout the movie. I'd heard the song before but never bothered to pay attention to it beyond how exciting it was to say "Niiiiiiiiiiiiiiineteen eighty-nine." But watching it as part of the movie, I remember hearing it, then thinking about Miguel. I called him on the house phone.[7]

I asked him if he'd ever seen the movie. He said no.

He asked me what it was about. I did a very bad job of explaining it.[8]

Then I asked him if he remembered the time we fought the two white kids in that parking lot. And he made fun of me for not knowing how to fight.

◆

HERE ARE SOME STATS ABOUT "FIGHT THE POWER" THAT ARE IMPRESSIVE, LISTED IN ORDER FROM MOST IMPRESSIVE TO LEAST IMPRESSIVE

"Fight the Power" was named one of the five hundred Songs That Shaped Rock and Roll by the Rock and Roll Hall of Fame. It was named the seventh best rap song of all time by *Rolling Stone*. It was named the greatest hip-hop song ever by VH1. It was named the best song of 1989 in the *Village Voice*'s annual Pazz & Jop critics poll. It was selected by *Time* as one of the one hundred most extraordinary songs of all time. It was named one of the best songs of the century by the Recording Industry Association of America. It takes samples from more than a

dozen different sources. It's been covered four times, and three of those times, one by Korn, one by Vanilla Ice, and one by the Barenaked Ladies, were, and remain to be, absolutely the worst things.

◆

OTHER PUBLIC ENEMY SONGS THAT ARE IMPORTANT, BUT NOT AS IMPORTANT, AS "FIGHT THE POWER"

1. **"Night of the Living Baseheads":** Don't do drugs because drugs are very bad.
2. **"Welcome to the Terrordome":** Every conversation about Public Enemy that lasts longer than two minutes will eventually approach their occasionally anti-Semitic rhetoric,

FIGHT THE POWER

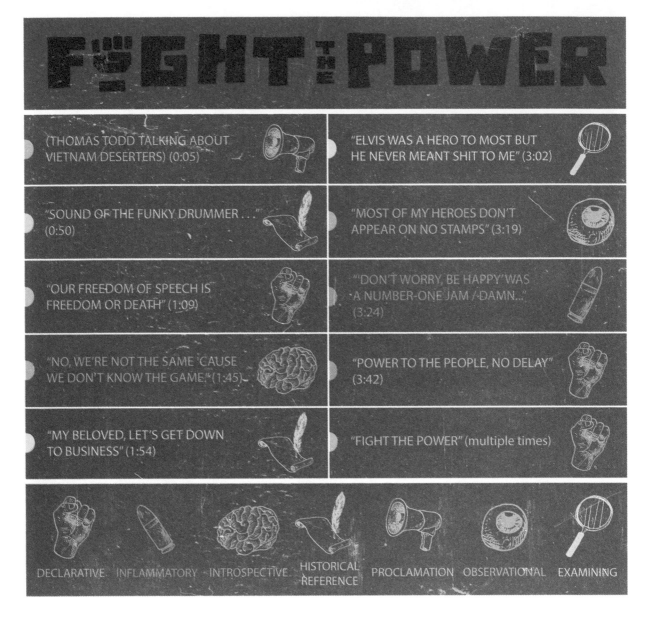

(THOMAS TODD TALKING ABOUT VIETNAM DESERTERS) (0:05)	"ELVIS WAS A HERO TO MOST BUT HE NEVER MEANT SHIT TO ME" (3:02)
"SOUND OF THE FUNKY DRUMMER . . ." (0:50)	"MOST OF MY HEROES DON'T APPEAR ON NO STAMPS" (3:19)
"OUR FREEDOM OF SPEECH IS FREEDOM OR DEATH" (1:09)	"'DON'T WORRY, BE HAPPY' WAS A NUMBER-ONE JAM / DAMN..." (3:24)
"NO, WE'RE NOT THE SAME 'CAUSE WE DON'T KNOW THE GAME." (1:45)	"POWER TO THE PEOPLE, NO DELAY" (3:42)
"MY BELOVED, LET'S GET DOWN TO BUSINESS" (1:54)	"FIGHT THE POWER" (multiple times)

DECLARATIVE   INFLAMMATORY   INTROSPECTIVE   HISTORICAL REFERENCE   PROCLAMATION   OBSERVATIONAL   EXAMINING

anti-gay rhetoric, or even their anti-women (quiet) rhetoric. This was the most famous version of low-key anti-Semitism, where Chuck howls, "Crucifixion ain't no fiction / So-called chosen frozen / Apology made to whoever pleases / Still they got me like Jesus." Important for a different reason than the rest, I suppose.

3. **"911 Is a Joke":** But not if you're white, I hear.

4. **"Burn Hollywood Burn":** Chuck D, Ice Cube,[9] and Big Daddy Kane all take swipes at Hollywood. The best part of the video: when they cut to clips of the three of them in a theater watching very racist old movie clips. Chuck D is the best.

5. **"Pollywanacraka":** Public Enemy titled a song about black men and black women dating out of their race "Pollywanacraka." That's just the most amazing thing.

6. **"Black Steel in the Hour of Chaos":** Opening lines: "I got a letter from the government the other day / I opened and read it / It said they were suckers." I have not received this letter but I would very much like to.

7. **"By the Time I Get to Arizona":** Arizona didn't officially recognize the MLK holiday until 1999. You gotta get your shit together, Arizona.[10]

8. **"Rebel Without a Pause":** The Bomb Squad did a lot of

amazing things while producing songs for Public Enemy, but maybe none of them were as blindingly and obviously perfect as the winding/screaming horn here.[11]

♦

MORE IMPORTANT THINGS ABOUT "FIGHT THE POWER"

Chuck D's voice is amazing. It's superheroic. It sounds like it's two miles wide. It sounds like God made a mistake because nobody should have a voice like Chuck D's rap voice. That's important.

Spike Lee asked Public Enemy to make "Fight the Power" for his movie *Do the Right Thing*. If he doesn't call them to do that, does "Fight the Power" ever get made? And if the answer is no, then is he granted lifetime immunity for all the ridiculous outfits he wears to Knicks games? Can we forgive him for *Girl 6*? CAN WE FORGIVE HIM FOR *OLDBOY*? That's important.

What's more: During Public Enemy's induction into the Rock and Roll Hall of Fame, Spike, the first person up introducing them, made mention of how the first song Public Enemy submitted wasn't quite what he was looking for. "Fight the Power" was their second try. WHAT HAPPENED TO THE FIRST VERSION? THAT'S IMPORTANT.

Chuck D was a revolutionary when people were kind of looking for one, even if he didn't want to be. That's important.

More on that: In his book *Can't Stop Won't Stop*, Jeff Chang writes about how Spike viewed Chuck, saying that the video Spike shot for "Fight the Power," which looked less like a rap video and more like a presidential rally, helped to "firmly establish Chuck's cultural authority." That's important.

More from Chang:[12] "Lee placed Chuck in the streets amidst the likenesses of Black power fighters, one new Black icon anointing another." That's important, too.

Semi-related to all of this: The last time I talked to Miguel was either right before or right after I graduated from college. I'd come home to visit my parents and had run into him at a store. I said hello and he said hello back, and we talked for a moment, and it was only a little bit weird. Then I asked him what he did and it got very weird, or great, depending on how you feel about prostitutes. He told me he was a pimp, and I laughed a little, and then I realized he was serious and I stopped laughing. I said something like, "Oh, that's pretty cool," because, I mean, what's the right thing to say in that moment? Last I heard he'd just gotten out of prison. I still don't know how to fight.

---

9. In Chuck Klosterman's 2013 book, *I Wear the Black Hat*, he begins an essay about N.W.A with the following quote from Ice Cube from a long-ago interview Cube did: "Chuck D gets involved in all that black stuff. We [N.W.A] don't. Fuck that black power shit: We don't give a fuck."
10. South Carolina was the very last state in the country to recognize MLK as a holiday. Up until 2000, residents were allowed to choose between celebrating MLK Day or one of three Confederate holidays. That's not a joke. That's 100 percent not a joke.
11. It's similar to the one on "Don't Believe the Hype" but somehow even more powerful.
12. Buy *Can't Stop Won't Stop*.

———————————————— REBUTTAL: "WILD THING" TONE LOC ————————————————

To stage a successful full-scale cultural offensive, you need at least one goofball. Actually, you usually need several: The ratio, roughly, is at least two goofballs to every one stern revolutionary. Anthony Smith, a.k.a. Tone Loc, came with a weighty past—he ran with the notorious Rollin 60s Crips, and once showed up to a studio session with a fresh bullet in his shoulder. But on record, he was a dry, witty, face-pulling libertine, and he is one of hip-hop history's most pivotal goofballs. "Wild Thing" was written largely by Young MC, with Fab Five Freddy in mind. But the song is irretrievably Loc's. The video, in which Loc mugs and leers at a row of alien-looking women imported from Robert Palmer's "Addicted to Love" video, while sporting a Delicious Vinyl shirt, gave Loc, and Delicious Vinyl, a fat, crossover hit. "Wild Thing" was the first rap song, after the Fresh Prince's "Parents Just Don't Understand," that I knew every word to at my elementary school lunch table. The album it came from, *Lōc-ed After Dark*, became the first album by a black rap artist to reach number one on the *Billboard* pop albums chart. Pretty revolutionary.

—JAYSON GREENE

BONITA APPLEBUM

—

A Tribe Called Quest

"Bonita Applebum" is the best rap love song that's ever been. It's also the first one that stepped away from the loverman style, and it did it without trying, and that's the only way that this sort of monumental change happens. Here are a dozen other rap love songs that are very good but not the best:

- **"I Need Love," LL Cool J (1987):** This wasn't the first rap love song, but it was the first one where the protagonist was actively trying to be cool, which felt cosmic at the time.
- **"Passin' Me By," The Pharcyde (1993):** This is a straight-line descendant of "Bonita Applebum," though it replaces Q-Tip's charismatic begging with self-deprecating measures ("Damn, I wish I wasn't such a wimp"). Each time one of the guys is rapping in the video he's shown hanging upside down, and that's (probably) supposed to be the literal version of the phrase "head over heels in love," because rappers from the late '80s and early '90s really loved hats and they also really loved being literal.
- **"Me & My Bitch," The Notorious B.I.G. (1994):** In the second line of the song Biggie says, "You look so good, huh, I'll suck on your daddy's dick," and when I heard it the first time I remember rewinding it to see if I'd heard it correctly, playing it again, confirming what I'd heard, then thinking, *Wow, that must really be an attractive woman.*[1]
- **"I'll Be There for You/You're All I Need to Get By," Method Man, featuring Mary J. Blige[2] (1995):** This is the second-best rap love song. Method Man is rugged but secretly smooth, and Mary J. Blige is smooth but secretly rugged, so they play against each other with zero of the stitches showing. It ends with the line "We above all that romance crap, just show your love," and that's the most sophisticated, simple understanding of love that I think I've ever heard.
- **"Renee," Lost Boyz (1996):** Here's a line: "She told me what she was in school for / She wants to be a lawyer / In other words, shorty studies law." I suppose rappers in the mid-'90s liked to be literal, too.

• **"Brown Skin Lady," Mos Def and Talib Kweli (1998):** I need for Macklemore and Mac Miller to record a cover of this called "White Skin Lady," if they're really real.

• **"How's It Goin' Down," DMX, featuring Faith Evans (1998):** This is for sure the only love song to start with a phone conversation where a man aggressively accuses his girlfriend of performing oral sex on another man. Here's a thing I can tell you: DMX is terrifying. Were I ever to find myself in the position of suspecting my wife of having fellated him, then that's just some shit that happened, is all that is.

• **"What You Want," Mase, featuring Total (1998):** Mase was perfect.

• **"You Got Me," The Roots, featuring Erykah Badu and Eve (1999):** True question: Has any artist ever been as offensively underappreciated as Erykah Badu?

• **"The Light," Common (2000):** I met Common while I was covering a concert in 2008. I was supposed to talk to him about the show and the album he had coming out. But I'd watched *Wanted*, like, probably two weeks before that night. So instead I asked him what it was like to get shot in the head by James McAvoy, because that's what happens to him in the movie. He looked at me, paused for a moment, then said, "It was fine. The bullets weren't real." He's very charming in real life.

• **"21 Questions," 50 Cent, featuring Nate Dogg (2003):** This is a song where 50 Cent asks his girlfriend a string of questions in an attempt to decipher whether she really loves him or only loves him because he is famous and rich. One of the first questions he asks is if she'd do a drive-by with him. It sounds ridiculous, but I don't know that I can immediately think of three things a woman could do to prove that she loves me more than actively participating in a drive-by with me.

◆

Let me tell you quickly about the beginning of Native Tongues, because that's important, but let me be as cursory as possible without being detrimental:

Native Tongues was a loose co-op of rap groups who shared ideas and opinions and, eventually, sounds and philosophies. It began with a New York trio called the Jungle Brothers, then from there it absorbed De La Soul, and then from there A Tribe Called Quest, and then Native Tongues was finally formed. This was in the late '80s to early '90s—Jungle Brothers released their first album in 1988, De La released their first in 1989, and ATCQ released their first in 1990. ATCQ became the biggest and the most influential of the three, though it's difficult to say they'd have even been anything were it not for the first two. Native Tongues eventually reached nearly twenty members, though at no time was it more exciting or inventive than in those first three years, when Jungle, De La, and Tribe combined to counterbalance the seismic anger of N.W.A and the political charge of Public Enemy, by putting something out there for consumption that was on the opposite end of the emotion/ideology scale.

◆

"Bonita Applebum" was the second single from ATCQ's *People's Instinctive Travels and the Paths of Rhythm*, and that was the first album to heavily incorporate jazz samples, which accidentally significantly altered rap's arc. Their commercial ascension wasn't immediate (*People's* didn't go gold until six years later, a result of retroactive buys that followed the success of their other albums), but their creative ascension was. ATCQ became pioneering rap stars who did not present themselves as rap stars, and so that's how "Bonita Applebum" became transcendent: because it felt 100 percent natural and agendaless, like the whole rest of that album.

The first rap love song was the Sugarhill Gang's "The Lover in You," and that was barely even a rap song. Mostly, it was an R&B and funk disco amalgamation. It's very strange to listen to now, and I imagine the only reason it wasn't all the way strange when they released it in 1982 was because everything was kind of strange in 1982. Still, "The Lover in You" was noticeably different than the Sugarhill Gang's other songs—sweeter, more lush, somehow softer—and that's the sort of pattern loverman rap followed; rappers or rap groups had their songs and then they had the songs they made for girls. Whodini's "One Love" was like that. Slick Rick's "Teenage Love" was, too.

LL Cool J's "I Need Love" appeared to attempt to sidestep the blatancy of the formula. It was sleek and (tried to be) perceptive, and also kinetic and impassioned, and that was close enough to the rest of his music that it didn't glow neon pink like

---

1. The line is a callback to Richard Pryor's "The Wino and the Junkie" bit. Richard Pryor was legit a gift.
2. Several others have songs called "You're All I Need," too. Mötley Crüe's is the best (or the worst, depending on your gauge). It's about a man who loves a woman desperately but she doesn't love him back, so he murders her. Vince Neil sings, "Killing you helped me keep you at home / I got so much to learn about love in this world," and yes, I would agree that he has a fair amount to learn about love (mostly, "Don't stab to death the person you love" seems like a good start).

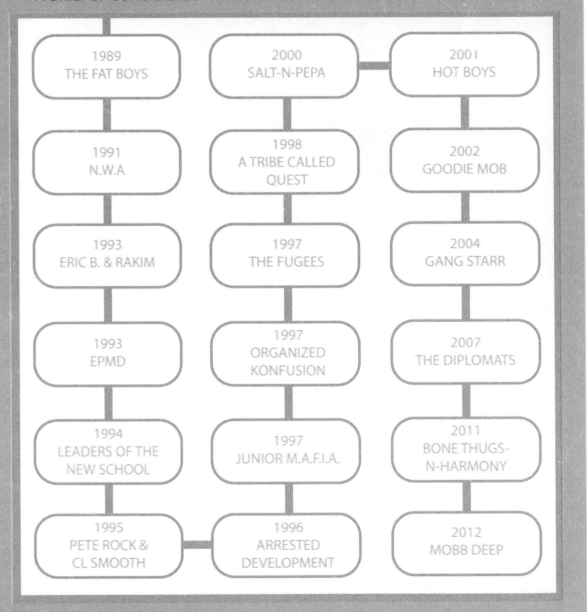

CAN I QUIT IT?

A BRIEFLY CONSIDERED TIMELINE OF 18 RAP GROUPS THAT BROKE UP

1989 THE FAT BOYS	2000 SALT-N-PEPA	2001 HOT BOYS
1991 N.W.A	1998 A TRIBE CALLED QUEST	2002 GOODIE MOB
1993 ERIC B. & RAKIM	1997 THE FUGEES	2004 GANG STARR
1993 EPMD	1997 ORGANIZED KONFUSION	2007 THE DIPLOMATS
1994 LEADERS OF THE NEW SCHOOL	1997 JUNIOR M.A.F.I.A.	2011 BONE THUGS-N-HARMONY
1995 PETE ROCK & CL SMOOTH	1996 ARRESTED DEVELOPMENT	2012 MOBB DEEP

the rap love songs that had come before it. But it was still him rapping for girls and not for just all humans, and you could tell because its seams still showed. He said things like "I hear my conscience call / Telling me I need a girl who's as sweet as a dove / For the first time in my life, I see I need love," and the only time a guy calls a dove "a dove" is when he's talking at a girl, not to her, or I guess also if he's John Woo, because John Woo fucking loves doves.

"Bonita Applebum" was not built like that, or at least not built with that purpose. It wasn't an addition to the group's persona, it was an extension of it.

In 2011, there was a documentary about ATCQ called *Beats, Rhymes & Life: The Travels of A Tribe Called Quest*.[3] I mention it because there are two things that Jarobi White, one of the group's original members, said that fit here.

1. While talking about the origination of the group, White said, "We were just trying to be fly. And make music. And be musicians. Be like Stevie and Marvin and Prince. Thelonious Monk and Mingus and Charlie Parker. We were trying to be those people." Two things: First, rap had already been popular for a decade, but he didn't mention any rappers. Even if it was a conscious decision, it's still telling. And second, the first three names, those are all guys who had essentially mastered singing to women without placating them or appearing condescending to anyone older than fourteen years old, which is exactly one of the things "Bonita Applebum" was able to do.

2. While talking about the dissolution of the group, which was primarily what the documentary was about, White attributed a portion of it to their general music-making process becoming outmoded. He said, "The largest difference between the hip-hop game now and back then is that people make songs. They don't do projects anymore. We did projects. Notice I didn't even say album, we did projects."

"Bonita Applebum" is a beautiful song. The way it saunters around in a circle, bordered in by that sitar's "bohm-bohm-bodhm-bodhm." The way Q-Tip talk-raps across the face of it at just the right speed, pursuing Bonita in a completely likable way, the way a guy who is very handsome and very good at making bedroom eyes does.[4] The way the beat falls out of the bottom of the song every so often, like when he says, "I like to tell ya things some brothers don't" after he prefaces it with "I like to kiss ya where some brothers won't."[5] The way the whole thing is built out like a scene from a movie. It's beautiful. All of it. It stands tall all by itself. But it also serves a bigger purpose than itself: It fits within the construct of the album seamlessly, blended in between a track called "Public Enemy" and "Can I Kick It?" and is usually close to over before you even realize it's playing, just like A Tribe Called Quest.

---

3. It was directed by Michael Rapaport, who has the unique distinction of having played a neo-Nazi who shot Tyra Banks in a movie once.

4. I am not very good at making bedroom eyes. My bedroom eyes look less like bedroom eyes and more like pre-pink-eye eyes.

5. The general assumption here has always been that Q-Tip is talking about Bonita's V, but a theory online asserting that he's talking about her B has gained popularity. I feel weird writing about this, but I also feel good writing about it because part of being a writer is trying to get people to think a thought they've never thought before, and Q-Tip eating a butt is probably up there.

REBUTTAL: "AROUND THE WAY GIRL" LL COOL J

I suppose you could have learned to kick game from "Bonita Applebum"—meager, mealymouthed, soothing "Bonita Applebum" for your meager, mealymouthed, soothing game. Good luck, guy. I'll take "Around the Way Girl" any day, and twice on days my hair looks good. This is peak pickup, talk so slick you could ice-skate on it. No one before or since has exuded the raw vigor of LL Cool J in this era, a cocksure lip-licker with a cherubic glow. And don't forget the song's video, a platform for James Todd Smith's Handycam perversions, teeming with graffiti'd clothing and doorknocker earrings and a swarm of handsy dancers with pendulum hips that wouldn't quit. Lisa, Angela, Pamela, Renée—I still love you. I'll never not love you.

—JON CARAMANICA

1991

MIND PLAYING TRICKS ON ME

on ME

—

Geto Boys

WHAT THIS SONG IS ABOUT

It's directly about paranoia, delusions, hallucinations, and schizophrenia, and it's indirectly a commentary on the structures that cause those psychoses.

WHY IT'S IMPORTANT

It's the best examination of mental health as it relates to rap. It was also the first.

In 1990, Geffen Records, the company that was going to distribute a remix album by the Geto Boys called *The Geto Boys*, decided the night before the album's release not to go forward. This is the explanation Bryn Bridenthal, who was the vice president of media and artist relations at the time, offered:

"I've never been frightened by a record before in my life, but for me the graphic details of the violence were really frightening. Finally we decided that we have a right as a private company to decide what kind of materials we want to be associated with, and this one, we decided, went too far."

His comments were somewhat focused on a song called "Assassins," which opens with Johnny C, a producer and ex–Geto Boys member, rapping about beating and then shooting a schoolteacher. But mostly he was talking about "Mind of a Lunatic," a six-verse nightmare starring Bushwick Bill, Scarface, and Willie D, the lineup that would eventually constitute the most substantial version of the Geto Boys.[1] Bushwick Bill, a Jamaican-born dwarf, is the first performer, and he lasts exactly three lines into the song before he's committed murder. The violence somehow increases exponentially from there; he spends the whole second verse talking about raping a woman he's seen through a window, murdering her, raping her corpse, then drawing his name on the wall and calling the cops on himself. And beyond just stating the particulars of his crimes, he presents them through some truly startling imagery ("She begged me not to kill her, I gave her a rose / Then slit her throat, and watched her shake till her eyes closed"). I can't say that I agree with Geffen's decision, but this was near the same time 2 Live Crew had been charged for indecency while performing some of their songs in a nightclub in Florida and Judas Priest had been blamed for the suicides of two men by their families, so I suppose I understand.

This whole thing—the controversy, Geffen Records refusing to release the album because the lyrics were so violent and threatening—was the first real exposure to the Geto Boys people outside of Houston had had en masse.

"Mind of a Lunatic" is a precursor to "Mind Playing Tricks on Me." It spoke of the particular psychoses each member of the group was dealing with, though it did so at the expense of sophistication. "Mind Playing Tricks on Me" angled the general idea of "Lunatic" (we are crazy motherfuckers) inward, making it less about the consequences they ascribed to insanity and more about the process of feeling insane. The self-examination was markedly more powerful than the hyperbolized violence. It was a completely new thing, and it was real and serious and real serious. It seemed unlikely that Bushwick Bill would ever have sex with a dead body and then draw his name across the wall for the police like he said he had on "Lunatic," but it was completely plausible he'd gotten into a fight with a person who didn't even really exist like he said he had on "Tricks."

◆

"Mind Playing Tricks on Me" samples a song called "Hung Up on My Baby" by Isaac Hayes. The song appeared in a 1974 movie called *Three Tough Guys* starring Isaac Hayes. There are a lot of very amazing parts in *Three Tough Guys*. One of them is a funeral scene for a pimp named Gator. As the funeral guests take turns viewing Gator's corpse, other pimps, the most spectacular of whom is a white man with pork chop sideburns wearing a jeweled eye patch and a bedazzled suit jacket, sprinkle cocaine on him. I suspect this is a way that pimps pay respect at funerals, but I'm not sure. I've never (knowingly) spent time with a pimp, so I've never been privy to that information. I Googled "Sprinkle Cocaine on Dead Bodies" but didn't find anything pimp-related.[2] One of the other pimps who shows up to the funeral—a rival pimp in a garish white fur coat holding a cane and a purple hat—spits on Gator. So I guess the good thing about inviting pimps to your funeral is that they will be dressed interestingly, but the bad thing is that they will either sprinkle cocaine on you or spit on you.

◆

OTHER SONGS THAT HAVE DEALT WITH BEING A NUT, DIRECTLY AND INDIRECTLY

"Somebody's Watching Me," Rockwell (1983): He thought people were watching him.

"The City Sleeps," MC 900 Ft Jesus (1991): This one is a first-person narrative told from the perspective of an arsonist. It's not that good of a song, but I'm including it here because we don't have any other arsonists on this list and I don't want to appear like I'm anti-arsonist, which I assume will be a hot topic by the time this book comes out because people get mad about everything so it's only a matter of time before someone starts talking about arson discrimination.

"Insane in the Brain," Cypress Hill (1993): It kind of feels like Cypress Hill maybe didn't know exactly what a membrane was.

"Suicidal Thoughts," The Notorious B.I.G. (1994): Biggie calls Puff, admits he is overcome with stress and is considering suicide, then talks himself into doing it.

"1-800-Suicide," Gravediggaz (1994): 1994 was a big year for suicide, I guess. (One of the ways the Gravediggaz say you can tell you're an insane person is if you're Sicilian but you don't like lasagna or the guy who delivers your pizza. I can't vouch for the authenticity of either of those claims.)

"Beautiful Night," Prince Paul (1996): This is Prince Paul in a therapy session admitting to sexually assaulting a girl, killing a bartender who refused to serve him because he was black, then killing a guy at a Beastie Boys concert who'd bumped into him, then sexually assaulting another girl with his friends. Paul is so casual in his description of the depravity that he somehow makes it enjoyable to hum "It's a beautiful night for a date rape" with the background singers.[3]

"Kim," Eminem (2000): By 2014, Eminem's turmoil had grown a chore to absorb. (It was uncreatively offensive, and that's way worse than being morally offensive.) But when he let it bloom fully in 2000 on "Kim," it was completely transfixing.

"Dance with the Devil," Immortal Technique (2001): The protagonist violently assaults and rapes a stranger with some other men as a way to prove he's tough and respectable. Turns out, the stranger was his mother. He kills himself by jumping off

---

1. The group was created by Rap-A-Lot founder J. Prince in 1986. He moved pieces in and out as he saw fit. J. Prince is as mysterious a figure in rap as has ever been. He's basically the southern version of Suge Knight, except he's about three times as small and ten times as smart. His most famous dodgery: In 1999, California congresswoman Maxine Waters and Attorney General Janet Reno made a federal drug investigation targeting Prince and Rap-A-Lot Records disappear.

2. Looking up information about pimps on Google is, were I to guess, not a very pimp-like thing to do. I can't imagine pimps use Google. Maybe they use Siri? They're probably very disrespectful to her. Siri doesn't deserve that.

3. FYI, it's enjoyable to hum, not to actually do.

the roof of a building after he sees who it was. The guys shoot the mom in the head. Eesh.

"Lemonade," Gucci Mane (2009): It doesn't deal with any slivers of mental instability directly, but, I'm saying, you kind of have to be crazy to make a song as perfect as "Lemonade" is.

"Devil's Son," Big L (2010): Spends the whole song talking about being the son of the devil. When he said, "When I was in preschool I beat a kid to death with a wooden block," that's when I knew I wasn't putting my kids in day care.

"What's Yo Psycho?" Tech N9ne, featuring Brotha Lynch Hung and Sundae (2010): The three take turns explaining their psychoses. In the third verse, Sundae explains, "It's dollars over dick," and that's the best summation of a business plan I ever heard.

◆

The most famous picture of Scarface + Bushwick Bill + Willie D is the one used for the cover of 1991's *We Can't Be Stopped*, where Willie D and Scarface are pushing Bushwick Bill down a hospital hallway on a gurney.

Willie D, the most physically imposing member of the group, looks slightly angry but also slightly urgent. Scarface, who later would explain that he had no interest in capturing that particular moment on film and certainly no interest in using it for the cover of their album,[4] looks discordant and disgusted. And Bushwick, who is sitting on the gurney pretending to be on a cell phone,[5] looks like he's just been shot in the face at close range with a .22-caliber derringer, because he had just been shot in the face at close range with a .22-caliber derringer. His right eye, which

hours earlier had been fine, is completely destroyed. It looks like a very unappetizing strawberry. This is the explanation Bushwick gave of the incident in a radio interview later that year:

"When I came home, my girl was asleep so I woke her up and told her to kill me 'cause I wanted to die. I was tired of my life. She said she didn't want to shoot me, so I shot at her and my [adopted] three-month-old baby first. Then I tried to beat her head in with a vacuum cleaner, but I missed. Then I gave her the gun and jumped at her. When I [saw] her hand reach the trigger I put my eye in front of it."

He did an interview on the Howard Stern show later, and his story expanded a bit. He explained that the reason he wanted to die was financially inspired: His mother needed money to pay a medical bill, he said, and, despite the success of "Mind Playing Tricks on Me," he didn't have the $500 she needed him to give her. He'd hoped that by getting himself killed she'd benefit from his life insurance policy. But he didn't want to be at odds with God, and suicide, he'd learned in Bible school, is an unpardonable sin, so he got very drunk and tried to goad his then-girlfriend into murdering him. He also explained to Stern that he'd picked up the baby and threatened to throw him out a window if she didn't shoot him.[6]

This is the sort of thinking that surrounded the Geto Boys when they were at their apex, and that's how you end up with a song as masterfully conspired and executed as "Mind Playing Tricks on Me," the finest examination of one's own psychoses in rap, and in all of music, really.

---

4. In 2010, Scarface told *Vibe*, "We took that picture at the actual hospital where Bill was at. And Chief, who was our manager at the time, said, 'Bill, take the eye patch down.' And I was like, 'Awww, fuck! Man, this is some bullshit.'"
5. I don't know who he could possibly be calling. Who do you call when your suicide-by-girlfriend attempt goes haywire? Your mom? The devil? Mark-Paul Gosselaar?
6. He tells this whole story in song on "Ever So Clear" from his 1992 album, *Little Big Man*. On a different song on the album he talks about how whenever he cuts off anyone's arms he donates the fingers to charity. Bushwick Bill is not that great at charity.

REBUTTAL: "CHECK THE RHIME" A TRIBE CALLED QUEST

The impact of the lead single from Tribe's sophomore album on the musical landscape of 1991 cannot be overstated. Within seconds, the listener is captivated by an Average White Band horn sample that is nothing short of iconic. The nostalgia of Q-Tip's opening lines is palpable. You may have never set foot in Queens, New York, but this song took your spirit there, right to Linden Boulevard, where you found yourself in that cipher with Tip and Phife as they ran through their fly routine. The subject matter, ranging from witty boasts to sage advice aimed at their aspirational peers, continues to resonate decades later. You would be hard-pressed to find an MC living who hasn't been counseled on Industry Rule #4080. The single would herald the arrival of *The Low End Theory*, a masterpiece of an album that would solidify ATCQ as one of the defining groups of a generation.

—eskay

MIND PLAYING TRICKS ON ME

"I sit alone in my four-cornered room staring at candles" (0:04)

"When I awake I don't see the motherfucker" (0:39)

"Candlesticks in the dark, visions of bodies being burned" (0:12)

"Every twenty seconds got me peeping out my window" (0:54)

"I feel I'm being tailed by the same sucker's headlights" (1:29)

"It's fucked up when your mind's playing tricks on ya" (1:05)

"I take my boys everywhere I go because I'm paranoid" (2:04)

"I keep looking over my shoulder and peeping around corners" (2:10)

"Day by day it's more impossible to cope" (2:30)

"This year Halloween fell on a weekend" (3:41)

"Now I'm feeling lonely" (3:21)

"Having fatal thoughts of suicide" (2:52)

"Then he disappeared and my boys disappeared too" (4:19)

"My hands were all bloody, from punching on the concrete" (4:29)

 INTROSPECTIVE

 POWERFUL

 EXAMINING

 INSIGHTFUL

 DESCRIPTIVE

 THRILLING

 PSYCHOLOGICAL

1992

NUTHIN'

BUT A

'G' THANG

—

DR. DRE

FEATURING

SNOOP DOGG

WHAT THIS SONG IS ABOUT

How Dr. Dre, Snoop Dogg, and the Death Row label (and all of the West Coast, really) were unfadeable, so please don't try to fade them.

· ·

WHY IT'S IMPORTANT

It was the origination of G-Funk, a strand of rap that was so intoxicating, it made California the most important place in rap, and that was the first time it had ever not been New York.

Dr. Dre does not seem like that fun of a guy to hang out with, and that's surprising considering that just about every other fake doctor seems like a real hoot to be around. There's Dr. J and Dr. Dunkenstein, and those guys are great if you're super into basketball. There's Dr Pepper, and he's great if you're super into sugary, carbonated, brown drinks. There's Aretha Franklin's Dr. Feelgood and Kiss's Dr. Love. There's Dr. Evil, whose name makes him seem bad but he's actually good. There's Doc Hudson from *Cars* and Doc McStuffins from lunch boxes, and she's just adorable. Dr. Phil is nerdy but also very positive, and very positive people are dope. Dr. Quinn, Medicine Woman would of course be a handy friend. Dr. Moreau seems a bit weird, but he'd make for good conversation, I'm sure.[1] So it's surprising Dr. Dre seems so wooden.

It's also surprising because the greatest thing he ever did musically was take the gangsta rap of the late '80s and early '90s, a subgenre of music that was poignant and powerful and provocative but also very heavy, and turn it into the grandest, most accessible party of all.

He did so in the third quarter of 1992 with "Nuthin' but a 'G' Thang," the first single from his debut album, *The Chronic,* the flagship track that introduced America to the G-Funk sound. G-Funk took the stripped-down, broken-glass harshness of gangsta rap and framed it with the liveliness and conviviality of '70s Afrocentric funk. The synthesis created a fusion that managed to be as modern and inventive as it was instinctual. Suddenly, the aggressively autobiographical lyricism that hard-core rap was driven by, and what ultimately earned it a very specific kind of popularity, was surrounded by a warmth

and lushness that was very nearly universal. And everything changed.

Dr. Dre seems very smart. It only requires a tiny amount of transitive logic to firm up that conclusion, what with him having been born into the breach of poverty and now being worth somewhere near a billion dollars.[2]

And he also seems very astute. In each of the interviews he's given that are available for viewing/reading on the Internet, his answers are almost exclusively insightful and forthright, even when he seems less than enthusiastic about responding to any particular question (him being asked about his oft-delayed *Detox* album, mostly).

But just not very fun.[3]

◆

SIX SONGS FROM 1992 THAT WERE NOT THE MOST IMPORTANT RAP SONG OF 1992

"Tennessee," Arrested Development: "Tennessee" was the Grammy-winning single from the group's debut album, *3 Years, 5 Months and 2 Days in the Life Of . . .* , which eventually went platinum four times over. When I was a kid there was this guy named Tennessee who lived in our neighborhood. He was INCREDIBLE at dominoes. There's a thing in *Teen Wolf* where the coach tells his basketball players that one of life's rules is to never play cards with a person named after a city, and I definitely think an addendum should be added about playing dominoes with guys named after states. He was unbelievable. He looked at the domino board like how Russell Crowe looked at the walls of newspapers and magazine clippings in *A Beautiful Mind*.

"Rump Shaker," Wreckx-N-Effect: This one wasn't ever really a contender, but the video for it featured a woman wearing a bikini fake-playing a saxophone on the beach, and that's just an image that we should talk about any chance that we get. We can never, ever let time push it into oblivion.

"Jump Around," House of Pain: Matched in its iconography only by its own annoyingness.

"Don't Sweat the Technique," Eric B. and Rakim: A big, lovably lyrical record that has aged into importance. "Don't Sweat the Technique" came in just as rap's (and New York's) boom-bap era was fading and its gangsta rap era was dominating. It was basically a basketball player hitting a seventy-foot buzzer beater at the end of the game with his team down ten points; impressive, but couldn't change the eventuality of the loss.

"Ain't 2 Proud 2 Beg," TLC: "Ain't 2 Proud 2 Beg" was the first single from TLC, and let me be clear when I say none of the women I have ever known begged to have sex with me. I had a girl beg me for $300 once, but that's not the same.

"Jump," Kris Kross: "Jump" is the single greatest rap song by children wearing their clothes backward to heavily promote aerobic activity that's ever been. It sold more than two million copies in 1992 alone, remarkable considering that neither Kris nor Kross was older than fourteen when it was released.

◆

This is Ice Cube on the opening verse of "Straight Outta Compton" (see page 64), the first single from N.W.A's seminal gangsta rap album *Straight Outta Compton*:

(see page 64)

---

1. The very first question I would ask Dr. Moreau is "Why did you ruin Val Kilmer's career?" and the second question would be "Can you please combine a tiger and an elephant? Because a tigerphant sounds like the most incredible thing."
2. In comparison, I was born into the lower middle class, and have only managed to not fall backward into total squalor.
3. While I was working on this book, I watched hours of video of Dr. Dre lasering through interviews from the past twenty years. I'd begun to assume he was some sort of advanced automaton. However, in a sit-down interview he did for Peter Spirer's 1997 documentary *Rhyme & Reason*, Dre responded to a question about what the then-future of hip-hop held by making an impromptu Dionne Warwick joke. I suppose this doesn't exclude the possibility of him being an A.I. machine, but it at least proves that he's trying to approximate a version of a human emotion, and that's close enough. The machines will provide a recognizable future for us. We can't ask for much more.
4. The verse is aimed at Eazy-E, whom Dr. Dre had decided to war against following his acrimonious departure from N.W.A.
5. Murdering a human is not that great of a thing to do, FYI. We should be clear on that.
6. Snoop actually wrote all of the verses on "Nuthin' but a 'G' Thang." He was twenty-one years old.
7. Snoop's own first album, *Doggystyle*, produced by Dr. Dre the year following *The Chronic*, went quadruple platinum.
8. The other ten: Afrika Bambaataa's "Planet Rock"; Arrested Development's "Tennessee"; the Beastie Boys' "(You Gotta) Fight for Your Right (to Party!)"; De La Soul's "Me, Myself and I"; Grandmaster Flash and the Furious Five's "The Message"; LL Cool J's "Mama Said Knock You Out"; Public Enemy's "Fight the Power"; Run-DMC's "Walk This Way"; the Sugarhill Gang's "Rapper's Delight"; U.T.F.O.'s "Roxanne, Roxanne."
9. "Nuthin' but a 'G' Thang" somehow lost to the Digable Planets' "Rebirth of Slick," a loss as unforgettable as Metallica losing Best Metal Performance to Jethro Tull at the 1988 Grammys, Elvis Costello losing Best New Artist to A Taste of Honey at the 1979 Grammys, and me losing at four square in 1991 to a kid that I'm pretty sure was blind.
10. Dr. Dre's first Grammy win came in the Best Rap Performance category for "Let Me Ride," also from *The Chronic*.

"When I'm called off, I got a sawed-off / Squeeze the trigger and bodies are hauled off / You too, boy, if you fuck with me / The police are gonna have to come and get me / Off yo ass, that's how I'm going out / For the punk motherfuckers that's showing out."

This is Dr. Dre on the first verse of "Fuck wit Dre Day (And Everybody'sCelebratin')," [4] a celebrated track from *The Chronic*:

"Used to be my homie, used to be my ace / Now I wanna slap the taste out ya mouth / Make ya bow down to the Row / Fuckin' me, now I'm fuckin' you, little ho / Oh, don't think I forgot, let you slide / Let me ride, just another homicide."

Both very plainly state that murdering a human is not altogether that big of a deal [5] or even really more than an arm's length of a departure from daily activities. But the first set of lyrics brought forth a locust swarm of criticism that carried with it radio bans, political protests, and more, while the second, its threats elbowed up next to an interpolation of Funkadelic's gorgeous "(Not Just) Knee Deep," inspired high fives and a very strong urge to stand near a barbecue pit.

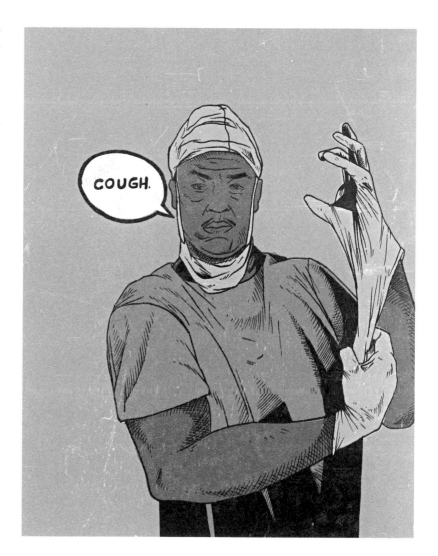

G-Funk's tranquility was instantly undeniable. "Nuthin' but a 'G' Thang" soared, doing lots of very impressive, very easy-to-categorize-and-celebrate things. It:

- Helped push *The Chronic* to triple platinum.
- Prominently featured a then-mostly-unknown Snoop,[6] helping to propel him into the rap stratosphere.[7]
- Reached number two on *Billboard*'s Hot 100 chart (it was on the chart for twenty-seven weeks) and number one on their Hot R&B/Hip-Hop chart.

- Was one of only eleven rap songs[8] selected by the Rock and Roll Hall of Fame as one of the "500 Songs That Shaped Rock and Roll."
- Was picked by *XXL* magazine as the best rap song of the '90s.
- Was picked by *Rolling Stone* as one of the 500 Greatest Songs of All Time, as well as one of the 50 Greatest Hip-Hop Songs of All Time.
- Was picked by VH1 as the third-best rap song of all time.
- Was named the third-best song of the '90s by *Pitchfork*.
- Earned a Grammy nomination for Best Rap Performance by a Duo or Group,[9] the first nod from them of Dr. Dre's career.[10]

"Nuthin' but a 'G' Thang" was transformative, and something larger than the song itself.

It took the anti-romance of gangsterdom and made it endearing, charming, almost insouciant. Even its video, which was built around a Day in the Life of Snoop and Dre premise, was perfect.[11] People pined for the lifestyle. Being a gangster wasn't dangerous, it was dope and wonderful, because you got to ride around in nice cars under ambient lighting from a perfectly warm sun and play volleyball with large-breasted women and pour beer on people if they weren't accommodating.

"Nuthin' but a 'G' Thang" did that. It took the nation's most aggressive, most polarizing movement, a movement born of racism and classism and confrontation and unrest and riots, and made it, quite simply, fun, which made it ubiquitous, which made it unavoidable.

Perhaps the most insightful measure of the influence of "Nuthin' but a 'G' Thang" came from Public Enemy's Chuck D, a forefather of gangsta rap. "We made records during the crack era, where everything was hyped up, sped up and zoned out," he told *Rolling Stone* in 2012. "Dre came with '"G" Thang' and slowed the whole genre down. He took hip-hop from the crack era to the weed era."

In 1997's documentary *Rhyme & Reason*, Dre talked about how *The Chronic* never wandered away from its Compton birthplace despite him having vacation homes in basically every affluent suburb in the country, saying:

"Gangstas like the album because the album is gangsta."

It was.

G-Funk bent the path of rap for all time, momentarily wrestling it away from New York's iron grip for the first time, and it did so without lending any of its power to anyone outside of the culture.

"Nuthin' but a 'G' Thang" did that, too, did that first, and did that best.

---

11. Dr. Dre directed the video "Nuthin' but a 'G' Thang." He did so over two days and with a budget of only $70K.

REBUTTAL: "SO WHAT'CHA WANT" BEASTIE BOYS

"Nuthin' but a 'G' Thang" is the monolith: preternaturally smooth, endlessly effortless, and quite possibly the closest that radio rap will ever get to platonic perfection. Which is exactly what makes "So What'cha Want," in all its scratchy, tossed-off brilliance, *way more important.* Note the three bored goofballs in the video, traipsing through the woods, nowhere in particular to go; note them mean-mugging, pogo-spazzing, balancing stalks of grass on their lips for that impromptu mustache effect. "Y'all suckers write me checks and then they bounce / So I reach into my pocket for the fresh amount"—is Mike D attempting to brag about being the victim of check fraud?!

This is a distillation of life lived not as we *want* it to be at its best—there are no fridges full of 40s here, oh no—but as it actually is at its best: fragmented, trifling, loose, confused, hopped-up, and hopeful. "Well just plug me in just like I was Eddie Harris / You're eating crazy cheese like you would think I'm from Paris"—does Ad-Rock believe he'd be made to feel comfortable by a host who confused Ad-Rock's origins to be Parisian in nature by said host eating a lot of *cheese* around him?!

According to the liner notes on the Beastie Boys' anthology *The Sounds of Science*, "So What'cha Want" was an afterthought: After two years of slaving over the rest of *Check Your Head*, the dudes tossed this one together at the last minute. Which of course they did. This is "true art" of the throwaway variety. If they'd thought too much about it, it wouldn't be this kind of classic.

—AMOS BARSHAD

NUTHIN BUT A 'G' THANG

THINGS IT'S LIKE	THINGS IT'S NOT LIKE
THIS THAT THIS AND UH	DOOR BEAR CELL PHONE

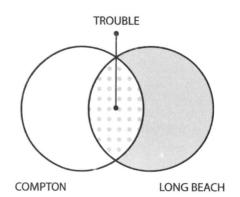

TROUBLE

COMPTON   LONG BEACH

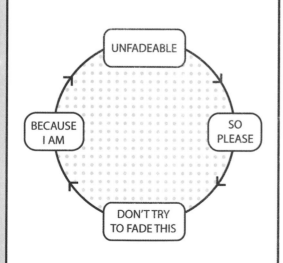

UNFADEABLE

BECAUSE I AM

SO PLEASE

DON'T TRY TO FADE THIS

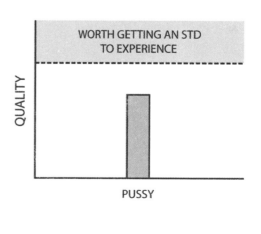

WORTH GETTING AN STD TO EXPERIENCE

QUALITY

PUSSY

C.R.E.A.M.
—
WU-TANG CLAN

The density and complexity of the universe Wu-Tang Clan built for itself was, remains today, and will forever remain exhilarating, exhausting, and exhaustive. Here is an example, and I'm just going to wholesale paraphrase the beginning of a brilliant Wu-Tang article by Brandon Perkins[1] from a 2007 issue of *URB* magazine called "Widdling Down Infinity":

There were 9 members of the Wu-Tang Clan. The number 9, "according to Supreme Mathematics—a Five Percent philosophy and belief of the Wu, used to describe the Earth's mechanics," means "to bring into existence." Each of those 9 members has a heart and that heart has 4 chambers, and 9 x 4 = 36, which represents the number of levels of mastery and also the title of their album, *Enter the Wu-Tang (36 Chambers)*, but also 3 + 6 = 9, and we're right back to where we started. There are 108 pressure points on the human body, and 1 + 0 + 8 = 9, but, also, of those 108, exactly 36 of them are deadly, and the 9 members + the 36 deadly pressure points = 45, and 4 + 5 = 9, and we're right back to where we started again.

The article goes on like that for a couple thousand words, and it only ever really examines the mathematical segment of Wu-Tang's spectrum. There are more cosmological layers, as well as superhero fantasies, chess metaphors, crime boss aliases, a clothing brand, and more, and more, and more. You could fill a book—lots of books—with information about them. And they have.[2] But that's not this, of course. So here is a mostly linear Wu-Tang primer:

There are nine members[3] of the Wu-Tang Clan. Sometimes when people talk about them there are more members.[4] And sometimes when people talk about them there are fewer members.[5] They are most often linked to Staten Island, a New York City borough, though not all of the members are/were from there. (Staten Island = Shaolin, FYI.) Though not the singular founder, RZA is the leader of the group, and, in addition to establishing their creative arc, he also set in place a five-year business plan that guided their professional dealings (more on this later). Their first single, "Protect Ya Neck," was an underground hit, and probably the first truly transcendent song to exist beneath the top layer of rap, which, by 1992/3, had firmed itself as a legitimate (very profitable) genre. Their debut album, *Enter the Wu-Tang (36 Chambers)*, is an unmitigated classic, and a handful of equally impressive projects followed.[6] They are now regularly cited as the greatest, most influential rap group of all time. And now you know about one percent of the history of the Wu-Tang Clan.

◆

Where "Protect Ya Neck," recorded for a few hundred dollars and sold out the backs of vans, sought to introduce Wu-Tang Clan into the rap conversation—any rap conversation, really—"C.R.E.A.M.,"[7] the standout song from *Enter the Wu-Tang, (36 Chambers)*, announced them as torchbearers.

"C.R.E.A.M." was dusty and intimidating and raw and unflinching, just as the album was, and it framed a very bleak economic realism in a handmade collage of bizarro tinks and thumps. It was the inverse to what had been happening in rap on the West Coast for the two years prior,[8] both sonically (Dr. Dre's G-Funk creation was unhurried and loping and a reflection of its own coolness; Wu-Tang's lo-fi bombast was frenetic and intricate and introspective) and ideologically (the whole first verse of "Nuthin' but a 'G' Thang" is about how Dr. Dre is unfadeable so please don't try to fade him; the whole first verse of "C.R.E.A.M." is about all the small-scale crime Raekwon had committed, only to realize he'd not advanced his station in life). It was a change matched in measure only by what Public Enemy had done five years prior with *It Takes a Nation of Millions to Hold Us Back*, and it was invigorating.

G-Funk certainly didn't disappear (Snoop Dogg's *Doggystyle* was released the same month as *Enter the Wu-Tang*) but the next direction of rap's evolution had been made obvious.

◆

There are three eventualities that spiral back toward "C.R.E.A.M.," which also means they lead back to *Enter the Wu-Tang (36 Chambers)*, which really means they lead back to Wu-Tang as an entity:

1. New York: I would argue that the strongest year in all of rap was 1994 (and, in fact, that's exactly what happens in the next chapter). There were groundbreaking tapes from UGK (Port Arthur, Texas); Common (Chicago, Illinois); Bone Thugs-N-Harmony (Cleveland, Ohio); Outkast (Atlanta, Georgia); Master P (New Orleans, Louisiana); and on and on. But 1994, expansive as it was, belonged 100 percent to New York. Rap leaned all the way toward the right side that year. You have to attribute that to Biggie's "Juicy" and Nas's *Illmatic*, for sure. But you also have to attribute it to what the Wu-Tang Clan accomplished in 1993.

2. The Inspiration for Moguldom: Puff, Jay, Master P, 50, any other rap mogul you care to name—that level of entrepreneurship was created by RZA.[9] Here's a quote from his

---

1. Brandon Perkins actually assigned me my very first long-form profile for a print magazine. He sent me to the Warped Tour to hang out with a DJ I'd pretended to know about so he'd give me the assignment. It was pretty bad. I blinked a lot during the interview, I'm sure.

2. This is a *Ratatouille* reference, FYI, and I'm proud to say that this moment right here is the first time *Ratatouille* and the Wu-Tang Clan have lived this close together in literature.

3. RZA, GZA, Ghostface Killah, Inspectah Deck, U-God, Masta Killa, Method Man, Raekwon, and Ol' Dirty Bastard.

4. There are a healthy number of associated acts. The closest affiliate: Cappadonna. The most bizarre affiliate: a rapper named Christ Bearer. He was loosely connected to the Clan as part of a group of guys signed to the Wu-Tang company out of the West Coast in the early to mid-2000s. Nobody ever paid any attention to him until April of 2014 when he cut off his penis and jumped off the balcony of an apartment building in a suicide attempt.

5. Ol' Dirty Bastard died in 2004.

6. Specifically, but not limited to, Raekwon's *Only Built 4 Cuban Linx* and GZA's *Liquid Swords*.

7. To be thorough, "C.R.E.A.M." was not released as a single from *Enter the Wu-Tang (36 Chambers)* until the end of January 1994. HOWEVER, the actual album came out in November of 1993, so "C.R.E.A.M." was available for consumption in 1993 and that's why it landed here. Otherwise this chapter would have featured "Who Am I? (What's My Name?)" by Snoop.

8. It was also counterintuitive to the jazzy style many East Coast rappers had been adopting in the early '90s, and thank goodness for that.

9. RZA has made an almost unfathomable amount of good creative decisions. His one bad one: playing the Blind Master in *G.I. Joe: Retaliation*. That was like if you took all of Lil Wayne's everything from 2010 to 2014 and mushed it up into a few minutes.

book, *The Wu-Tang Manual*: "I told them, 'If y'all give me five years of your life, I promise you in five years I'm gonna take us to the top.' And so we gave each other our word. The Wu-Tang Clan was born." RZA's plan was actually super-involved. In those five years, along with the albums, he'd push to build the Wu-Tang "W" into broadband recognition status, including a proper Wu-Tang video game and clothing line in their portfolio. His most ingenious move, though: He arranged for the group to sign with an independent record label (Steve Rifkind's newly formed Loud Records) that offered a unique clause in the contract: While the group as a whole was exclusive to Loud Records, each member was allowed to secure a solo deal with a competing label. GZA signed with Geffen Records. Ghostface went with Sony. Method Man went with Def Jam. It was the first time anything like that had ever been pulled off. RZA viewed the Wu-Tang Clan as a wide-based corporation, and so he positioned them as such.

(Note: Wu-Tang released their second album, *Wu-Tang Forever*, right at the end of RZA's proposed five-year plan. It shipped more than four million copies in its first six months.)

3. Cheese Wagstaff: That's the name of the character Method Man played on HBO's *The Wire*, which I'm assuming you knew already because you paid money for this book and so that's probably the sort of thing you'd know. I still can't believe Cheese set up Prop Joe to be killed like that. I just really can't. I almost threw away all my Method Man CDs after watching that scene. Top seven deaths on *The Wire*, ranked by emotional distress caused: 7. Prop Joe; 6. Snoop; 5. Bodie; 4. D'Angelo; 3. Stringer; 2. Omar; 1. Wallace. Oh great, now I'm crying again.

◆

Ol' Dirty Bastard does not have a verse on "C.R.E.A.M." He represents the duality of it as well as any of the members of the Clan do, though, and he probably does so more than most, really.

During the State of the Union address in 1994, President Bill Clinton talked about a lot of things, as presidents tend to do during State of the Union addresses. Here's a thing he said

about government assistance: "We have to end welfare as a way of life and make it a path to independence and dignity." He said more, but that's a fine enough summation of his premise.

During 1995, Ol' Dirty Bastard, the most erratic and unpredictable member of the group, did a lot of crazy things, as bastards who are old and dirty tend to do.[10] Here's a thing he said about government assistance: "The people that wanna cut off the welfare, man, I think that's terrible. You know how hard it is for people to live without nothin'?" He said it during an interview with MTV. Everyone thought it was funny because it came after he'd ridden in a limousine with MTV to pick up the food stamps he'd been allotted that month by New York.

ODB had of course earned more than enough money to disqualify himself from aid—*Enter the Wu-Tang* sold more than a million copies, plus he'd been given a $45,000 advance from his record label, Elektra, for his own solo album.[11] But he'd not filed his taxes for the year yet, so the state was using his previous year's income reporting, so, in that particular moment, he was eligible. "I'm glad to get the food stamps. Why wouldn't you want to get free money? . . . You owe me forty acres and a mule, anyway."

---

10. In a separate interview with MTV, John Norris asked ODB if he was a fan of Drew Barrymore. ODB said he didn't know who she was, though he definitely used the F word in there. Norris told ODB that she was in *E.T.* ODB said yes, that he remembered, she was the little bald-headed girl who played E.T. HE THOUGHT E.T. WAS DREW BARRYMORE AS AN ALIEN. I love you and I miss you, ODB.

11. ODB used his welfare card as the cover art for his album. That's really why he invited MTV along with him that day.

C.R.E.A.M.

"I GREW UP ON THE CRIME SIDE, THE *NEW YORK TIMES* SIDE" (0:23)

"IT'S BEEN TWENTY-TWO LONG, HARD YEARS OF STILL STRUGGLING" (1:37)

"SO THEN WE MOVED TO SHAOLIN LAND" (0:31)

"A MAN WITH A DREAM WITH PLANS TO MAKE CREAM" (1:48)

"A YOUNG YOUTH, YO ROCKIN' THE GOLD TOOTH" (0:34)

"LIFE AS A SHORTY SHOULDN'T BE SO ROUGH" (2:05)

"STICKING UP WHITE BOYS IN BALL COURTS" (1:03)

"READY TO GIVE UP SO I SEEK THE OLD EARTH" (2:28)

"MY LIFE GOT NO BETTER, SAME DAMN 'LO SWEATER" (1:08)

"STRAY SHOTS, ALL ON THE BLOCK THAT STAYS HOT" (2:39)

 DECLARATIVE DESCRIPTIVE LIFESTYLE INTROSPECTIVE INSIGHTFUL GET MONEY AUTOBIOGRAPHICAL

REBUTTAL: "PASSIN' ME BY" THE PHARCYDE

Many great rap albums came out in 1993, by Wu-Tang, Snoop, Tupac, and more. For the average-Joe white dudes in a Washington, D.C., suburb, those records were great and all, but we really didn't *get* them. We *said* we did. But we didn't. High school kids don't really understand much and West Coast rap was definitely not something we got.

But outside that domain, that's where the Pharcyde's "Passin' Me By" was. It was different than most rap we were listening to. It was a rap song that anyone could identify with—any high school dude, that is (which I was). We wanted girls to like us. We struggled to get girls to like us. The Pharcyde got real with us and told us that it wasn't going to happen. "Damn, I wish I wasn't such a wimp," Fatlip exclaims in the third verse, followed by an exasperated "Damn." Damn, indeed.

The Pharcyde never had another hit like "Passin' Me By." Ironically, the world kept passin' them by. Maybe it's because most of us grew up and found out girls don't always have to pass you by. Maybe it's because we took their rhymes and turned them into a cautionary tale. Getting passed by sucks. But we knew what it felt like. Like all important music.

—MIKE AYERS

Juicy

The
Notorious
B.I.G.

Here are nineteen of the twenty best rap albums that came out in 1994, which is, in no
uncertain terms, one of the three best years in this history of hip-hop.[1] They are ranked
because only a human with a spine made of fiberglass would ever put together a list and
use a variation of the phrase "in no particular order":

20. Method Man, *Tical*

19. Various Artists, *Murder Was the Case:
The Soundtrack*

18. O.C., *Word . . . Life*

17. Pete Rock & C. L. Smooth, *The Main
Ingredient*

16. Eightball & MJG, *On the Outside
Looking In*

15. Warren G, *Regulate . . . G Funk Era*

14. Organized Konfusion, *Stress: The
Extinction Agenda*

13. The Roots, *Do You Want More?!!!??!*

12. Digable Planets, *Blowout Comb*

11. Jeru the Damaja, *The Sun Rises in
the East*

10. Various Artists, *Above the Rim*
soundtrack

9. Gang Starr, *Hard to Earn*

8. Da Brat, *Funkdafied*

7. UGK, *Super Tight*

6. Common, *Resurrection*

5. Bone Thugs-N-Harmony, *Creepin' on
ah Come up*

4. Outkast, *Southernplayalisticadillacmuzik*

3. Scarface, *The Diary*

2. Nas, *Illmatic*

One of two things just happened right now. You (a) appreciate Nas and respect Nas and understand that Nas's place in rap history is near the top but have never truly found his hyperaware ability to unpack a particular setting or situation especially compelling and so you read that *Illmatic* was the second-best album of 1994 and said, "Yup," because you knew what the first best album of 1994 was as soon as you started reading this book; or, you (b) are a very big Nas fan and so when you read that *Illmatic* was the second-best album of 1994, your eyeballs exploded in your skull, in which case I am sorry about your eyeballs and also, wow, congratulations on being able to read without eyeballs.

If you are in the first group, I am going to move on, because re-explaining something to you that you already understand is dumb. If you are in the second group, I am also going to move on because trying to convince a Nas fan that *Illmatic* is anything short of God's will is no different than trying to explain to a fish how to climb a tree, in that both would be neat to see but neither are very likely to happen. And so:

Here is the best album of 1994:

1. The Notorious B.I.G., *Ready to Die*

♦

Ready to Die was the Notorious B.I.G.'s proper debut, and the only album he put out while he was still alive. It was a master class in paranoia, depression, death contemplation, the unfamiliarity of legitimate success, and the intersection of all four of these things. It is regarded by some as a completely perfect recording. "Juicy" was the album's first single and its most important moment.[2]

"Juicy" did four things well:

"Juicy" was gorgeously produced, albeit (probably) unoriginally. The build and the tinks and the weightlessness and the every little detail. All golden. And also swiped. Poke[3] and Puff Daddy are credited with having produced "Juicy," sampling a track called "Juicy Fruit" by the funk/soul band Mtume. But producer Pete Rock has long asserted that he came up with the original version and that it was lifted from him. Still, even if that's not true, even if Rock is lying (which seems unlikely), San Francisco's Dre Dog released a song in 1993 called "The Ave." that also sliced out a sliver of "Juicy Fruit" and turned it into its foundation. The origination is murky but the point is not: The most famous version of the beat featured in "Juicy" was not the first iteration of it.

"Juicy" was eager. It was, in effect, the song that gave the Puff Daddy Rap Vehicle perpetual motion, the one that first fueled his Diddy Bop across history. Its success helped legitimize Bad Boy Records,[4] and it helped rocket Puff toward moguldom, and that was definitely not an accident.

"Juicy" was impeccably timed. Its most important immediate effect was that it counterbalanced Snoop's *Doggystyle*, which had arrived from California just ten months prior and obliterated everything. "Juicy" helped pin rap down again in New York for a little bit longer as the West Coast continued yanking it back across the country.

"Juicy" was nuanced/insightful/incisive/culturally perceptive in a manner that allowed it more wiggle room than fundamentally equally menacing tapes. It was an examination of the existence of the disenfranchised black man in America disguised as a pop-rap track for anybody with ears. You could argue that its top was the moment when hip-hop

---

1. The three best years in the history of rap for America are: 1988 (Public Enemy, *It Takes a Nation of Millions to Hold Us Back*; N.W.A, *Straight Outta Compton*; Run-DMC, *Tougher Than Leather*); 1993 (Snoop Dogg, *Doggystyle*; Wu-Tang Clan, *Enter the Wu-Tang (36 Chambers)*; A Tribe Called Quest, *Midnight Marauders*); and 1994 (The Notorious B.I.G., *Ready to Die*; Nas, *Illmatic*; Scarface, *The Diary*). The three best years in the history of rap for me are: 1992 (Wreckx-N-Effect release "Rump Shaker," and the video features an attractive woman pretending to play the saxophone on a beach, and that's the first time I'd ever seen that in my eleven years on earth); 1992 (while rapping his verse on "Rump Shaker," A-Plus compliments a woman on her body, then tells her he has an award for her, and then that award turns out to be his penis, and up until then I didn't know you could give your penis out as an award); and 1992 (I called into the radio station and asked them to play "Rump Shaker" and the DJ said okay and then a few minutes later they played it and I was like, "Wow, I just made thousands of people listen to 'Rump Shaker'").
2. Not its "best." Its best was "Big Poppa," a song so mind-bending that it almost became cool to be overweight.
3. Poke is part of a production team called the Trackmasters. They worked on a bunch of stuff in the '90s and 2000s, including but not limited to Nas's "If I Ruled the World" and Method Man and Mary J. Blige's "You're All I Need to Get By," maybe the best rap love song that's ever been.
4. Bad Boy Records was a brand-new label at the time. *Ready to Die* was its first album release, which is as good a start to something as anyone has ever had to anything. It eventually sold more than four million copies. Seventeen of Bad Boy's first twenty album releases achieved platinum sales, with Biggie's *Life After Death* selling more than ten million copies. Puff Daddy helped Black Rob sell a million copies. BLACK ROB. Puff was not dicking around.

sprinted out from the shadows of popular American culture, from its dirtiest and most threatening corners, and began absorbing all of its energies and dollars, shaping the schema into the earliest version of what we know it to be today.[5]

But here's what "Juicy" did that no other song like it had ever managed to do, and really what B.I.G. eventually proved he was going to do well on basically every song he ever recorded ever in his whole life ever: It took all of these very specific feelings and observations and thoughts he had and turned them into ideas that were very familiar and common. He pushed sentences out through that humidor he had for a voice box, floating those humid clouds of words that had just the right blend of plump confidence and plumper insecurity out into the atmosphere, and it emboldened you. You always knew exactly what Biggie was talking about, even if sometimes you didn't know *exaaaactly* what he was talking about.

When he talked about listening to *Rap Attack*, a radio program on New York's WBLS 107.5, on Saturdays; when he talked about having to eat sardines for dinner; when he expressed feelings of disbelief and self-doubt ("I never thought it could happen, this rapping stuff"); when he talked about the pivot his love life made after his name began to ring out ("Girls used to diss me / Now they write letters 'cuz they miss me") and the pivot his financial life made, too ("Birthdays was the worst days / Now we sip champagne when we thirsty"), you knew.

I understand what you're saying, Biggie. I feel it, too, Biggie. I am also nervous and happy and scared and excited and confounded by the complexities of life, Biggie. We are unified, Biggie. Everything is one, Biggie. Thank you, Biggie.

The only other song from 1994 that could've possibly stolen this spot on the list from "Juicy" was Nas's "N.Y. State of Mind," *Illmatic*'s fire-and-brimstone street sermon. And it is a technically amazing song. It's a sword slice right down the middle of your fucking chest. But Nas has mostly always been a selfish[6] genius.[7] He didn't share it with you on "N.Y. State of Mind," he just showed it to you. He brought you inside of his head to show you that he was a superhero. Biggie veered in the opposite direction. He opened your skull up and showed you that you weren't a superhero, but that he wasn't either, and that maybe nobody was, really. Nas was popular. Biggie was a populist. He brought you to him, and then he took you both into the cosmos.

That's the very best, most influential thing a rapper (or human) can do.

The shakings from "Juicy" will echo forever in the canon. It dwarfs everything else.

---

5. I wrote a little about this for Grantland in 2014.
6. This sounds more negative than it actually is.
7. (The above footnote absolutely shouldn't be necessary. But that's how wacko Nas fans are. They will read that sentence, A SENTENCE THAT REFERS TO HIM AS A GENIUS, and be mad that it didn't fellate him enough.)

REBUTTAL: "THUGGISH RUGGISH BONE" BONE THUGS-N-HARMONY

"Thuggish Ruggish Bone" is the most important rap song of 1994. It took the multisyllabic, tongue-twisting flow that had been a staple of the South and Midwest for years and changed it from a gimmick in the eyes of the hip-hop nation (back when the hip-hop nation still thought of itself in those terms) into a legitimate style and a cultural and commercial force.

In the proud tradition of Snoop's "Who Am I (What's My Name)?" and, later, Eminem's "My Name Is," "Thuggish Ruggish Bone" told you everything you needed to know in one song about a group you'd likely never heard of before. Like those records, the hook is built around the group's name (takeaway: the shit works), but "Thuggish Ruggish" goes one step further, winding down with Shatasha Williams singing all of BTNH's members' names and then shouting out the home market, Cleveland. Here was an entirely new sound by an entirely new act from an entirely new place, and after this one record, you wanted to know and hear a whole lot more. —**BENJAMIN MEADOWS-INGRAM**

TIMELINE: TUPAC ·AND· BIGGIE

1993: Tupac Shakur meets the Notorious B.I.G. while filming *Poetic Justice*. They become friends.

November 1994: Tupac gets shot outside of a recording studio in New York. He sees Biggie, Puffy, and Andre Harrell once he makes his way fully inside.

February 1995: Biggie releases "Who Shot Ya," a song that very much sounds like a jab at Tupac. Biggie explains that he'd written and recorded it months before Tupac's shooting.

October 1995: Tupac gets out of prison. He signs with Death Row, which had become a premier label behind Dr. Dre's *The Chronic* in 1992 and Snoop Dogg's *Doggystyle* in 1993.

August 1995: Suge Knight, CEO of Death Row, makes fun of Puff Daddy at the Source Awards for always showing up in his artists' videos.

April 1995: Tupac gives an interview to *Vibe* while in prison. He very strongly implies that Biggie, Puffy, and Harrell were responsible for the shooting.

March 1996: Tupac's entourage gets into a verbal altercation with Biggie's entourage at the Soul Train Awards. A gun is pulled, though no shots are fired.

May 1996: Tupac releases "2 of Amerikaz Most Wanted," featuring Snoop Dogg. In the video's opening, a person imitating Puffy has a meeting with a person imitating Biggie. They talk about how they'll be the main figures once Tupac is gone.

March 1997: Biggie is shot and killed while in the passenger seat of a car in Los Angeles. (The song playing while he was shot was "Going Back to Cali," which starts with a conversation between him and Puffy where Biggie implies that maybe that's not the best idea. Shortly after his burial, the bulletproof car he'd ordered arrives at his house.)

June 1996: Tupac releases "Hit 'Em Up," a massively crushing diss song aimed at Biggie's forehead.

October 1996: Tupac is shot and killed in Las Vegas following a boxing match between Mike Tyson and Bruce Seldon. Nobody is ever charged, let alone convicted.

1995

Dear Mama

—

Tupac

There's a great scene early in *Juice*, Ernest R. Dickerson's brilliant 1992 film about a series of events that unfold among four friends in Harlem.[1] It takes place in an arcade run by Samuel L. Jackson, who is playing a bit part in the movie, because he has at least a bit part in every movie if you pay close enough attention.

In the scene, Tupac, playing a character named Bishop who eventually evolves into the movie's terrifying antagonist, glides up next to Steel, one of *Juice*'s other stars (he's played by Jermaine "Huggy" Hopkins, whom you might more readily remember as "the fat kid" from *Lean on Me*). He challenges Steel to a game of Street Fighter.

Steel, effervescent and confident, laughs. "What makes you think you can beat me? Tell me. I'd like to know." Shakur's bright eyes briefly lose all of their light. He pauses just long enough to establish that his mood is flickering. "Two reasons," he begins. "For one, if I lose, I'ma beat that ass. For two, if I lose, I'ma beat that ass. So if you don't put two motherfucking quarters in and get this goddamn game started . . ."

Steel relents.

Truant officers rush into the arcade shortly after, forcing an unfinished end to their game.[2] However, the dynamic of Tupac's character has already been established, and it is a metaphor that extends beyond the role Tupac plays in just that movie and into his real life: He doesn't lose; not even when he's bound to lose. Which is how he took what was (it would appear to be) a turbulent relationship with his drug-addicted mother and turned it into "Dear Mama," one of the greatest rap songs that's ever been.[3]

◆

Quick aside: Tupac was named after Túpac Amaru II, a rebellious Peruvian leader who was eventually sentenced to death by his captors. He had his tongue cut out and his arms and legs each tied to a separate horse and yanked from his body. They removed his head, too. This all came after he'd watched his family get executed. Don't break any laws in Peru, is basically what I'm telling you.

♦

Given that this chapter is about a song that's about Tupac and his view of his mother when he was growing up, it seems to make sense to at least have a section here about Tupac growing up, so that's what this section is. I will try to keep it as direct as possible:

Tupac was born of an affair between Afeni Shakur and Billy Garland, both then-members of the Black Panther Party.[4] He arrived in 1971, one month after Afeni had successfully argued on her own behalf and was acquitted of 156 counts(!!)[5] of conspiracy against the U.S. government.[6]

Garland disappeared when Tupac was five years old, marrying another woman and losing contact with Afeni. In a 2011 interview with XXL, Garland explained that he'd actually not even seen Tupac after he left Afeni until he watched him in Juice,[7] somehow managing to sound slightly charming about the whole thing. "I'm sitting here watching Juice, and I am crying. I saw the advertisement. I didn't know which kid was mine until I saw him."

Afeni struggled to raise Tupac and his younger half sister, Sekyiwa Shakur, moving from city to city—from New York to Baltimore to Marin City, California. They were impoverished, but that was mostly an extension of Afeni's drug addiction, which was especially devastating to her son. She was, as she's said in numerous interviews, almost to the point of being considered an absentee mother much of the time. And from that, Tupac culled and cultivated the angst that propelled him.

Jada Pinkett Smith, whom Tupac befriended while attending the Baltimore School for the Arts and whose own mother was also a drug user, explained the schism Afeni's chaotic lifestyle had on Tupac in Michael Eric Dyson's 2006 book *Holler If You Hear Me*. "Your mother is your pulse to the world. And if that pulse ain't right, ain't much else going to be right. I don't think he ever reconciled [that] within himself."

♦

"Dear Mama" was the first single from *Me Against the World*, the third album from Tupac and one that managed to go double platinum that year despite his being in the thick of serving a prison term when it was released.[8] While he'd already shown a superheroic ability to process a milieu that extended beyond himself and produce from that a compelling arc—particularly with regard to women, 1991's "Brenda's Got a Baby" and 1993's "Keep Ya Head Up," most courageously—"Dear Mama" outpaced everything he had previously achieved.

The song was produced by Tony Pizarro, and it splices together the Spinners' "Sadie" (1974), which also happens to be about mothers, with Joe Sample's "In All My Wildest Dreams" (1978), which doesn't have any words in it but still might also be about mothers.[9] It is warm and nearly sunburnt and definitely emotive.

---

1. I saw *Juice* for the first time shortly before I started middle school. I watched it with my mom and dad, because that's how you're supposed to watch it, I'm pretty sure. The first day of sixth grade, when my mom dropped me off, she spied an older Mexican kid wearing a hoodie. She called me close. "You see that boy over there?" she said, eyeing him. "Remember that movie we watched? The one about juice? He looks like he was in it. Stay away from him, okay? You don't need his juice." Moms are so clutch, man.

2. Near the end of the movie, Tupac shoots Steel in the gut. It was not because of Street Fighter, FYI.

3. It really is beautiful. Oddly enough, in a 1995 interview with Bill Bellamy at MTV, Tupac explained that he wrote it one morning while he was on the toilet.

4. Tupac's godfather, Elmer "Geronimo" Pratt, was also a very famous member of the Black Panther Party. He was convicted in 1972 of kidnapping and murder, though after he'd served twenty-seven years in prison his murder charge was "vacated," which is just a nicer way to say that it was erased because of unscrupulous tactics used by the prosecution to get him convicted in the first place.

5. Afeni has mentioned that she'd previously been pregnant but had not been able to carry a baby past three months. Embryo Tupac not only made it past the three-month mark but also made it through a prison sentence his mother was serving as well as a court case against the government of the United States. My sons were eighteen months old before they could even walk. Shameful.

6. Allegedly plotting to blow stuff up, as it were.

7. Garland didn't meet Tupac again in person until 1994. He visited him in the hospital after he'd been shot five times outside of Manhattan's Quad Studios. In the 2002 documentary *Biggie & Tupac*, Garland jokes about how Tupac responded to reports that he'd had a testicle shot off by flashing his junk at his father. It was only the second time they'd seen each other in nearly two decades.

8. Tupac became the first artist to have an album atop the *Billboard* charts while in prison.

9. *ALL* things are probably about mothers, really.

Despite the obvious complexities of the relationship between Afeni and Tupac, "Dear Mama" is a gorgeous, entirely gripping matriarchal appreciation.[10] In the song's most expository moment, and maybe the most famous line of his career, Tupac floats out the bar "And even as a crack fiend, Mama / You always was a black queen, Mama."

This, more than any other lyric, more than any other truth, was undeniable to Tupac.

Sweep aside the statistical merits "Dear Mama" collected. It: was certified a platinum single months after its release; was number one on *Billboard*'s Hot Rap Singles chart for five straight weeks (again: Tupac was in prison while this was happening, and he only gave one interview the entire time); was picked by *Rolling Stone* as the eighteenth greatest hip-hop song of all time; earned a Grammy nomination (Best Rap Solo Performance); and was added to the National Recording Registry for preservation by the Library of Congress for its cultural significance, of which had only happened thrice before for rappers.[11]

But move all that out of the way. And you're left with Tupac, those big eyes and bigger teeth and emotions that are bigger still.

His succinct, crucial explanation of the song that I just spent two thousand words talking about and that countless others have written countless more words about:

"It's a love song to my mama."

Fewer things are simpler. Fewer still are more complex.

♦

Quick couple of notes about the video, which was an achievement in itself because they filmed it without Tupac there: (1) In it, two guys and a girl sit around a kitchen table playing a board game called Thug Life, which is a variation of the real board game Life. (2) It opens with just this wonderful quote from Afeni: "When I was pregnant, in jail, I thought I was gonna have a baby and the baby would never be with me. But I was acquitted a month and three days before Tupac was born. I was real happy, because I had a son." (3) An adolescent Tupac, who is supposed to be on his way to school in the video, ditches his books by placing them under a tree in the front yard. That's adorable. This seems like a good time to point out that Tupac never had any true issues with the police until after he became a rapper. This was addressed indirectly in the most endearing fashion in the 2003 documentary *Resurrection*, where Tupac talks about the time he attempted to be a drug dealer: "I tried selling drugs for maybe two weeks. Then the dude was like, 'Aw, man. Gimme my drugs back.' 'Cuz I didn't know how to do it!" A drug dealer told Tupac Shakur "Gimme my drugs back." I've never heard of a thing so perfect.

---

10. "Dear Mama" was so good that it made me mad at my mom for not being addicted to crack. I wasn't that smart as a kid. I'm still not, I suppose. :-/
11. The other three: Grandmaster Flash's "The Message" (see page 28), Sugarhill Gang's "Rapper's Delight" (see page 10), and Public Enemy's "Fear of a Black Planet."

REBUTTAL: "SHOOK ONES PT. II" MOBB DEEP

Something happens when "Shook Ones Pt. 2" comes on. Keep your eye out next time you're in a bar and you hear it. Glasses will shatter, grown men will grip each other for support, and everyone's head starts nodding like it's being choreographed by some kind of higher power. The opening sounds, sampled from Quincy Jones's "Kitty with the Bent Frame," is like some kind of *Manchurian Candidate* signal that programs people to wild out. It starts out feeling like it was beamed in from another planet, but when the beat drops, and Prodigy says, "I got you stuck off the realness, we be the infamous," you know this could only come from the bottom of a stairwell, somewhere on the 41st side of Queensbridge.

You remember where you were the first time you heard it, you remember how you felt when *8 Mile* opened with it, and every time you think of it, you need to hear it as soon as possible. 1995 is one of the high-water marks in hip-hop history, but no song from that damaged, beautiful year has had the staying power of "Shook Ones Pt. 2."

—CHRIS RYAN

Dear Mama

"When I was young, me and my mama had beef" (0:11)

"I shed tears with my baby sister" (0:29)

 "Ain't a woman alive that could take my mama's place" (0:21)

"I reminisce on the stress I caused" (0:42)

"And who'd think in elementary, hey, I'd see the penitentiary one day?" (0:51)

"And even though we had different daddies, the same drama" (0:35)

"And even as a crack fiend, mama, you always was a black queen, mama" (1:00)

 "I needed money on my own so I started slangin'" (2:01)

"No love from my daddy 'cause the coward wasn't there" (1:40)

 "I hope you got the diamond necklace that I sent you" (2:14)

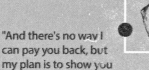

"Everything will be alright if you hold on" (3:49)

"And there's no way I can pay you back, but my plan is to show you that I understand" (2:44)

"To keep me happy there's no limit to the things you did" (3:18)

POWERFUL   HOPEFUL   INTROSPECTIVE   INSIGHTFUL   CONSIDERATE   AUTOBIOGRAPHICAL   DESCRIPTIVE

1996

CALIFORNIA LOVE

—

TUPAC

FEATURING

DR. DRE

AND

ROGER TROUTMAN

WHAT THIS SONG IS ABOUT

How much fun it is to live in California.

• •

WHY IT'S IMPORTANT

It was the reverse engineering of the gangsta rapper, who was—at this moment—styled in Tupac's mold. It also married gangsta rap and G-Funk.

The first proper single of Tupac's career was "Brenda's Got a Baby" in 1991, and that's kind of insane to think about, and it's insane in two different ways: (1) because of what it is about, and (2) because of what Tupac eventually came to represent in rap.

"Brenda's Got a Baby" is about an illiterate twelve-year-old girl who gets impregnated by her older cousin,[1] secretly gives birth to the baby on a bathroom floor,[2] puts the baby in a Dumpster,[3] gets kicked out of her house,[4] attempts to become a crack dealer,[5] gets robbed,[6] becomes a prostitute,[7] then gets murdered.[8] It's as "socially conscious" a rap song as has ever been written.

The singles that followed either replicated the tone (though rarely to such extremes) or spun in the other direction altogether. Over one very eager stretch of six months in 1993, he released "Holler If Ya Hear Me," a frustration anthem and his very best Public Enemy impersonation, followed by "Keep Ya Head Up," a female empowerment song, followed by "I Get Around," which is about having lots of sex with lots of females. The contradiction was an early indication of the kind of in-the-moment, emotionally reflective artist Tupac was, and would become, and that's how we get to what Tupac came to represent:

Distilled down to its pith, the entirety of gangsta rap imagery is Tupac; he is the archetypal gangsta rapper, and he has come to stand in for any and all other rappers in the subgenre. That's an easy claim to make because he, in fact, perfected gangsta rap,

and weighed and measured by Dre's steadiness. All three parts play perfectly together. Examined free of the context of Tupac's career, it would have lived a perfectly pleasant life, and likely even still managed to become critical to the rap genre.

But it arrived to an almost unfathomably perfect orchestra of circumstance, and so it is endlessly important today, and forever, on earth and in heaven and anywhere else they listen to rap. To wit:

- It was the first song Tupac released when he got out of prison in 1996, and that would've been gigantic all by itself. But the insanity surrounding his court case at the time of his sentencing had grown his indestructible gangster myth tenfold,[9] so Tupac getting out of prison was less him getting out of prison and more him rolling away the stone and stepping up out of the tomb.
- It was the first song from his new album, *All Eyez on Me*, which was coming behind *Me Against the World*, his most successful album to that point, commercially (it moved more than 3.5 million units) and critically ("Dear Mama"; see page 106).
- It was the first thing he delivered under Death Row, a label that was, at that moment, the biggest and baddest and most overwhelming in rap.[10]
- It was produced by Dr. Dre.
- And his amazing film run from 1992 to 1994 (*Juice*, *Poetic Justice*, *Above the Rim*)[11] stretched his name well beyond the parameters of just rap, and even just music.

but it's also slightly tricky. He was so convincing in the role that he effectively rendered all other portrayals obsolete, or, worse still, uncool. (Nearly) all of the images we've come to associate with gangsta rap are images he presented. And the origination of that version of him was him on "California Love," when Dr. Dre stood back behind him in the Thunderdome and framed his mania, and it was so exciting and obvious when it happened.

◆

"California Love" is a great song. It's a funky, chirping, fever of noise, the sonic weirdness is boxed in by Roger Troutman's robo charm, pummeled into acquiescence by Tupac's fury,

You can imagine the sort of fervor that surrounded this song when it dropped. It was his biggest song figuratively, because of its commercial success, but also literally. Up to that point he'd mostly been an insular artist, with ideas and thoughts aimed in specific directions. "California Love" gave him the wide-screen treatment we'd watch the Notorious B.I.G. get later. It was a glimpse at what he was going to do as a proper superstar, and also pointed toward where Puff Daddy would eventually take rap.[12]

♦

"California Love" was not originally Tupac's song. There are two conflicting stories on how he nabbed it. One comes from Chris "The Glove" Taylor, who claims he helped produce the track (though he received no credit for it), and the other from Death Row's cofounder and former CEO Suge Knight, who is like if an angry rhino began morphing into a human and then stopped halfway through and so that's just how he was stuck.

The parts that they quibble about are the parts you'd expect (Taylor says he helped piece together the track with Dr. Dre at his house, while Knight tells some overly complex story about a stylist wearing a leather suit and that's where the *Mad Max* theme for the video came from, or something), but they both agree on one point: It belonged to Dr. Dre before it belonged to Tupac. Taylor says he and Dre made it at Dre's house during a get-together, and then Tupac showed up and was in the studio so he recorded a verse for it. Knight says that the song had been written for Dre, but since *The Chronic* had already been out, and since Tupac's album was on its way, Suge thought the song should go to Tupac. There's a moment during Suge's explanation where he basically congratulates himself for not blatantly stealing the whole song by allowing Dre to remain on it, and it's easy to see how Suge eventually pile-drove Death Row into nothingness.

♦

There are thirteen reasons you should visit California and celebrate California, according to Tupac and Dr. Dre in "California Love."

GOOD REASONS

1. **Lots of opportunities for sex:** If you are in charge of promoting tourism for your state, you should 100 percent include that your state has a higher sex rate per capita than other states, if that happens to be the case.
2. **Bomb-ass hemp:** "Bomb ass" is slang for "very good," and "hemp" is slang for "marijuana." I remember reading this thing about how when you want to add a new word to your vocabulary, you have to use it two times out loud, so I'd recommend that here for you so that you can get comfortable saying this. For example, if your friend's mother passes away, you might try consoling him or her by commenting on the high quality of the event: "Susan, hi, I just want to say real quick that this is a bomb-ass funeral. Your mother, also bomb-ass, would've been pleased."
3. **Dance floors busy with bodies:** "Ecclesiastes assures us . . . that there is a time for every purpose under heaven. A time to laugh . . . and a time to weep. A time to mourn . . . and there is a time to dance." —Kevin Bacon, *Footloose. Footloose* is so much fun.[13]
4. **Hoochies, likely screaming:** Hoochies who like to scream are better than, say, hoochies who like to stab, or hoochies who like to steal your identity.
5. **Chucks:** This is in reference to the Chuck Taylor Converse. Chucks are timeless.

---

1. This.
2. Just.
3. Keeps.
4. On.
5. Getting.
6. Worse.
7. And.
8. Worse.
9. He was shot five times on December 1, 1994, the night before the sentencing. He rolled himself right TF into the courtroom the next day.
10. The first five albums Death Row released: Dr. Dre's *The Chronic*, Snoop's *Doggystyle*, the soundtrack for *Above the Rim*, the soundtrack for *Murder Was the Case*, and Tha Dogg Pound's *Dogg Food*.
11. I can't think of four actors who had a better back-to-back-to-back run, seriously.
12. I meant this generally—the big videos, the budgets, all that—but in this case it's also specific: Puff re-created the desert scene from "California Love" in his "Can't Nobody Hold Me Down" video. He just replaced the *Mad Max* cars with a very expensive one for him and Mase.
13. The original version, I mean. Not the 2011 remake. The 2011 remake was a real chore, the one clear exception being Miles Teller as Willard. He wasn't nearly as complex as Chris Penn, but he was still a total gem.

6. **Dark sunglasses and khaki suits:** This seems a lot like something that a murderer would wear, because it's difficult to picture a sane person shopping in a store and asking where the khaki-suit section is. But dark sunglasses and khaki suits are always cool.

7. **Caution:** This is from the line "Flossin', but have caution," and, really, being cautious while flossin' is smart, and it's the way I'd floss were I ever in a position to do so. (It's also probably counterintuitive to the spirit of flossin'. Still, it's a good reason, just to be safe.)

8. **The potential to bump and grind like a slow jam:** I am a very big fan of bumping and grinding, be it like a slow jam or any other jam, really.

9. **Bomb beats from Dre:** Sure.

10. **Serenades:** Okay.

BAD REASONS

1. **Pimps:** I've only ever met two pimps in my life. Neither of those times was that great of an experience. The pimps were not anywhere near as entertaining as the flamboyant pimps you see in movies from the '70s. They were more like the pimps from *Taken*.

2. **Fiends:** What's happening right now?

3. **Riots (not rallies):** No, thank you. But you have fun at your riot full of pimps and fiends.

That's ten good and three bad. California seems okay.

◆

Roger Troutman's Zapp band had a very clear influence on G-Funk. Dr. Dre choosing to use him for the hook on "California Love" indicates a new stage in rap: having precedents and heroes and the ability to incorporate them into the new music being made from their seeds. That he was being featured on a song that was connecting gangsta rap with G-Funk for this new thing feels significant, too, as does the fact that this celebration of Cali counterculture was happening while the ground was still vibrating from the police batons and boots that had swung at and stomped on Rodney King. "California Love" was Tupac's turn as the biggest gangsta rapper in the world. He was dead nine months later.

REBUTTAL: "THA CROSSROADS" BONE THUGS-N-HARMONY

As with most Bone songs, keeping up with the lyrics of Bizzy Bone, Wish Bone, Krayzie Bone, and Layzie Bone to "Tha Crossroads" and singing them word for word is damn near a fool's errand, but the somber mood of the track (produced by their in-house producer DJ U-Neek), which samples the Isley Brothers' soul ballad "Make Me Say It Again Girl (Parts 1 and 2)," is all we need to feel the song's weight. Dedicated to Eazy-E, the man who signed them to Ruthless Records and brought them to national prominence, "Tha Crossroads" was ironically their biggest hit ever. The song not only reached number one on the *Billboard* Hot 100, it also gave the group a Grammy for Best Rap Performance by a Duo or Group.

No song since has ever been able to speak about sudden death and loss the way Bone did on "Tha Crossroads." Considering the tragic circumstances that made the song possible (Eazy-E's sudden passing), that's probably a good thing. "Tha Crossroads" is a song that matches an unexplainable feeling we all have either experienced or will go through at least once in our lives. That is why, in a weird way, it's the song we never want to have to hear, because it usually means we have been overcome with some terrible news. "Tha Crossroads" is the perfect song for the shittiest feeling, but whether we want to admit it or not, we all need a song like it.

—JOZEN CUMMINGS

CALIFORNIA LOVE

"Now let me welcome everybody to the wild, wild west" (0:46)

"I been in the game for ten years makin' rap tunes" (1:05)

"Pack a vest for your jimmy in the city of sex" (0:53)

"Throw up a finger if ya feel the same way" (1:22)

"Diamonds shinin', lookin' like I robbed Liberace" (1:13)

"Out on bail, fresh out of jail, California dreamin'" (2:18)

"Fiending for money and alcohol" (2:21)

"In L.A. we wearin' Chucks not Ballys" (2:35)

"Flossin', but we have caution" (2:40)

"Bumpin' and grindin' like a slow jam" (2:48)

"Let me serenade the streets of L.A." (2:54)

"Give me love" (3:01)

CONSIDERATE   PROCLAMATION   THRILLING   NAME BRAND   AUTOBIOGRAPHICAL   INSIGHTFUL   COMPARATIVE

1997

CAN'T NOBODY HOLD ME DOWN

PUFF DADDY featuring **MASE**

It's nearly impossible to discuss Puff Daddy without mentioning one of three things, and most of the time at least two of them, and occasionally all three if you happen to be having a very long conversation about him. There's:

The City University of New York Tragedy. In 1991, nine people were trampled to death at an overcrowded celebrity basketball game at the City University of New York, organized, in part, by Puff. This one generally only comes up if you happen to be writing about him or producing a documentary about him. But if you do happen to be doing one of those two things, it comes up a lot. It's part of his complicated history with death, which he always appears to be trying to outrun.

The Name Changes. This one generally comes up sarcastically, and usually in a way that's meant to be funny but never, ever is. It's often in a sentence that ends with some form of ". . . or *Diddy* or *Puffy* or *Puff Diddy* or *Diddy Pops* or whatever it is he's calling himself these days." It's usually delivered by a mom or a dad or a friend who nobody likes.

The Notorious B.I.G. This one comes up all the time. And it should, because it's the most important. Puff and Biggie are tied together in history almost inextricably. The exchange of influence and skill and ideas that occurred between them, especially as it relates to the West Coast–East Coast rap rivalry that punctuated the mid- to late '90s and all of the tributaries that stem off that, is a labyrinth, and a true chore to attempt to detail

within the confines of a chapter in a book, and basically impossible in just one paragraph in the intro of a chapter.

Here are the very general, very generic, very basic details of their relationship:

Puff Daddy interned at a company called Uptown Records. He was brought on as an employee. He was fired. He attempted to start his own label. He backed his way into finding the Notorious B.I.G.[1] He heard him. He loved him. He signed him. They put out *Ready to Die* as the first album on the new label (Bad Boy Records). It eventually went quadruple platinum. More Bad Boy albums came. And they sold very well, too. None were ever as impactful as Biggie's, though. To be stylistic about it: Puffy was the face, but Biggie had become the voice of Bad Boy. And then he was murdered.[2]

Puffy had been a successful producer, and had operated as the head of a successful label, and had even rapped a tiny amount, but nothing he'd done *without* Biggie touched anything he'd done *with* Biggie. Plus, for as much as he'd made himself visible in his artists' videos, he'd never been a solo act. That's why when Biggie was gunned down, most assumed Puff's career was going to shrivel up and die right along with him.

Then "Can't Nobody Hold Me Down" came out.

◆

"It looked like Puffy was finished a hundred times; it don't make no difference. No matter how many times you stab him, Puff ain't gonna lay down. He's a survivor. He'll reinvent himself."
—Russell Simmons, cofounder of Def Jam Records and V-neck sweater devotee, talking about Puff Daddy's success after being fired from Uptown Records

"Can't Nobody Hold Me Down" was Puff's first solo song. It sold more than four million copies and was a *Billboard* number one for six weeks. Part of the reason it was so successful is that it was so instantly likable, and part of the reason it was so instantly likable is that it was instantly recognizable. To make it, Puff doctored up Grandmaster Flash's 1982 hit "The Message"

(see page 25). Ice Cube had tried something similar with "The Message" on 1992's "Check Yo Self," and that was a fine enough song,[3] but even over that very pop-oriented production he still sounded too rugged. Puff's talk-rap style was perfect for it. His version was warmer, smoother, easier to digest. And he doubled down on the nostalgia, too: In addition to sourcing "The Message," "Can't Nobody Hold Me Down" also incorporated part of Matthew Wilder's 1983 hit "Break My Stride"[4] for the chorus. He even aligned himself with the ideological core of the song.[5]

To wit: In the opening of "Break My Stride," Wilder sang about an unfavorable exchange he had with a woman (he dreamt he sailed to China to be with her, but that she said she had laundry to do[6]), and he did so as a way to say that he was a strong person and this wouldn't break him ("Ain't nothin' gonna break my stride / Nobody's gonna slow me down"). Puff's initial argument was the reverse (I'm great and people are envious of me), but the end point was the same (others couldn't stop him).

The video for "Can't Hold Me Down" was an opulent ode to itself, which is to say it was a standard Bad Boy video. The most memorable portion was Puff and Mase driving around the desert in a Rolls-Royce looking not all that impressed with driving a Rolls-Royce around in the desert. Later, they blow the car up because they get bored with it. And then in the next scene they're dressed in all white in an all-white room with no furniture or furnishings, because colors and chairs are boring, too. The whole thing felt like the inverse of Tupac and Dr. Dre's "California Love" video, a *Mad Max*–themed ode to anarchy that consisted of makeshift cars being driven around the desert (see page 112).

So for his first song Puff just redid what he'd done as a producer (sample famous songs people recognized) and redid what he'd done as a video coordinator (spend a lot of money), and I think we're all feeling pretty foolish for having not been able to see that he was going to be just fine without Biggie.

◆

---

1. A writer gave Biggie's demo tape to Puff after featuring him in *The Source*'s Unsigned Hype column.
2. He was killed sixteen days before the release of his second album, *Life After Death*.
3. Cube's version shipped more than a million copies.
4. Wilder did an interview in 2012 where he talked briefly about Puff sampling "Break My Stride" for "Can't Hold Me Down." "That was the first I'd ever heard of [rappers sampling songs]. They came to us with the finished product and said, 'We've used your song,' followed by, 'Can we use it?' And I was like, 'You're kidding, right?'"
5. Neither "The Message" nor "Break My Stride" makes mention of anything hanging out of anyone's anus, though, money or otherwise, as Puff did in "Can't Nobody Hold Me Down." Puff is a trendsetter in that respect, too.
6. This is unacceptable behavior on her part. It takes about four months to sail to China on a small boat from San Francisco.

PUFFY HAD CAMEOS IN NO LESS THAN 35 MUSIC VIDEOS BETWEEN 1991 AND 2005

Heavy D, "Don't Curse," featuring Kool G. Rap, Pete Rock & CL Smooth, Big Daddy Kane, Grand Puba, Q-Tip + Mary J. Blige, "Reminisce" + The Notorious B.I.G., "Juicy" + The Notorious B.I.G., "Warning" + Craig Mack, "Flava In Ya Ear (Remix)," featuring The Notorious B.I.G., LL Cool J, Busta Rhymes, Rampage + Total, "Can't You See," featuring The Notorious B.I.G. + The Notorious B.I.G., "Big Poppa" + Mobb Deep, "Survival of the Fittest" + Total, "No One Else (Puff Daddy Remix)," featuring New Edition and Missy Elliott + MC Lyte, "Cold Rock a Party (Bad Boy Remix)," featuring Missy Elliott + The Notorious B.I.G., "Hypnotize" + Mase, "Feel So Good" + The Lox, "We'll Always Love Big Poppa" + Black Rob, "Whoa" + Big Pun, "It's So Hard" + Lil' Kim, "No Matter What They Say" + Busta Rhymes, "Break Ya Neck" + G-Dep, "Special Delivery (Remix)," featuring Ghostface Killa, Keith Murray, Craig Mack, Puff Daddy + Usher, "U Don't Have to Call" + Faith Evans, "Burnin' Up (Bad Boy Remix)," featuring Missy Elliott and Freeway + Jay Z, "La La La (Excuse Me Miss Again)" + Mary J. Blige, "Love @ 1st Sight," featuring Method Man + Da Band, "Bad Boy This, Bad Boy That" + Da Band, "Tonight" + Loon, "Down For Me," featuring Mario Winans + Loon, "How You Want That," featuring Kelis + T.I., "Rubberband Man" + 8 Ball and MJG, "Forever," featuring Lloyd + 8 Ball and MJG...

The dominance of Puffy: The song that followed "Can't Hold Me Down" on top of the *Billboard*'s Hot 100 was "Hypnotize" by the Notorious B.I.G., which is the most perfect example of Bad Boy's We Have Money, Life Is a Party mission statement. It was there for three weeks. Hanson's ridiculous "MMMBop" ba-duba-dopped its way to the top for three weeks (Puff did not produce that one, turns out). After that, it was "I'll Be Missing You," a tribute song to the Notorious B.I.G. by Puff, Faith Evans, and 112. It was at number one for eleven weeks. "Mo Money Mo Problems" was next (by the Notorious B.I.G., Puff, and Mase). It was there for two weeks. And then "Honey" by Mariah Carey came after. It was there for three weeks. Puff produced that one, too. That's a stretch of twenty-five out of twenty-eight weeks where Puff Daddy was, in part, responsible for the number-one song in the nation, and he'd spread it over five songs. It had never happened that way before. It hasn't happened that way since.

If we can go broader: "Can't Nobody Hold Me Down" was the first single from Puff's debut album, *No Way Out*. The album sold more than seven million copies. The six albums that had come before it on the Bad Boy label: the Notorious B.I.G., *Ready To Die* (4x platinum); Craig Mack, *Project: Funk Da World* (gold); Faith Evans, *Faith* (platinum); Total, *Total* (platinum); 112, *112* (2x platinum); the Notorious B.I.G., *Life After Death* (10x platinum).

And the next twenty that came after *No Way Out* on the Bad Boy label were also all certified gold, platinum, or multi-platinum.

Puff even managed to sell six hundred thousand–plus copies of Da Band's album. That's the most amazing thing. Do you remember Da Band? They were a group formed on a reality TV show called *Making the Band* on MTV. The only thing anyone seems to know about them today is that Dave Chappelle made fun of one of the members[7] one time. Puff Daddy is a genius.

◆

There are two ways to view Puff Daddy's legacy.

He is either (a) one of the most successful persons in rap, with an influence and an impact on music history that is unquestioned and unending, and that is incredible. Or he is (b) one of the most successful persons in rap, with an influence and an impact on music history that is unquestioned and unending, and that is incredible, but a steadier look outside of the jet stream of his propulsion toward the sky shows a littering of discarded acts who are irrelevant,[8] broke,[9] incarcerated,[10] or dead,[11] and that is not incredible.

Either way, "Can't Nobody Hold Me Down" plays an essential role in his legend, and his legend is essential to rap.

7. Dylan Dilinjah.
8. Mase, Craig Mack, Total, Jodeci, 112, Carl Thomas, etc.
9. Black Rob, Da Band, Shyne, etc.
10. G. Dep, Loon, etc.
11. The Notorious B.I.G.

REBUTTAL: "THE RAIN" MISSY ELLIOTT, FEATURING TIMBALAND

Supa Dupa Fly, Missy Elliott's debut album, is a seventeen-track duet with Timbaland's beats. "The Rain" starts out with a delicate boast and back-and-forth with a sample from Ann Peebles's "I Can't Stand the Rain": "Me, I'm supa fly, supa dupa fly, supa dupa fly," Missy raps, countering Peebles's plucky timbale backing track. She sets the expectation for her sound: "Me and Timbaland . . . / We so tight that you get our styles tangled." Later: "BEEP! BEEP! Who got the keys to the Jeep? *VROOOOM*." There's no point in imagining these lyrics coming out of another rapper's mouth, over another producer's beat, because no other duo would be so audacious to try that shit, and no one else on the planet could make it sound and look so purely cool—dressed in a trash bag and under a fisheye lens, to boot. "The Rain" is an iconic song with an iconic (Hype Williams) video, featuring the best tangled styles in hip-hop.

—EMMA CARMICHAEL

1998

RUFF RYDERS' ANTHEM

—

DMX

DMX is maybe the most compelling person I have ever considered. He's not especially complicated, nor is his history. But that helps build his case instead of working against it.

He was abused and abandoned as a child. That led him to emptiness. Then that led him to crime. Then that led him to rap. And then compulsions (drugs/fame/anarchy) turned all of those into the same thing, and that was eventually the foundation for his unraveling. And this, the whole everything, all of the hurt and the anguish, he's viewed it through the belief that his suffering was/is/will remain God's will. It's a perpetual torment. He absorbed and processed the absence of truth and love[1] early in life, the two things he coveted the most but was rarely able to find, and eventually interpreted that absence as beneficial to others in their own lives, so long as he spoke on it. He's addressed this indirectly and also directly, most admirably on a track called "Prayer (Skit)" from his first album, *It's Dark and Hell Is Hot*: "So if it takes for me to suffer for my brother to see the light / Give me pain till I die, but please, Lord, treat him right."[2]

Lots of people have compared DMX to things before (a dog, mostly, due to his branding and a variety of other things). The most auspicious comparison was in the book *Hip-Hop Redemption: Finding God in the Rhythm and the Rhyme*. In it, Ralph Basui Watkins rhetorically asks if God really was communicating through X, wondering, "What if God is using DMX as his weeping prophet?" I don't know if He is, but I know I'd have gone to church way more often if it involved more contemplation of God as He relates to Dark Man X.

(probably) because X, fed up with a history of abuse and a lifetime of fear and uneasiness around anybody bigger than himself, had decided to bark back.[3]

DMX is certainly not the first person to associate reckless behavior with a favorable outcome (it's basically the impetus behind every immoral act committed by coherent humans), but it was an important moment for him here, so much so that two decades after it happened, after he'd had that single thought, he felt the need to highlight it in that chapter, and then eventually extend it to become the thesis for the entire book. Because it's been the thesis of his entire life.

A TERRIBLE THING DMX HAS EXPERIENCED (ONE OF THE MANY, AS IT WERE)

DMX's early existence was built largely around isolation. The most overt and literal case involves his mother quarantining him as a young child alone in his room for thirty days straight with the door closed as a punishment. He was only allowed to leave to get water and use the restroom. I can't imagine what kind of impact that has on the psyche of a person, particularly a child, or how that feeling mutates with maturity. But others have:

In a documentary series called *Biography Late Night*, Ted Kaczynski's[4] mother told a story about how when her son was a nine-month-old baby, he

A THING THAT DMX HAS THOUGHT

"Oh, so this is how it goes down? I zap out and then you want to talk. A few minutes ago, you were coming to whip my ass, now you want to ask me what's wrong? Hmmm. Maybe getting reckless is not such a bad thing after all."

That's a passage from DMX's autobiography, *E.A.R.L.: The Autobiography of DMX*, which came out in 2002. For context: It's DMX, as a child, thinking to himself, when he finds his mother and her then-boyfriend sitting at the kitchen table waiting to talk to him. In the minutes prior, the then-boyfriend had gone to X's room, belt in hand, intending to beat him for some trouble he'd caused. But the then-boyfriend welshed on the threat

suffered through extended isolation during a hospital stay (his body had become covered in hives and nobody knew why, so nobody was allowed to visit with him). The experience had, she felt, eroded him. "I took that baby home and I rocked and coaxed and cajoled and hugged and sang to him, and it took days before he would look at me. And when he looked, it was a sober look. He became a sober baby." I'm not saying DMX is Ted Kaczynski. But still.

A THING SOMEONE HAS SAID ABOUT DMX

"I could hear the breaking of the wires."

That's a quote from Lyor Cohen, remembering watching DMX perform for him in 1997[5] when Cohen was with Def Jam Records. X had suffered a very crucial beating prior and had to have his mouth wired shut. Still, given the opportunity to perform for a contract, he rapped with such ferocity and fervor that he nearly pulled the brackets holding his mouth together apart. Cohen signed him that night.

DMX's first five albums all released at number one, and two of those, *It's Dark and Hell Is Hot* and *Flesh of My Flesh, Blood of My Blood*, came out the same year. It was the first time in the history of music that someone had released five consecutive number-one albums, and only the second time a rapper had released two albums the same year and both debuted at number one.[6]

A THING DMX HAS SAID ABOUT VISITING A NEW CITY

"I go straight to the grimy part, you know, the unattractive parts of the city. You know, a lot of abandoned buildings, you know, stray dogs and cats running all over the place. I know that area; never been there before but I know it."

He said that in 1999 during an episode of MTV's *Diary*.

HOW ALL OF THIS RELATES TO "RUFF RYDERS' ANTHEM"

"Ruff Ryders' Anthem" is the second track on *It's Dark and Hell Is Hot*, and the album's fourth and final single. While it's largely recognized as an anthem track (meaning "Let's turn it on to get everyone to wild the fuck out"), it's also philosophical, and glances at nearly all of the parts of DMX that make DMX "DMX."

Consider the first twenty seconds of him rapping, where he manages to touch on his twisted history . . .

"All I know is pain / All I feel is rain"

. . . And how the aftereffects will narrate his Rap Charts Pillage and Plunder but will never let him escape himself, no matter how high into the stratosphere he ascends . . .

"How can I maintain with mad shit on my brain?"

. . . And how his first instinct will always be the wrong one . . .

"I resort to violence."

. . . And how none of the introspection or self-loathing or self-sacrifice or good intentions matter because, truly, if someone has something that he wants, he is going to take it without concern, and then he is going to tell you that he took it and dare you to attempt to recover your property . . .

"You want it? Come and get it / Took it then we split / You fuckin' right we did it."

The most commercially successful song of DMX's career was "Party Up (Up in Here)" from . . . *And Then There Was X*. The most trenchant was "Get at Me Dog" from *It's Dark and Hell Is Hot*. The most self-aware was "Slippin'"[7] from *Flesh of My Flesh, Blood of My Blood*. But the most well-known one, the most important one, the one that cemented everything DMX would become in the pop culture canon into place, is "Ruff Ryders' Anthem."[8]

HOW "RUFF RYDERS' ANTHEM" INVERTED RAP

This is every song that reached number one on *Billboard*'s rap singles chart the year before DMX became a superstar, before he'd released "Ruff Ryders' Anthem," and how long it was there:

• **"No Time," Lil' Kim, featuring Puff Daddy** (two weeks): This song is about only having time to drink very expen-

---

1. Maybe the most devastating DMX anecdote (excluding the childhood stuff) is the one about him crumpling into a pile after a very big concert, crying out to God, asking why He'd made him successful but only ever prepared him for failure. "I didn't know how to take the love," DMX said afterward, remembering the moment. "I didn't know how to interpret the love." :'(
2. DMX said this particular prayer was "burned in my head" while he was in jail in 1994.
3. There's another section in the book where he talks about how when he was eleven his mother took him to visit a reform school for all the worst kids. But it turned out he wasn't there to visit; she was there to drop him off. She told him in front of a group of other kids. She had not even mentioned the possibility to him beforehand. "It was one of the hardest things I've done in my life, to this day, was to just say 'All right' and keep a straight face," X said during his *Behind the Music* documentary, of when his mother told him she was leaving him there. "Another side of me was born right then and right there. A side that . . . enabled me to protect myself. That let me know that I had to protect myself. Because no one else would protect me."
4. The Unabomber.
5. Producer Irv Gotti says he arranged the meet-up between X and Cohen the day he (Gotti) was hired by Def Jam.
6. The other artist was Tupac.
7. There's a part here where he talks about how a crack addiction upended his life and how people made sure to mention it whenever they could. He follows that by talking about getting sober for his kid and how important that is and also about getting right for his woman and how important that is, too, which is just basically the saddest thing when you trace his history from the moment that song came out to today.
8. The beat, of course, was amazing. It was always amazing that Swizz Beatz, then an unknown, managed to twist a sitar string into a sound that changed rap forever. He gets a lifetime pass. Even the Alicia Keys debacle is forgiven.

sive beverages with friends and count money. Also, Puff Daddy spends a whole verse talking about how good he is at sex,[9] because I guess he wasn't paying attention to the chorus.

- **"Cold Rock a Party," MC Lyte** (two weeks): This song is about how cool MC Lyte is, according to MC Lyte.
- **"Can't Nobody Hold Me Down," Puff Daddy, featuring Mase** (twelve weeks): This song is about how Bad Boy is so effervescent that nary a person is capable of suppressing any of its members. Also, they are in possession of an automobile that is bulletproof. (For more, see page 118.)
- **"Hypnotize," The Notorious B.I.G.** (seven weeks): In the video for this song Puff and B.I.G. are on a yacht being chased by helicopters (but it's a chase that's more funny than dangerous, so much so that B.I.G. smiles during the chase, which is a thing he'd never done in a video before then). Later in the video, Puff and B.I.G. are in a convertible Mercedes[10] being chased by men on motorcycles and also some men in a Hummer. In the last part of the video, mermaids rap the chorus to the song underwater. Nobody had more fun having money in the late '90s than Puff Daddy.
- **"I'll Be Missing You," Puff Daddy and Faith Evans, featuring 112** (eight weeks): This song was about B.I.G. dying and how terrible it was.
- **"Mo Money Mo Problems," The Notorious B.I.G., featuring Puff Daddy and Mase** (four weeks): This song was about how being rich was troublesome, although it kind of seemed like the problem with being rich was that others weren't, which seems okay to me. (The one specific issue Puff mentions is that if you wanted to reach him, you had to call him on his yacht. Do yachts have great reception? I don't know. I've never been on one. I was on a barge once. My cell phone worked fine. But if you're missing important phone calls due to excessive yachting, then I admit, yes, that is a true problem.)

- **"Up Jumps Da Boogie," Timbaland and Magoo, featuring Aaliyah and Missy Elliott** (eight weeks): I don't know what this song is about and nobody else does either but everyone knows that it's all-caps AMAZING.
- **"Feel So Good," Mase** (six weeks): This song is about how good it feels to be rich.
- **"Been Around the World," Puff Daddy & the Family, featuring the Notorious B.I.G. and Mase** (three weeks): This song is about how there are people all over the world who hate Bad Boy because they have so much money and also because Puff has sex with attractive women (and how he prefers ones who are cinnamon-colored).

Rap in 1997 (the most prevalent[11] form of it, anyway) was aspirational. "Ruff Ryders' Anthem" helped fracture that, helped turn one of its eyes away from the moon and down into the dungeons. DMX had had other successful songs before, but "Ruff" did what they couldn't: It was menacing enough to maintain X's energy and fire, but scalable enough that it reached far out beyond his established fan base,[12] comparable to the balance Public Enemy found on "Fight the Power" (see page 70).

Puffy wanted a plane made of diamonds to fly him to a private island where the beach was also made of diamonds and the natives were big-bottomed women and, guess what, they had diamonds for nipples. DMX did not want a plane. DMX wanted a father. DMX wanted a mother who didn't abuse him.

DMX wanted peace in his heart, but felt fated to emptiness.

Puff wanted a dollar because he wanted to be rich.

DMX wanted your dollar because he wanted you to be poor.

---

9. If I had to guess, I'd assume him to be average. I don't have any facts to base that off of, though. I've never had sex with Puff Daddy.

10. Puff drove the car in reverse the whole time. He's very good at driving in reverse. In the "I'll Be Missing You" video he drove a motorcycle forward and crashed it on the open road. Perhaps he should've tried driving the motorcycle in reverse, too?

11. Puff Daddy was involved in whatever song it was that was at the top of the charts for forty-two of the fifty-two weeks in 1997.

12. We saw this on an even greater scale with "Party Up (Up in Here)," which turned X into a worldwide star. "Party" was not nearly as intimidating as "Ruff," but it was still coarser around its edges than some realized. There was a movie in 2001 called *Hardball* where Keanu Reeves tried to save some black kids by coaching baseball. In it, they play "Party" during one of the game sequences, which is very weird when you consider there's a line in it where DMX tells all the men who have been to jail before to S his D.

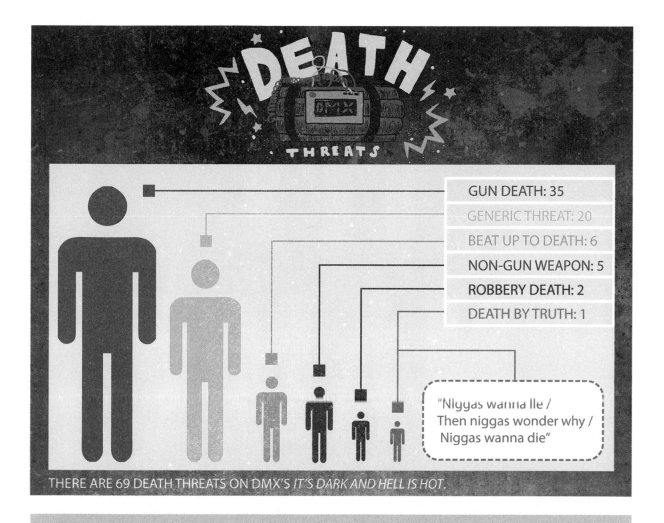

THERE ARE 69 DEATH THREATS ON DMX'S *IT'S DARK AND HELL IS HOT.*

REBUTTAL: "HA" JUVENILE

Shea's going with "Ruff Ryders' Anthem" as his top song of 1998. I'm going with Juvenile's "Ha." The reason is simple: If I'm going to give props to a southern record, it's actually going to be a southern record. Not a regional hybrid of a song—over a track produced by a New Yorker who lived in Atlanta for a while—but a gritty, unrefined window into where the rap game was going. It was uncompromising—to the point where the unfamiliar couldn't understand half of the lyrics—at a time when southerners were expected to apologize for not being "real" hip-hop. It was grimy but still relied on one of the catchiest hooks you'll ever hear. And it came with the best video anyone's ever made for a rap song.

Yeah, it's played out to call something "real," but how else would anyone describe "Ha"? It was simple and street, the good and bad of being a gangster—a series of unfortunate confluences that did a better job of what Alanis Morissette was going for on "Ironic." None of it sounded like fun, but all of it sounded like life. And with only hints of the bounce music that first made him a name, it sounded like Mannie Fresh, the best producer the Gulf Coast had produced.

So yeah, I see why someone would go with "Ruff Ryders' Anthem." But compared to "Ha"? It's like drinking Crown Royal with Diet Coke.

—BOMANI JONES

MY
NAME
IS
—
EMINEM

WHAT THIS SONG IS ABOUT

It's about an insecure guy who understands he's insecure but is having trouble processing it. Also, he very much wants to tell you his name.

WHY IT'S IMPORTANT

Because it was the launch song to the unprecedented hyper-success of Eminem, which carried with it the validity of the White Rapper and the true commodification of satirical wit and self-deprecating humor in rap.

There were a couple of times when I was in Los Angeles while working on this book. On one of those occasions, in December of 2014, I wandered around downtown for a bit, and I eventually ended up at the movies because I couldn't find a taxi to take me to see where they filmed the hilltop fight scene from *Blood In, Blood Out*.

The theater I walked into was mostly empty—there were, maybe, fifteen to twenty other people scattered throughout. We were there to watch *Top Five*, a movie written and directed by Chris Rock.[1] One thread running through the movie is that at different points different characters give their picks for the top-five rappers of all time. At the end, as Rosario Dawson's character (the woman Rock is considering leaving his fiancée for) is walking away in tears,[2] Rock calls to her. He asks, "What's your top five?"

Now, up to that point, the theater had been relatively quiet, as theaters tend to be. But when that scene happened, a woman down at the front immediately shouted, "Eminem! Eminem!"

Of all the different top-five lineups proffered in the movie theretofore, nobody had yet listed Eminem in their grouping. Jay Z was mentioned, of course. So was Notorious. Tupac was there, and Nas, Scarface, Ice-T, Big Daddy Kane, on and on. But Eminem—the guy who sold more albums than any artist in any genre of music in the 2000s; the guy who (as of this writing) has thirteen Grammys, including an unmatched run of five Best Rap Album awards over an eleven-year period;[3] the guy who was the first rapper ever to win an Academy Award; the guy who has the two biggest opening-week album sales numbers of any rapper in

she looked like, because, I mean, how could I not? I thought maybe she was going to be actually sitting with Eminem or at least be wearing an Eminem T-shirt or have the Detroit Tigers logo tattooed on her neck or have short, peroxide-blond hair or whatever. She didn't have any of that, though. She was just an average-sized, average-faced, non-neck-tattooed woman.

Sometimes L.A. can be boring.

♦

Eminem is white and that's a thing that everyone knows, but it's still a part of any Eminem discussion because that's just how things are, particularly when you consider that he is the most successful artist in rap, a genre that is largely non-white. Here are three things that have to do with his whiteness:

1. **Talent:** His whiteness is almost always brought up as a positive aside to his skill level as a rapper.[5] The only other act that received a similar sort of praise was the Beastie Boys, though they were always more likably sincere than lyrically deft.[6] But that's why "My Name Is" proved to be critical: It established the validity of the white rapper. The clever part is, he did so without attempting to peddle immersion ("Look how many black people I know!") or imitation ("Listen to how much I sound like a famous black rapper you already know!"), as those who'd come before him had.

history;[4] the guy who was picked as *Rolling Stone*'s "King of Hip-Hop," *Vibe*'s "Best Rapper Alive," MTV's "Hottest MC in the Game," and *Billboard*'s "Artist of the Decade" all within a two-year stretch—his name had not come up. And so I guess that woman was upset about that.

Dawson gave her list very dramatically, and each time she paused that same lady shouted. Dawson said a name. "Eminem!" Dawson gave another one. "Say Eminem!" Dawson gave her fourth. "EM! EH! NEM!" Dawson gave her fifth. It wasn't Eminem. The woman was flabbergasted. "What?!"

When the movie ended, I waited for the woman who'd been shouting to get up and leave because I wanted to see what

2. **Authenticity:** With "My Name Is," Eminem presented a new kind of whiteness in rap by parodying the normative version of it. To wit: In the video, he very clearly shows different versions of white that have been derided by rap (trailer-park white, famous white, nerdy white, powerful white, weirdo white, etc.), then very deliberately places himself opposite them. The effect is/was startling: By doing so, he created a new faction, one that could exist within the largely non-white rap world as an ally and contemporary instead of a novelty.

3. **Threat:** I'm going to reuse an Ice-T quote from the N.W.A

chapter where he was talking about one of the ways gangsta rap was being viewed as a problem. "The real problem here with the one side versus the other is not that my homeboys are hearing [this music]. If only my friends were hearing these records, nobody'd care. It's that [affluent] kids are buying more rap records than our kids. And the white kids now from suburbia are listening to N.W.A and the parents don't know what to do about it. If only the brothers in the neighborhood listened to it, nobody'd care." I mention it again as a supplement to this quote, which is what Carson Daly said about Eminem in 2011: "Here's a white kid saying stuff that rappers had said for years before. But they looked at it as a problem that was happening over there. And now you've got this guy who looks like your son—you have suburban white American kids who are buying the records. He's the new spokesman for a generation saying these controversial things. And I think all of a sudden it's a problem."

Eminem is not a gangsta rapper. But he *is* a philosophical extension of gangsta rap, especially with regard to the existential conundrum that white people consider white youth experiencing offensive music to be.

♦

TRUE THINGS ABOUT "MY NAME IS"

A lot of people remember it as Eminem's first song, but that's not a true thing. Eminem had an entire album that came out before "My Name Is." The album, *Infinite*, was not a major-label release, though, and it also wasn't very good, so it gets either lost or disregarded during discussion, which is for the best either way.

Slim Shady is the alter ego of Eminem. The idea for an alter ego came out of the premise of D12, the rap group Eminem is a part of. Each member had to come up with one. Eminem came up with his while he was using the restroom, which probably makes a lot of sense.

"My Name Is" won the Grammy for Best Rap Solo Performance. It beat out "Gimme Some More" by Busta Rhymes, "Vivrant Thing" by Q-Tip, "Changes" by Tupac, and "Wild Wild West" by Will Smith. The album it was on, *The Slim Shady LP*, won the Grammy for Best Rap Album.[7]

Eminem and Dr. Dre recorded "My Name Is" during their inaugural studio stint. It was one of a handful of songs they recorded that evening. According to them, it took somewhere near an hour. AN HOUR. It took Jean-Claude Van Damme more time to win the Kumite than it did for "My Name Is" to be made.

In addition to producing "My Name Is," Dr. Dre also codirected the video for it. The song and the video were built solely to serve as an introduction to, and the trademarking of, Eminem. (Slim Shady is said eighteen times during the song.) Dr. Dre did the exact same thing six years earlier with Snoop Dogg on his first single. That song, which also employed name recognition, was called "Who Am I (What's My Name)." ("Slim Shady" was said twenty-five times in it.) Dr. Dre is smart.

"My Name Is" samples a piece of "I Got the (Blues)" by a man named Labi Siffre. Siffre, an openly gay man, let them use it, but only after they'd made changes to a few of the lyrics that Siffre felt were offensive. Example: "My English teacher wanted to have sex in junior high. / The only problem was, my English teacher was a guy" became "My English teacher wanted to flunk me in junior high / Thanks a lot. Next semester, I'll be thirty-five."

"My Name Is" was the B side to a song called "Guilty Conscience," where Dr. Dre and Eminem were presented with three different scenarios (a potential robbery, a potential date rape, and a potential murder) and each argued a side, Dr. Dre the good conscience and Eminem the bad. "Guilty Conscience" is masterfully done, and the third verse on it was probably the single most captivating music moment of 1999.[8]

---

1. Top-five Chris Rock acting roles: 5. Detective Lee Butters in *Lethal Weapon 4*; 4. Marty in *Madagascar*; 3. MC Gusto in *CB4*; 2. A rib joint customer in *I'm Gonna Git You Sucka*; 1. Pookie in *New Jack City*.
2. All of the pieces that led up to this moment are too complex to relay, inasmuch as romantic comedy can be complex.
3. Kanye has won four over a seven-year stretch. Nobody else has more than two (Outkast).
4. *The Marshall Mathers LP*, 2000 (1.76 million); *The Eminem Show*, 2002 (1.31 million). Only 'N Sync and the Backstreet Boys have sold more during their first week in America.
5. In 2010, Scarface, considered one of the very best rappers on earth, was asked if he'd do a song with Eminem. His response: a laugh. Then: "I'm not fixin' to go in there fuckin' with that white boy, man."
6. "You know why I could fuck with them? They don't try to be black. They know they are white, trying to do this rap shit, and they're fans of it." —Q-Tip, August 1994 issue of *Vibe*
7. Grammys are good to use when you want to argue something is good, but they're also good to use when you want to argue something is bad. For example, right here, I'm using it to say that "My Name Is" is good. The year prior, though, Will Smith's "Gettin' Jiggy Wit It" beat Busta's "Dangerous," Wyclef's "Gone till November," Jay Z's "Hard Knock Life," and Lauryn Hill's "Lost Ones." Bad.
8. Other contenders: Elton John appears on *The Simpsons*; Britney Spears releases . . . *Baby, One More Time*; Sisqó makes "Thong Song."

Women have served as Eminem's rage source material for the entirety of his career (mom, daughter, girlfriend then wife then ex-wife then wife again then ex-wife again).[9] It's one of the overarching themes in his music. We get traces of that in "My Name Is." There's the bit about Pamela Anderson (tearing off her breast implants and then smacking her), and also . . .

Eminem's mother, Debbie, took a real beating in the song. Em accused her of being a druggie, not providing for him, and being incapable of breastfeeding him because she didn't have breasts. In response, she sued him for $10 million. She was awarded $25,000. Legal fees ate up most of it. She ended up getting $1,600. That's .00016 percent of what she was hoping for. That's the highest percentage of disappointment I've ever heard of.

To extend the point, some: Eminem's rage, while often aimed at women, is not exclusively so. He is equally fond of lampooning celebrities, be it men, women, clowns, cripples, rappers, reality TV stars, civil rights figures, or any variation or combination of either of those. There's a direct relationship between how funny or clever or insightful his barbs are and the dates he delivered them (they were enjoyable in 1999 and have gotten only more and more tiresome since then), and there's also a whole infographic with examples of some of his more pointed barbs right on the next page. You should look at it.

◆

Eminem is, on regular occasion, rated the most powerful rap tactician, and a seamless example of the intricacy and brilliance with which he stitches his rhymes together happened on the TV show *60 Minutes* when they ran a segment on him in 2010. During the interview, he and Anderson Cooper were sitting in a studio talking about how Eminem bends words to get them to do what he wants. The word "orange" came up. "What rhymes with 'orange'?" Cooper asked. "I'm trying to think of some and I can't figure out any." Eminem explained that nothing rhymes with "orange" exactly, but that you can mold it into a two-syllable word—*oh-range*—and all of a sudden, "I put my *oh-range*, four-inch door hinge in storage and ate porridge with George." I don't even know.

9. The best example (and worst example, too) of the kind of reactionary existence in which Slim Shady lives came via a song called "Just the Two of Us," which is a take on Will Smith's "Just the Two of Us," a song he delivers to his son about how he will always love him even though Smith and his son's mother divorced. In Eminem's version, he delivers it to his daughter, and it's about them taking a trip out to a lake late at night to dispose of her mom's body because Eminem murdered her.

REBUTTAL: "WHO DAT" JT MONEY

One-hit wonder JT Money's "Who Dat" is one of the initial bread crumbs on the path to mainstreaming southern rap. Number one on the *Billboard* rap chart for eight weeks—the longest-running hold at the top that year—and reaching number five on the Hot 100 (which is eleven places higher than where "My Name Is" peaked) gave evidence to the region's potential for dominance. It belongs in a category with Master P's No Limit posse cut "Make 'Em Say Uhh" (1997) and the Hot Boys' collaboration with the Big Tymers, "I Need a Hot Girl" (1998), as part of the fabric. But not only did "Who Dat" bring Miami booty, bass–informed rap into homes dominated by East Coast and West Coast sounds, it brought Tricky Stewart into the fold for the very first time. Stewart has since become a wizard of production, helming things like Rihanna's star-making "Umbrella" and Beyoncé's iconic "Single Ladies." Without "Who Dat," who knows?

—CLAIRE LOBENFELD

EMINEM PICKS ON PEOPLE

"Won't Back Down" – "Girl, forget remorse, I'mma hit you broads with Chris's paws"

"Welcome 2 Hell" – "Bruce Willis on his death bed / Last breath with an infection / Fighting it while he's watching Internet porn / About to meet his death with an erection"

"The Real Slim Shady" – "Will Smith don't gotta cuss in his raps to sell records / Well, I do / So fuck him and fuck you, too"

"Stir Crazy" – "I'm sicker than Boy George picturing Michael Jordan in little boys' drawers shopping at toy stores"

"Role Model" – "My mind won't work if my spine don't jerk / I slapped Garth Brooks out of his rhinestone shirt"

"Rap Game" – "I'm all for America, fuck the government / Tell that C. Delores Tucker slut to suck a dick"

"Purple Pills" – It's Mr. Mischief with a trick up his sleeve / Roll up on you like Christopher Reeves"

"Psycho" – "Beat the Octomom to death with a Cabbage Patch Kid"

"No Apologies" – "I am not failing, you fuckers are not ready / 'Cause I got jelly, like Beyoncé's pot belly"

"It Ain't Nothin' But Music" – "If Affleck can get his licked how come I can't / Shit, goddamn, bitch, I'm rich, I can't understand this"

"Chemical Warfare" – " . . . While I watch Whoopi Goldberg scissor with Oprah"

"Berzerk" – "All I know is I fell asleep and woke up in that Monte Carlo / With the ugly Kardashian, Lamar, oh, sorry, yo"

2000

Big Pimpin'

—

JAY Z

featuring UGK

WHAT THIS SONG IS ABOUT

Impulsive living.

. . . .

WHY IT'S IMPORTANT

Jay Z was, by then, a certified star. UGK, while heralded in rap, was still largely unknown outside of their core fan base. Their pairing here, and the success that came from it, helped rearticulate the northern and southern rap conversation.

The very first thing we see in the video for "Big Pimpin'" is a very big yacht, and all through the video the party that happens on it and away from it is a very big spectacle, and the very last thing we see in the video for "Big Pimpin'" is the very big yacht, and that was all a deliberate move to relay the following:

Jay wrote "Big Pimpin'" shortly after he'd been charged with assault for stabbing record producer Lance Rivera in the stomach during an altercation at a nightclub.[1] Had he been convicted, he might have seen upward of fifteen years in prison. That possible reality served as the impetus for the world he built in "Big Pimpin'": "The contrast between the million-dollar extravagance of the 'Big Pimpin'' video and the potential of being behind bars for years behind a mindless assault wasn't lost on me. Both were about losing control." Jay Z wrote that in his 2010 book, *Decoded*. He further explained: "It's a song that seems to be about the purity of the hustler's thrill—pleasure cooked down to a crystal." And even further: "If the price is life, then you better get what you paid for. There's an equal and opposite relationship between balling and falling." He anticipated a catastrophic fall, so he balled stratospherically. His pimpin' was the biggest it ever was, and ever got, really.

When the actual trial date neared, though, Jay hedged his bet. Nervous he'd catch the violent reflex of a justice system that'd attempted and failed to lock up Puff Daddy the winter before for a shootout he was involved in at a separate New York nightclub, Jay settled ("No way was I going to allow myself to be a sideshow for the state"). He pled guilty to the charge and received three years probation,[2] and that is 100 percent a fair trade.[3]

It's a weird thing to be thankful that someone was stabbed, but I am grateful to Rivera for taking that I, as we all should be.[4] Without that happening, (maybe) Jay isn't motivated to live through the "most paranoid and hedonistic" period of his life, and so we (maybe) don't get "Big Pimpin'." That would've been a real tragedy. He should've stabbed five or six more people. He might've written the most transcendent rap album of all.[5]

Jay Z had twenty career singles before "Big Pimpin'." Of those, only three were RIAA certified gold ("Dead Presidents," "Can I Get a . . . ," and "Hard Knock Life"). "Big Pimpin'" was his first platinum single.[6] "Big Pimpin'" was also UGK's first career platinum single. The song was produced by Timbaland (a true hero), and the video, which became the first rap video featured on MTV's *Making the Video*, which carries with it its own knot of supplemental offshoots, was directed by Hype Williams (also a true hero). The song was included in *Rolling Stone*'s countdown of the 500 Greatest Songs of All Time (number 467) as well as their countdown of the 50 Greatest Hip-Hop Songs of All Time (number 16). It was nominated for a Grammy (Best Rap Performance by a Duo or Group) and an MTV VMA (Best Rap Video). In totality, it was the most successful pairing of a rapper from the North with rappers from the South[7] that had occurred up to that moment, and its brilliance lent itself as inspiration for others to try, even if they never could quite match the glow.

◆

Quick aside: Rap videos with less impressive boats.

2nd Place: The Notorious B.I.G.'s "Hypnotize," featuring Puff Daddy (1997) The boat here is the second most impressive rap video boat. Biggie's bowler hat is the first best bowler hat, though.

3rd: Young Bleed's "How Ya Do Dat," featuring C-Loc and Master P (1997) Young Bleed put nine hundred people on this boat, and that's way too high a population density. I figure this boat capsized about fifteen minutes after Master P's verse.

4th: Big Tymers' "Oh Yeah!," featuring Boo and Gotti (2002) They were on a boat that cost a few hundred thousand dollars to rent per week, and they brought a portable basketball goal on board with them. I miss the Big Tymers so much.

5th: B.G.'s "Bling Bling," featuring Hot Boys and Big Tymers (1999) I MISS THE BIG TYMERS SO MUCH.

6th: 2 Chainz's "I'm Different" (2012) This boat never even made it to the water. 2 Chainz just hung out in it while it was being carted around on the streets. What royalty.

7th: The Fugees' "Ready or Not" (1996) Lauryn Hill. ☺. But also ☹.

8th: Pusha T's "Can I Live" (2011) This was a total misplay. He was just on a boat rapping, not doing anything else. Pusha T is a drug-dealer rapper. His name is literally "Pusha." Give this man the yayo and let's make a proper drug-transporting video, please.

9th: Theophilus London's "I Stand Alone" (2011) It was a rowboat. Like, a real, for real, actual rowboat.

◆

Jay Z avoiding a fifteen-year prison sentence is a monumental *What if . . .* moment in rap. SO MUCH stuff would've been different. It's a string of possibilities superseded by only two other potentialities:

What if Tupac had not been murdered in 1996?

What if Biggie had not been murdered in 1997?

Others on the *What if . . .* list that fall somewhere below those top three: What if the Hot Boys never disbanded? What if DMX favored cats instead of dogs? What if *BET: Uncut* never existed? What if Patrick Ewing didn't miss that finger roll? What if Lauryn Hill didn't go crazy? What if Chris Tucker made *Friday 2*? What if Plies used his government name?[8] What if Suge Knight was two feet shorter?[9] What if Dr. Dre was Mr. Dre? What if Halloween didn't fall on that weekend? What if Kanye never had his heart broken? What if the Fresh Prince's dad hadn't abandoned him? What if Lil Wayne was from, say, Rhode Island? What if Snoop didn't beat his murder charge? What if Soulja Boy never

---

1. He did so because he'd been told that Rivera was responsible for *Vol. 3 . . . Life and Times of S. Carter* leaking a month before the official release date.

2. Jay was sentenced in December of 2001. Four months before that, he'd released "Izzo (H.O.V.A.)," the first single on the album that followed *Vol. 3*. On "Izzo," which he'd written after the charges came down but before the sentencing, he rapped, "Cops wanna knock me, D.A. wanna box me in / But somehow, I beat them charges like Rocky." This was (highly likely) a miscalculation on his part—he (probably) thought he actually was going to beat the charge. Or, I guess I suppose he could also have been talking about the first *Rocky* movie, where Rocky loses at the end but really he wins.

3. This is an easy assertion to make when it's not your abdomen being gouged into.

4. To be clear: I don't want anyone to be stabbed. But if we can detract the violence of the event from what came after it, then, yes, I am for real thankful.

5. Please see footnote 4.

6. From "Big Pimpin'" to 2014, he's had twenty-one singles that were gold or platinum.

7. The least successful was when Jay Z tried to co-opt Juvenile's free-form flow on the "Ha (Remix)." Oh, man. That was a sad day.

8. Algernod. ALGERNOD. That's not a rapper's name. That's the name of a mischievous elf in a Disney movie.

Supermanned any hoes? What if Lil' Kim didn't do that to her face? What if Master P's tank was just a normal-ass tank?

But to the original point: Originally, Pimp C didn't want to record for "Big Pimpin'." It wasn't in line with the sound he and Bun B had built for UGK.[10] "We put the ['Big Pimpin'']reel on and we hear these flutes and this happy music . . . and I'm like, *maaan*. I'm not doing it. I called [Jay Z] and said, 'Hey, man, are you trying to sabotage me?' He said, 'Look, fam, it's gonna be the biggest record of your career.'"[11] Eventually, he was convinced to do it. Bun B was glad. "It was probably the biggest chance that we took in our career, but it ended up being the biggest payoff as well."[12]

So, what if UGK passes again on Jay's invite to be on one of his songs? They never do "Big Pimpin'" together. What happens? Does Jay Z just keep it moving and do it with Three 6 Mafia instead? Or maybe Jay takes offense at having been turned away twice.

And maybe Jay, already short-tempered from having Nas gnawing at him, attempting to goad him into war—maybe Jay snipes at Pimp C and Bun B in a song instead of how he went for Nas's neck. And so then instead of getting the historic "Takeover" vs. "Ether" 2001 battle (see page 142) we get a true North vs. South rap war, because there is a zero percent chance that if Jay says Pimp C's name in a song, Pimp doesn't spend a planet's worth of energy attempting to unravel Jay Z's career. How does that play out?

Is it Biggie and Tupac again—an uncontrollable firestorm that ends in tragedy? Or does the fight stay on tape like how the Jay Z vs. Nas feud did? And if Jay never calls out Nas by name on "Takeover" then Nas never records "Ether," right? And if he doesn't record "Ether," then which direction does his legacy point? Because "Ether" is for sure a critical part of the Nas legend. And how does he use his extra time? Do we get to Nas's reggae period ten years earlier, and is rap even ready for that in 2000?

Or maybe Nas, having watched Bun and Pimp throw salt on Jay as two vs. one, teams up with Jay behind some home-team allusion? And so we get Jay Z and Nas vs. Bun B and Pimp C? When it's over, do Nas and Jay Z release a duo album together? Is it any good? Or maybe the two couldn't get their styles to congeal and it flops and so they both just sort of fizzle around in New York, local titans but that's it? Oh my god: WHO MARRIES BEYONCÉ IF SUCCESSFUL JAY Z ISN'T THERE? Is it Kanye? Or does Jay Z somehow still end up with Beyoncé except now it's not really a power couple, it's more of a Britney Spears and Kevin Federline couple? Does Beyoncé spiral into insanity? Does Britney Spears end up recording "Single Ladies"? Whaaaaat issss happppppening?

"Big Pimpin'" is the representation of a time in Jay Z's life that almost wasn't. But it's also a linchpin in history, keeping the reality line from sprigging out into all sorts of weirdo directions.

---

9. That puts him somewhere near as tall as George Costanza, and fucking NOBODY would've been afraid of Black George Costanza.
10. In 1998, Jay extended an offer to UGK to be on a song called "A Week Ago" from *Vol. 2 . . . Hard Knock Life*. Pimp C opted against it and they passed.
11. This quote comes from a book called *Third Coast: OutKast, Timbaland & How Hip-Hop Became a Southern Thing*.
12. This quote comes from a 2014 interview with BET.com.

REBUTTAL: "SO FRESH, SO CLEAN" OUTKAST

"Big Pimpin'" is not a bad song. It's a very, very good song. "So Fresh, So Clean" is just superior, that's all.

To be great, "Pimpin'" requires the aid of not only UGK's Pimp C and Bun B but also a "mutilated" sample from an Egyptian film whose makers are still suing for the way Jay Z and his producers butchered it. Not saying overstacking is always a damning quality (see "Monster," page 198, which is clearly the correct choice for 2010), but in this case, the muses are clearly on the side of "Clean," which careens into Classicsville with its slick, timeless, endlessly applicable simplicity. Big Boi and Stacks float on a carefree wave of well-tailored

greatness, and the fact that they did this much without featured artists or problematic samples (they use Joe Simon's "Before the Night Is Over," and *possibly* an unconfirmed riff from Funkadelic's "I'll Stay," neither of which has garnered a lawsuit) speaks to "Clean"'s exceptional nature.

I mean, I still have absolutely no idea how to process the line "I love who you are / I love who you ain't / You're so Anne Frank," but considering the rest of the song, I'm gonna just maintain that comparing a lover to an optimistic Jewish child hiding from and eventually caught and murdered by Nazis is a singular compliment. **—DEVON MALONEY**

BIG PIMPIN'

 "You know I thug 'em, fuck 'em, love 'em, leave 'em" (0:14)

 "First time they fuss I'm breezing" (0:23)

"Many chicks wanna put Jigga's fists in cuffs" (0:36)

 "I'll be forever macking" (0:49)

 "Gettin' blowed with the motherfuckin' Jigga Man" (2:31)

"Go read a book you illiterate son of a bitch and step up your vocab" (2:00)

"Coming straight up out the black barrio" (1:40)

 "Smoking out, pouring up, keeping lean up in my cup" (3:01)

 "Everybody wanna ball, holla at broads at the mall" (3:10)

 "Chroming, shining, sipping daily, no rest until whitey pays me" (3:21)

"All my car got leather and wood" (3:05)

 "My stamina be enough for Pamela Anderson Lee" (3:58)

"It'll sell by night" (4:12)

 "We got bitches in the back of the truck, laughing it up" (4:23)

 OBSERVATIONAL INFLAMMATORY DEADLY EXAMINING LIFESTYLE PSYCHOLOGICAL HOPEFUL

2001

TAKEOVER

vs.

ETHER

JAY Z vs. NAS

WHAT THESE SONGS ARE ABOUT

Destroying the other person by discrediting the other person.

. . . .

WHY THEY'RE IMPORTANT

Because the two together represent the Homeric intersection of real life and art, and are one of the greatest-ever testaments to the role that ego plays in rap music.

. . . .

Note: This is the only chapter in the book that's about two songs. It had to be this way.

Today, Jay Z is very famous. He's very famous inside of rap and he's also very famous outside of rap.[1] Nas is considerably less famous outside of rap but equally famous within it. This, it would appear, is a reflection of what was at the very center of their very famous feud, which culminated in "Takeover" vs. "Ether," the most electrifying rap battle that's ever occurred and that will ever occur.

In the interest of space, I'm going to move forward under the assumption you understand three things:

1. Jay Z and Nas are two of the very most influential rappers of all time. It's as true now as it was in 2001 and as it will be in 2101.

2. Jay Z and Nas were equally at risk during their war. That's a large part of the reason the feud ended up being so important. This wasn't LL Cool J vs. Canibus, where one guy is a star and nobody really knows who the other one is. This was two boss-level bosses. And that meant that the loser was going to be unfavorably remembered forever. That is a terrifying thought, for sure. It's why these sorts of things happen so rarely, really. It's just, like, why risk it? Think on it like this: Ja Rule and 50 Cent were equal stars relative to one another when they started going at each other (2002–2003). Ja could've avoided it. He didn't. So 50 Cent crushed him. Now 50 Cent is worth about half a billion dollars and Ja Rule works at Arby's.[2]

3. Jay Z and Nas both wanted the same thing (to be the best rapper) but were trying to get there in different ways; Jay thought stacking up credits could get him there;

Nas thought layering art on top of art was the way there.

Here is a timeline of the six years it took for Jay Z and Nas to go from spark to nuclear war:

1995: Nas is a no-show for a recording session with Jay Z. Producer Ski Beatz, still wanting Nas's voice on the track, lifts the line "I'm out for presidents to represent me" from Nas's "The World Is Yours," then uses it as the spine for Jay Z's "Dead Presidents." Despite "Dead Presidents" being an amazing song—tempered, insightful, perfectly pitched—Nas isn't that happy about being included without actually being included.

Sidebar: *There's a scene in the video for "Dead Presidents" where Jay, the Notorious B.I.G., and Dame Dash, who used to be Jay Z's manager and business partner but is now only in the news anymore when people want to talk about how much financial trouble he's in, sit at a table and drink alcohol and play Monopoly. Given what we know now about his business acumen, I have to assume Jay Z won this game handily.[3] I also have to assume Dame Dash spent all his efforts trying to land on the railroads and Baltic Avenue to buy them. There's no land more useless in Monopoly than Baltic Avenue.*

1996: Nas says the line "Lex with TV sets [are] the minimum" in his song "The Message." It lives in disguise at first, but is eventually revealed as a masked swipe at Jay Z, who Nas says he'd seen riding around in a Lexus with TVs in it. (Nas also once said, "I got rid of my Lexus at that point and I was looking for the next best thing." NAS THREW AWAY A CAR because he saw someone he was upset with driving a similar one. One time I ate half of a donut that I found on the floor in the bathroom at my house. He and I live in different worlds.)

1997: Following the death of the Notorious B.I.G., Jay Z attempts to anoint himself replacement royalty on *In My Lifetime, Vol. 1*. On "The City Is Mine," Jay raps, "Don't worry about Brooklyn, I continue to flame / Therefore a world with amnesia won't forget your name / You held it down long enough, let me take those reins."

1998: Jay releases *Vol. 2 . . . Hard Knock Life*. It debuts at number one on *Billboard*'s Top 200, and eventually sells more than five million copies and earns him a Grammy for Best Rap Album. Some people are upset because it seems pretty clear that the album's main goal is success instead of art. Jay Z is not upset because he is only a handful of smart business moves[4] and ten years away from marrying Beyoncé.

Sidebar: *Jay Z has proved to be driven by commercial success, specifically the accelerated advancement of his brand within whichever corridors he feels offer the greatest ROI. He's certainly not alone in this philosophy—Ice-T, for example, though slightly less interested in shaking hands with Prince William, has always talked about his career in music as an enjoyable byproduct of his desire to become impactful—Jay Z's just the very best at it. In 2014, Forbes estimated his net worth was greater than $520 million.*

1999: Nas releases "We Will Survive," a song that is, in part, an ode to the Notorious B.I.G. It includes this: "It used to be fun makin' records to see your response / But now competition is none now that you're gone / And these niggas is wrong, using your name in vain / And they claim to be New York's king? It ain't about that." Nas has always appeared more interested in artistry,[5] which is a trait that nearly everybody who is familiar with rap attributes to him, even if he did go

1. Jay Z is one of six rappers that my mom can name. The other five: Tupac (he's her first mention always), Slim Shady (though she doesn't know that he and Eminem are the same person because she is adorable), Vanilla Ice (this one is my fault—I really, really liked "Ice Ice Baby" when I was in elementary school), Snoop (he's my dad's favorite rapper, inasmuch as a fifty-plus-year-old Mexican man can have a favorite rapper), and Pitbull (though she will always ask, "Is he a rapper?" when she names him).
2. Probably.
3. The dream Monopoly rapper showdown: Jay Z, Dr. Dre, Puff, Master P, and DMX. The first four because they've amassed fortunes in rap and other ventures, the last because I really just want to see what DMX says when he draws the Go to Jail card.
4. A noncomprehensive list of Jay Z's endorsement deals: Budweiser, Samsung, Reebok, Hublot, Hewlett-Packard, Rhapsody, and Bing. If Jay Z couldn't make Bing cool, nobody can.
5. Nas actually has a long string of endorsement deals as well. It's not impossible that his philosophical stance is a restriction imposed by poor business skills and not by morality, I suppose.

on to record "Braveheart Party."[6] That discrepancy in purpose was the point of his barb here, and really the whole philosophical reason for their fighting. After he rapped it, everyone looked at Jay Z to see what he was going to do. Jay Z responded by looking at his very expensive watch to see if he was late for a meeting.

1999: Nas pokes Memphis Bleek in the eye. Bleek, who is closely associated with Jay Z, responds in 2000 on "My Mind Right," saying, "Your lifestyle's written / So who you supposed to be? Play your position." It's a tame assault (it references Nas's album *It Was Written*), but it was at least proof that Nas had Jay's ear. (The most important thing Memphis Bleek did in his career was exist so Nas could pick on him, which eventually led to Jay Z responding to Nas. Bless you, Bleek.) [*Note:* Mobb Deep, Nas allies, also began inserting themselves into all of this around this point, though never to any real effect beyond being close enough to Nas to encourage him.]

2000: Nas, (probably by this point) frustrated he's not goaded Jay into a direct response yet, gets louder, more confrontational, more unavoidable: "Y'all niggas all hail, the King is dead / He running like a bitch with his tail between his legs / 'Stillmatic,' still eye for an eye, wanna be God / You're just the next rapper to die, fucking with Nas." He makes it impossible for Jay Z to ignore him. So Jay Z stops ignoring him.

Sidebar: *This feels like a good time to mention that in an interview that ran in a 2003 issue of XXL, Nas said that when he heard Tupac diss him on "Against All Odds," it made him cry. Nas is great for a lot of reasons, but one of the ones near the top is that he's always seemed aware of his emotions, even if he doesn't explicitly speak about them all regularly.*

2001: FINALLY, Jay Z responds. While performing at Hot 97's Summer Jam concert, Jay performs a previously unheard song called "Takeover." The first verse is aggressive, though it doesn't specifically name names. The second verse calls out Mobb Deep, doing so while showing adorable pictures of Mobb Deep member Prodigy as a child on the stage's big screen. Everyone laughs. Jay ends the song with the line "Ask Nas, he don't want it with Hov, no!" Everyone goes, "*Whhhhaaaaaaaaaaaaaaaaaaaat!*" It's all the provocation Nas needed.

2001: Nas releases "Stillmatic (Freestyle)," which is just full-on war mode. He attacks several of Jay Z's label mates, then Jay himself, calling him, among other things, a liar and a homosexual and a copycat. All of a sudden, two of the most terrifying rappers on the planet are missiling toward each other at a trillion miles per hour. "Exciting" isn't the word. Nothing else matters.

2001: Jay releases the full version of "Takeover," which includes a whole section dedicated to the mathematical annihilation of Nas. This is the most crushing part:

> *You said you been in this ten, I've been in it five.*
> *Smarten up, Nas. Four albums in ten years, nigga? I can divide.*
> *That's one every, let's say two.*
> *Two of them shits was due.*
> *One was . . . "Nahhh."*
> *The other was Illmatic.*
> *That's a one hot album every ten year average.*
> *And that's so . . . laaaaammmme!*
> *Nigga, switch up your flow.*
> *Your shit is garbage, but you try and kick knowledge? (Get the fuck outta here.)*

Everyone assumes Nas is going to put his head in an oven. He does not.

6. The generally accepted Worst Nas Song is "Who Killed It?" from 2006's *Hip Hop Is Dead*. That's incorrect, though. "Who Killed It?" is a bad song. But it's bad in a pretentious way. (It's Nas talking about rap being dead, and that's no new thing, but he's doing it in a cartoonish Al Capone accent, and that was a real mistake.) *Stillmatic's* "Braveheart Party" is a failed grasp at radio play, and that's way more offensive. The song was so upsetting that Mary J. Blige, who sang the hook, asked that it be removed from further pressings of *Stillmatic*.

7. Biggie told *Vibe* that he'd written that song well before Tupac was shot, which is either proof that he didn't intend this as a diss song or proof that it is a diss song and also that he knew Tupac was going to be shot. And even if it wasn't originally intended as a diss song, the timing of the release certainly wasn't an accident.

8. When Tupac took aim at Biggie on "Hit 'Em Up" it starts with "That's why I fucked your bitch, you fat motherfucker." Tupac and Jay Z did not handle things the same way.

2001: Nas releases "Ether" and all of the birds in the sky die and all of the fish in the ocean die, too. It's full of salt, but the worst is when Nas strips away the bluster:

My child, I've watched you grow up to be famous.
And now I smile like a proud dad watchin' his only son that made it.
You seem to be only concerned with dissing women.
Were you abused as a child?
Scared to smile?
They called you ugly?
Well, life is harsh.
Hug me, don't reject me.
Or make records to disrespect me, bla-tant or indirectly.

The saddest thing, too, about my whole life is Little Kid Jay Z being called ugly. ☹

◆

Seven questions:

1. Is this the best rap battle that's ever happened?

Yes. It's one of only two rap battles that was as mesmerizing to experience as it is to talk about today, which is how everyone knows that it's very important. The other one is Tupac vs. Biggie, which matched Nas and Jay Z's star power. But Tupac vs. Biggie was never even truly a battle. There was confrontation, yes (see page 105), and there were of course two clearly defined sides, yes. But "Tupac" and "Biggie," at least in the context of "Tupac vs. Biggie," were always just avatars for "West Coast" and "East Coast." The closest Biggie ever even came to addressing the animus of the situation was releasing "Who Shot Ya," which showed up a few months after Tupac was robbed and shot in New York in 1994. But Biggie never said Tupac's name in it, and he never publicly acknowledged that it was even about Tupac.[7]

Tupac's "Hit 'Em Up" is a crucial and critical blow. But there was never reciprocation.

2. What's the best "Takeover" vs. "Ether" piece of trivia?

Here it is: There was a third part to all of this: "Ether" was so damning when it hit that Jay Z, nearly impossible to rattle, offered an impromptu response on Hot 97 called "Super Ugly." In it, he said that he and Allen Iverson slept with Nas's then-girlfriend, an allegation he alluded to on "Takeover" ("You-know-who did you-know-what with you-know-who"[8]). He also said he left a used condom on Nas's baby's car seat. Jay Z's mother was so offended, she made Jay Z apologize to Nas and his girlfriend and all other women.

3. Which song is sonically better?

"Takeover" sampled the very rugged "Five to One" by the

Doors, and it sure was fun and surprising, and I definitely do enjoy Jay Z's ability to bend sentences around corners to fit into whatever cadence it is he's trying to make. But "Ether," a testament to Nas's superheroic skill, was as rotund as it was slicing, and that's a pair of traits nobody else on earth has figured out how to match up yet. "Ether" got it.

4. Which song has the better disses?

"Ether" was very, very ruthless. It covered all the bases.

Destructive: "Blowed up, no guts left; chest/face gone"

Self-congratulatory: "Name a rapper that I ain't influenced"

Directly hurtful: He called Jay a camel, and that's so sad.

Indirectly dismissive: "What's sad is I love you 'cuz you're my brother / You traded your soul for riches"

But Jay Z's above-referenced math class was too real to overcome. "Takeover" got it.

5. Wait, so who won, then?

Everyone did, actually.

Jay Z won because he thrust himself further into the true rap canon than he could have had he avoided confrontation. No matter how famous he gets, how many endorsement deals he does, or how many times he hangs out with the president, he will always be one-half of the most exciting, realest rap battle in history. His name couldn't carry as much weight in rap without it.

Nas won because it reinvigorated him and revitalized his career.

And humans with functioning ears won because we got "Takeover" and "Ether" and all of the excitement that surrounded the battle while it was happening. Also, nobody died, which is always preferable.

6. Yeah, but who *really* won?

Well, "Ether" was technically better than "Takeover."

7. Got it. So Nas won?

Kind of, but really no. It's hard to say Nas won because we know how each of their lives turned out. I mean, Nas literally worked for Jay Z when he signed to Def Jam Records in 2006.[9] At the end of everything, we're back at their core dispute: art vs. success.

In 2001, Nas won. But for the rest of time, Jay will win.

I suspect that's how they prefer it, too.

---

9. Jay Z was president of Def Jam Records by that point.

REBUTTAL: "RENEGADE" JAY Z, FEATURING EMINEM

Jay Z engaged in a rivalry more subtle, but no less significant, on *The Blueprint*. Well, "rivalry" implies that the competition between Jay and Eminem on "Renegade" was close. But just as Sean Carter was bested by another smiling nihilist on an infamous freestyle six years earlier, so too was he dominated by his album's only guest. Eminem was coming off the best record of his career, one that made him "the king of these rude, ludicrous, lucrative lyrics." Aside from being Jay's main competition commercially, Em had inherited hip-hop's mantle of the underdog: Even when on top, he came across as an outsider. On *Blueprint*, Jay established himself as the twenty-first-century rap overlord. But Em, more mercurial, and ultimately more self-destructive, hijacked "Renegade" with a jaw-dropping display of the raw talent that allowed him to dominate the next five years, as well as the overwhelming fury that eventually doomed his music.

—JONAH BROMWICH

Rivalries

SOMETIMES RAPPERS DON'T GET ALONG WITH OTHER RAPPERS, THINGS

Jay Z vs. Nas + Common vs. Drake + Snoop Dogg vs. Looking Like Abraham Lincoln's Skeleton +

Eazy-E vs. Dr. Dre + Ice-T vs. Soulja Boy + Lil B vs. Kevin Durant + Lupe Fiasco vs. Aliens + The

Real Roxanne vs. Roxanne Shante + LL Cool J vs. Canibus + Nelly vs. Chingy + Chingy vs. Having

to be Chingy + Jermaine Dupri vs. Timbaland and Dr. Dre + Charles Hamilton vs. That Girl Who

Punched Him in the Face + Boogie Down Productions vs. Juice Crew + 50 Cent vs. Ja Rule +

Busy Bee vs. Kool Moe Dee + Rakim vs. Daddy-O + J. Cole vs. Everlasting Corniness +

Run-DMC vs. Sucker M.C.'s + Lil Wayne vs. Guitarist Tha Carter III + Memphis Bleek vs. Nas

+ Pimp C vs. Master P + MC Eiht vs. DJ Quik + T.I. vs. Lil Flip + Lil Flip

vs. Whomever It Was Who Convinced Him to Pose with Shaun on That One Album

Cover + Future vs. Rich Homie Quan + Suge Knight vs. Being a Very

Despicable Person + Soulja Boy vs. Lil Kim + Lil Kim vs. Cosmetic

Surgery + Iggy Azalea vs. Ears + N.W.A vs. Havoc Vs. Prodigy + Tyler, The Creator vs.

B.o.B. + DMX vs. Going Insane + Gucci Mane vs. Going to Prison + LL Cool J vs. Not Licking His

Own Lips + Joe Budden vs. Raekwon + Ol' Dirty Bastard vs. Welfare + Young Jeezy vs. The Plug

+ Jackie O vs. Foxy Brown + LL Cool J vs. Those Sharks in *Deep Blue Sea* + Method Man and

Redman vs. Acting in *How High* + Coolio vs. Weird Al Yankovic + Eminen vs. Every Woman on

the Planet + Mos Def vs. His Facial Hair + Missy Elliott vs. Whomever Had the Keys to the Jeep

GRINDIN'

—

The Clipse

WHAT THIS SONG IS ABOUT
Dealing drugs.

● ●

WHY IT'S IMPORTANT
It evolved gangsta rap, thumbing it into coke rap, a subgenre of a subgenre of rap that was rooted primarily in talking about dealing drugs in clever ways, which became a dominant trend in rap. (Also, it became the North Star for the Neptunes, an affluential production duo.)

The following names are of characters from a TV show called *The Wire*, which ran on HBO from 2002 to 2008 and examined the caustic effects of drugs in Baltimore. Their quotes are scattered throughout this chapter.

> **Omar Little:** He is a self-employed mercenary. He sticks up drug dealers for a living.
> **Avon Barksdale:** He's the leader of a fiercely successful drug operation.
> **Cutty:** He's a reformed enforcer from the drug trade. He runs a boxing gym now.
> **Bunk Moreland:** He's a detective in the homicide unit of the Baltimore PD.
> **Slim Charles:** He mostly works as an enforcer for whichever drug cartel needs him.
> **Bubs:** He alternates between being a drug addict and a recovering drug addict.
> **Stringer Bell:** He's second-in-command in the Barksdale organization.

This is not a comprehensive list of the people on the show, and the descriptions here can hardly really be called descriptions. But they will do.

◆

"The game is out there, and it's either play or get played." —Omar Little
Pusha T is one of two members of the Clipse, and just that quickly you know that Pusha T spends a lot of his time talking about drugs, because his name is Pusha, referencing "pusher," which is slang for "drug dealer." The other member of the Clipse used to call himself Malice, and just that quickly you know that he spent a lot of time talking about bad things, drugs and the such, because his name was Malice. In 2012, Malice changed his name to No Malice, a reflection of his conversion to Christianity. The religiosity was largely inspired by the 2009 arrest and eventual incarceration of Anthony Gonzalez, the group's former manager. Gonzalez admitted to being the leader of a $20 million drug ring that had moved a half ton of cocaine, a full ton of marijuana, and hundreds of pounds of

heroin to different parts of the United States. He received thirty-two years in prison. No Malice still raps about the bad things, the drugs and such, and he does so with the same concrete resolution he'd flexed before, but now it's of a different tone—a no-thank-you tone; a good-bye tone.

Pusha T admires *The Wire*.[1] This makes sense because *The Wire* is wonderful and largely considered the finest television of its time and all time. But it also makes sense because the way you would talk about it—an unflinching, nuanced, steadied drug drama set in a city in the northeastern United States that forgoes celebrating drug culture and drug dealers in favor of positioning them as a reflection of that culture—is the exact same way you would talk about the Clipse's music. They make drug records. More accurately: They make coke rap records. They did so in the '90s to moderate success, but after linking up with production team the Neptunes, they did it in 2002[2] better than anyone had ever done it before,[3] specifically with "Grindin'," and effectively legitimized the coke rap trend that would come to dominate rap in the years that followed.

♦

"We gon' handle this shit like businessmen. Sell the shit, make the profit, and later for that gangster bullshit." —Stringer Bell

At the beginning of "Grindin'," Pharrell, one-half of the Neptunes,[4] introduces everything by saying, "Yo, I go by the name of Pharrell, from the Neptunes, and I just wanna let y'all know the world is about to feel something that they've never felt before," and as far as boasts go, it was similar to most,[5] but also as far as boasts go, it was truer than most.

The Neptunes are maybe the most influential production team of the last fifteen years,[6] and they were definitely that from 2000 to 2010. They built up large, large hits for Snoop ("Drop It Like It's Hot"), Nelly ("Hot In Herre"), Justin Timberlake ("Señorita"), Kelis ("Milkshake"), Britney Spears ("I'm a Slave 4 U"), Jay Z ("I Just Wanna Love U"), and more. But none matched the weight, the ingenuity of sparseness, of "Grindin'." It sounded like someone was beating on a garage door, which connected it to the past, but it also sounded like someone was trying to make a phone call from outer space, which connected

it to the future, and that's exactly what it represented, both in production and rap.

♦

"I'm just a gangster, I suppose. And I want my corners." —Avon Barksdale

There's a scene in the final episode of the second season of *The Wire* where a plan Stringer Bell laid gets tangled up and a hit man he hired named Brother Mouzone ends up getting shot but not killed. Stringer visits him in the hospital, and while there he asks Mouzone who shot him. Mouzone doesn't say. When Stringer mentions the exchange to Avon, he says he asked Mouzone who shot him. Avon, flabbergasted, asks him why, but in a voice that lets him know it's less a question and more an admonition. "Why, what?" Stringer asks. "How you gonna ask a soldier like Mouzone a question like that?" Avon barks. "Either he's gonna say or he's gonna work it out. Either way, you ain't got to be asking him for shit." Watching it unfold, I had no idea Stringer had done anything wrong, but as soon as Avon explained it I understood. Watching *The Wire* is great, but it always reminds me that I am not a gangster.

There's a part in the third verse of "Grindin'" where (No) Malice says, "Four and a half will get you in the game / Anything less is just a goddamn shame." It's an easy bar to learn, and it's fun to say, but I didn't have any idea what it meant for the whole twelve years between when the song came out and when I wrote this paragraph right here. I didn't know if "four and a half" meant hundreds, dollars, or guns or crack rocks or hot dogs. When dealing with cocaine, an eighth of a kilogram is the minimum amount considered to be major weight (an eighth of a kilogram is 4.5 ounces). Isn't that interesting? Listening to the Clipse is great, but it always reminds me that I am not a drug dealer.

♦

"The game done changed." —Cutty

Pusha T and Malice are from Virginia Beach, Virginia. There's an argument to be made that their prominence signaled the potentiality for other cities not known for rap to become known for rap (Memphis, Seattle, Baltimore, Washington, D.C., etc.). There's also an easier argument to be made that the success of "Grindin'" was the continuation of the radio dominance of the

---

1. "I felt like it was so authentic, man." –Pusha T, talking about *The Wire* with MTV in 2012
2. The same year *The Wire* started, I'd like to remind you.
3. And better than anyone's done it since, FYI.
4. Pharrell Williams + Chad Hugo.
5. In fact, it's a direct homage to Slick Rick's very similar claim on 1985's "La Di Da Di" (see page 46).
6. Oh, hey, Timbaland.

GRINDIN'

"I sell it whipped, un-whipped, it's soft or hard" (0:21)

"Call me subwoofer 'cause I pump base like that, Jack" (0:28)

"Gucci Chuck Taylor with the dragon on the side" (0:44)

"Watch it, like my whip, like my chick, topless" (1:28)

"Legend in two games like I'm Pee Wee Kirkland" (0:53)

"Cocky, something that I just can't help" (1:47)

"I'm just grinding, man, y'all never mind me" (1:58)

"My grind's 'bout family, never been about fame" (2:41)

"Filthy, the word that best defines me" (1:55)

"Four and a half will get you in the game" (2:46)

"I move 'caine like a cripple" (3:01)

"Glock with two tips, whoever gets in the way" (2:53)

"One eye closed I'll hit you, as if I was Slick Rick my aim is still an issue" (3:08)

DESCRIPTIVE

INTROSPECTIVE

HISTORICAL REFERENCE

SELF-REFLECTIVE

THRILLING

NAME BRAND

COMPARATIVE

Neptunes, Missy Elliott, and Timbaland, all also from Virginia, and all interested in evolving rap into etherealness.

◆

"Thin line between heaven and here." —Bubs

Right around the time that Malice was deciding to become No Malice, Pusha was deciding to join Kanye West's GOOD Music label. No Malice found Jesus. Pusha T found Yeezus. I'm glad everything that's ever happened in the whole history of the world has happened because it led to me being able to write a No Malice/Pusha T, Jesus/Yeezus couplet. This book is a success, as is history. Sometimes the universe serves this stuff up right in your face and all you can do is be thankful.

◆

"If it's a lie, then we fight on that lie." —Slim Charles

There have been stages to gangsta rap, which definitely is what coke rap is rooted in. Early gangsta rap, tied to the crack epidemic of the '80s and early '90s, was not an uplifting narrative; it didn't have any Horatio Alger in it. It was meant as the loudest kind of analysis, an unsettling look at the aftershocks caused by the drugs and the drug war.[7] It grew from there into what Dr. Dre and Snoop turned it into, which is to say a perfectly stylized version of itself. Then came the American outlaw Tupac, and after his death things started to tip. Crack, while still a nasty problem, wasn't the rampant epidemic it was anymore, and so the

violence that had been attached to it tapered off. ("In 1991, 50.4 African Americans per 100,000 were killed. By 2000, that number had halved itself. Actual murders committed by young black males dropped from 244.1 per 100,000 youths in 1993 to 67.3 in 1999."[8]) Biggie had turned the lens inward, examining the effect the drug trade had on a person philosophically and intrinsically (Jay Z occasionally did this, too, though never as well), and Nas sat on his stoop and reported on the entirety of his universe like no one else had or could. But, absent a sense of true urgency, gangsta rap floundered otherwise. Puff showed up and yanked rap in the direction he took it, commodifying commodities, commercializing everything with light-speed, slapping Cîroc stickers on everything and swapping out bandannas for velour Sean John sweatpants. And then the Clipse walked onto the radio with "Grindin'," and *Oh my goodness, what TF is this???* It was back to drug dealing, but it was this new thing, from this new perspective. There was no romanticizing, no upsell, just d-boy rap championing d-boy rap. The post-crack, post-Tupac gangsta rappers were supplementing true chaos with charisma, and the result was an inescapable feeling of secondhandedness.[9] The Clipse were the opposite. There was no charisma. They had reverse charisma. The Clipse anesthetized the process. They removed the emotion. They were workaday hustlers. It was perfect.

---

7. In 1985, Toddy Tee released a song called "Batterram." It was about the armored vehicle battering ram the police had started using in Los Angeles to bust through the walls of suspected drug houses. It was the first diss track aimed at a mode of transportation.
8. This is from Ta-Nehisi Coates, who is brilliant.
9. We didn't see another large-scale gangsta rapper until 50 Cent showed up in 2003 (see page 156).

REBUTTAL: "WORK IT" MISSY ELLIOTT

Not to be that guy—Ack! The nos*talg*ist!—but as wrong as hip-hop could have gone in 2002, it mostly kept going crazily, awesomely right, week after week after week. 2002 was so good that "Grindin'" never went higher than eight on the *Billboard* rap songs chart. *Eight.* On the rap chart. 2002 had "Pass the Courvoisier Part II (Remix)" and "My Neck, My Back" and "Hot in Herre" and "Lights, Camera, Action!" and, uh, "Mama's Baby, Poppa's Maybe." But, look, this amazing thing happened at the end of the summer that year. This woman rapping, in inimitable cadences, about how awesome sex with her would be: so good that you'd have to resort to onomatopoeia to describe it, so good that *she's*

gotta speak in tongues, so good that you have to laugh—and it's never not funny. "Badonkadonk"? *Hahahaha!* This was Missy and Timbaland in the age of sexual eruption. Hip-hop had never been more graphically horny, more headed to spring break, more likely to leave you praying for that Clearblue minus to never go plus. This song doesn't sound like the future or the past or even the present. It keeps on operating in its own surrealist universe of clocks melting in the rocks and pipes not being pipes. Missy did it at the Super Bowl 41, and the song shot back up the *Billboard* chart. In 2015! Don't doubt "Work It." It still works.

—WESLEY MORRIS

2003

IN DA CLUB

---

50 CENT

"People love the bad guy. I watch movies all the time and root for the bad guy and turn it off before it ends because the bad guy dies. It's cinematic law: the bad guy has to die. But sometimes the bad guy gets a record deal and becomes a superstar like 50." —50 Cent, *The Guardian*, 2003

Right around the middle of the aughts, there was a pushback against Oprah Winfrey by several rappers, the most famous being Ludacris, 50 Cent, and Ice Cube. All three asserted she had an agenda against rap.

Ludacris was invited on her show in 2005 with the rest of the major cast members of the movie *Crash*, but that's where his ire was born; he told *GQ* that his inclusion was a last-minute addition, that he felt his interview was acrimonious and unfair, that she took the opportunity to lecture him about his music even though he'd gone on the show to talk about his film role, that she told him privately she wasn't comfortable with giving rappers the sizable platform an appearance on her show afforded. Following that, 50 Cent extended Luda's complaint, telling the Associated Press she'd been making television for old white women so long that she'd become one.[1] He also got a dog and named it after her, and that's pretty terrible but also kind of funny.[2] Ice Cube was mad she'd invited cast members of *Barbershop* to her show but left him out, which was certainly strange given he was the star of the movie, so he took potshots at her, too.

After receiving the three swipes, Oprah, queen, told MTV she didn't have a problem with rap, she had a problem with the way that it can/will/had/has marginalized women. Ice Cube had a song in 1990 called "It's a Man's World" that opened with "Women, they're good for nothing—no, maybe one thing / To serve needs to my ding-a-ling," and there are about one billion other examples of similar viewpoints from rappers, so her criticism of rap made/makes sense. In a 2006 interview with Ed Lover, though, she admitted she wasn't above listening to it, that she liked some of it. The one song she mentioned specifically: "In Da Club."

"I've been accused of not liking hip-hop and that's just not true. I got a little 50 in my iPod. I really do. I like 'In Da Club.' Have you heard the beat to 'In Da Club'? Love that."

She called 50 Cent "50," and that's cool. She's probably danced to "In Da Club," and that's cooler.

♦

50's origin story is the sort of thing an uncreative person would come up with if he or she were trying to manufacture a gangsta rapper.[3] A fact-and-effect version of it:

FACT: He was an underprivileged youth who never knew his father.
EFFECT: This would give him the long-form mistrust and disregard for authority he'd need.

FACT: His mother was a neighborhood drug dealer.
EFFECT: This would give him the eventual agency he'd need to become a criminal himself.

FACT: His mother was murdered early in his life and the case was never solved.[4]
EFFECT: This would give him the broken and blackened heart he'd need.

FACT: He was raised by grandparents but felt the need to take care of himself, so he became a drug dealer at age twelve.
EFFECT: This would help him hone his business acumen under the most severe kind of stress.

FACT: He was arrested as a young boy.
EFFECT: This would either help him fully understand the stakes or extinguish any remaining fear he had in him—in this case, it was the latter.

FACT: He dropped out of school.
EFFECT: This would almost entirely wipe away the ability to attain wealth through legitimate means, making his lawlessness even more urgent.

FACT: He rose to the top of his deadly drug dealer–based eco-system.[5]
EFFECT: This would foster the endless self-belief he'd need.

FACT: He was shot some terrible amount of times[6] in an attempted assassination but didn't die.
EFFECT: This would establish hyperauthenticity while also creating a He's Indestructible myth.

FACT: He was dropped by his record label because he was deemed too big a liability.
EFFECT: This would propagate the idea that he was so dangerous that even standing near him was too big of a liability, which magnifies the aforementioned myth.

FACT: He was picked up off the wire and championed by the most successful rapper of all time and the most influential rap producer of all time.[7]
EFFECT: This would give him insta-credibility, both artistically and commercially.

FACT: He was hand-delivered to the radio with "In Da Club," an unstoppable and seismic single.
EFFECT: He "puts the rap game in a choke hold," as he explains it.

The whole thing, it's predictable and uninteresting in any fictional capacity. As a work of nonfiction, though—as a work of nonfiction it was the single most compelling story arc any rapper presented for a decade in either direction. 50 arrived to us fully formed and absolute. He was the best villain in rap since Eminem, but he was about twice as likable and two hundred times scarier, and "In Da Club," the first single from his first album *Get Rich or Die Tryin'*, managed to package everything together. It became the spire of free-enterprise rap. Nobody's been able to re-create that moment since (not even 50). For perspective: Only eight albums in the history of all of rap have sold more copies than *GRoDT*, and no rap album that's come after it has sold as many.

---

1. He said so during an interview he did with *Elle* magazine. *ELLE* MAGAZINE.
2. He also got a cat and named it after Gayle, Oprah's longtime friend. 50 Cent excels at pickling his enemies.
3. He or she would almost certainly use the phrase "gangsta rapper" in their notes. He or she would also probably be wearing annoying shoes.
4. 50 was eight years old when his mother was murdered. Someone put something in her drink that knocked her out, then that someone closed all the windows and doors in the house, turned on the gas, and left her body there to inhale all the everything.
5. At his peak, 50 says he was making $5,000 a day selling crack and heroin.
6. 50 was shot nine times in 2000, including once in the face, which knocked a chunk of his gums out and gave him a permanent soft slur.
7. Eminem and Dr. Dre.

◆

"I've never really felt anticipation on an artist like that and I've dealt with Biggie and watched Dr. Dre and Snoop. This is a new type of beast."—Puff, talking to MTV about 50 Cent after "In Da Club" was released and exploded Jupiter with the vibrations it made

"In Da Club" was the first single from *Get Rich or Die Tryin'*, a very real classic that was as successful as an album as "In Da Club" was an individual song.[8] "In Da Club" was number one on *Billboard*'s Hot 100 chart for nine weeks. (That's one week for every time he was shot.) In total, it was on the chart for thirty weeks. "In Da Club" received Grammy nominations for Best Male Rap Solo Performance and Best Rap Song.[9] *Billboard* picked it as one of the one hundred hottest songs of the decade. *Rolling Stone* did, too. *Rolling Stone* also picked it as one of the 500 Greatest Songs of All Time. VH1 had it on their 100 Greatest Hip-Hop Songs list. It broke *Billboard*'s "most-listened-to song in radio history within a week" record, which is a thing I didn't even know they kept track of.

◆

Did you know that after Columbia dropped 50 from their label, the first person who called him to come work was Puff Daddy?[10] Did you know DJ Quik played percussion on "In Da Club"? Did you know Eminem's group D12 was actually given the beat to "In Da Club" first but they passed on it because they weren't sure what to do with it? Did you know 50 Cent told rapper Tech N9ne he bought Mike Tyson's mansion off the success of "In Da Club"? Did you know four of 50's first ten singles went platinum, and seven of them went either platinum or gold? Did you know in the history of rap only Kanye, the Notorious B.I.G., and Drake have done anything similar?[11] Did you know before 50 recorded "In Da Club" he met with Eminem, and he was so nervous that he barely talked and that made Em nervous that 50 didn't like him and that's basically the exact same thing that happened when Dr. Dre met Em before they recorded "My Name Is" in 1999?

◆

50 Cent is a good businessman. That's easy to see now because when *Forbes* writes about the wealthiest rappers, he is always included and there are always nine numbers by wherever his name is on the page. But it was easy to see before he was rich, too. The two most obvious examples:

1. While in jail during his drug-dealer life, 50 made acquaintances with a group of stickup men. When they got out of jail, he hired them. He had them go around and rob competing drug dealers. He'd give them the info they needed, they'd rob the dealers, keep the cash and whatever else they got, but give 50 the drugs. As a result, the drug dealers who were being robbed had to start carrying guns, and that meant that when the police popped up they had to run away, which is a thing they'd avoided previously because they never had guns or actual drugs on them while they were dealing. Even in drug dealing, consistency is vital. While the other dealers would periodically be forced to abandon their posts, 50 was always available. What's more, he was packaging the stolen drugs with his drugs and offering them as two-for-one deals.

2. In 1999, 50 released a song called "How to Rob," which was him rapping for four minutes about all the different ways he'd rob different people. Among those listed was Jay Z, who was by then well into propping himself up as a superstar. Jay Z responded on a song called "It's Hot," saying, "I'm about a dollar, what the fuck is 50 cents?" This was before 50 had even released an album, and before he'd teamed up with Eminem and Dr. Dre, and before he was shot and so on. 50, willing opportunist, began using it to open his shows.

There's no string of reality where 50 Cent isn't successful.

---

8. It moved 872,000 copies its opening week despite being released five days early because of bootlegging. That was the most for a debut album by any artist. It's since sold twelve million copies worldwide.

9. Eminem's "Lose Yourself" won both. 50 Cent also lost the Grammy for Best New Artist that year. Evanescence won. 50 walked up onstage during their presentation as a matter of silent protest, then walked back off. Nobody made a big fuss about it like they did when Kanye did it to Taylor Swift at the 2009 VMAs. That's because Taylor Swift is adorable and Evanescence is like if a headache was alive.

10. He wanted him as a songwriter, but after 50 showed up in a bulletproof vest holding a cocked gun, he didn't want him as a songwriter anymore.

11. Kanye did 8/10, Biggie did 7/10, and Drake did 9/10. Drake's only misstep was "Fancy," which makes sense because Swizz Beatz was on it and Swizz Beatz is always dicking up everything.

IN DA CLUB

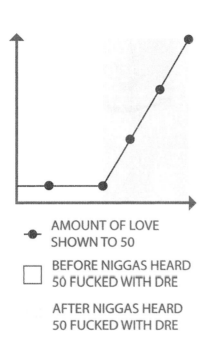

AMOUNT OF LOVE SHOWN TO 50

BEFORE NIGGAS HEARD 50 FUCKED WITH DRE

AFTER NIGGAS HEARD 50 FUCKED WITH DRE

"IN DA CLUB" COMPONENTS MEASURED IN ENERGY EXPENDED

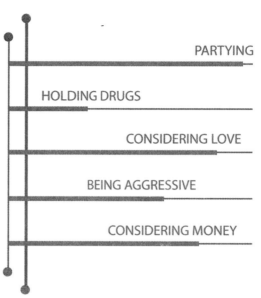

PARTYING

HOLDING DRUGS

CONSIDERING LOVE

BEING AGGRESSIVE

CONSIDERING MONEY

REBUTTAL: "MADE YOU LOOK (APACHE REMIX)" NAS

Of all the cuts that crushed us in '03, "Made You Look" stayed with us from when it dropped at the see-your-breath February parties in dank Chicago warehouses until the year was out. It was a time when songs were no longer concrete. They were mutating, rife with remixing, mating, and meme-ing with novelty—Jay got Grey'd, "Beware of the Boys" went unavoidable, and "Work It" arrived in new weekly itera-tions in time for each weekend's set. Yet "Made You Look" remained virgin and intact—no use trying to temper it, and no reason to. Nas flexes with exceptional fearlessness over that Apache sample that doesn't quite resolve itself, string-ing it with a new tension that is only punctured with that startle of the shot. *Click click boom*. The sheer lethality of it telegraphed the unease of the time. Released a month before the U.S.'s invasion of Iraq—"Y'all appointed me to bring rap justice"—this was our song, an anthem of seduc-tive, rectifying might with Nas, trigger hand standing in for that reckless, justifying hand of America, moving with the surety and machismo assured by armament, of hot control, of a USA 4-ever cocked and ready.

—JESSICA HOPPER

STILL TIPPIN'

MIKE JONES

featuring SLIM THUG

and PAUL WALL

WHAT THIS SONG IS ABOUT
It's a lifestyle song, stuffed fat with meta Houston rap references and slang.

• •

WHY IT'S IMPORTANT
It turned Houston into the epicenter of rap in the months following its release. The city's influence in rap has yet to wane.

There were only four songs that were in contention for this chapter, but really there was only ever one.

The four: "Roses" by Outkast; "Drop It Like It's Hot" by Snoop Dogg and Pharrell Williams; "Jesus Walks" by Kanye West; and "Still Tippin'" by Mike Jones, Slim Thug, and Paul Wall.

The most fun song of 2004 was Outkast's "Roses," a song so transfixing that you kind of forgot that Andre 3000 makes twenty-five separate references to poop in it. But "Roses" wasn't even the most important song on 2003's *Speakerboxxx/The Love Below*. That was "Hey Ya!," possibly the best rap song ever with an exclamation point in the title.

The most mesmerizing song of 2004 was Snoop's "Drop It Like It's Hot," a song so hypnotic it managed to prop Snoop atop *Billboard*'s Top 100 chart for three straight weeks, a thing that had somehow never previously happened during his career. But Snoop had been rapping for sixty-five years[1] by the time he released "Drop It Like It's Hot." He'd long been a star. It didn't establish him. Nor did it establish Pharrell. Pharrell actually wrote for, and helped produce, Wreckx-N-Effect's "Rump Shaker" in 1992. That's how long Pharrell had already been around.[2]

The best song of 2004 was Kanye West's "Jesus Walks," a song so perfectly constructed I have to assume it is, and will remain forever, the high point of Jesus's rap career. But it gets nixed, too, because while it was/is/will remain truly magnificent, it (mostly) didn't accomplish anything broader than its own success.

The most important song of 2004 was "Still Tippin'." It managed to not only create insta-superstars out of Mike Jones, Slim Thug, and Paul Wall (and Chamillionaire, albeit indirectly), but, more permanently, it legitimized Houston as a viable rap city, which in turn led to the adoption and mutation of the city's music styling, a sound still prominent in rap today.

◆

life, in general it's usually Stephon Marbury's fault. A semi-related, 100 percent true thing: In 2003, I received an autographed Stephon Marbury basketball. By 2005, the skin on the ball had nearly completely flaked away. In 2003, I met David Robinson and he signed a separate basketball for me, too. I still have it. The skin is in perfect condition. I'm left to conclude that Stephon Marbury's touch is enough to chemically destabilize leather. I'm also left to conclude that I was super-uninteresting in 2003 because I was apparently collecting autographed basketballs.

Lindsay Lohan starred in *Mean Girls. Mean Girls* is secretly a very advanced, very powerful movie of the generation. A lot of people refer to *Godfather II* as the *Mean Girls* of the '70s. I actually heard that Lohan read for Al Pacino's part in *Heat* but that the director was nervous about giving it to her because she was a nine-year-old girl. Ageism is real in Hollywood.

None of these, of course, has any tie-in to Mike Jones or Kanye West or any rap from 2004 or even rap music at all, for that matter. They're just some things that happened. But there's no way I will ever write anything about 2004 without *at least* mentioning *Mean Girls.*

I suppose that means I am still super-uninteresting.

♦

These are some things that happened during 2004 that were memorable, and so maybe you'd like to remember them:

Facebook launched. That meant we were all only six years away from the Facebook movie and then from there only a few days away from a bunch of Well, Actually conversations about how the Facebook movie wasn't actually titled *The Facebook Movie.*

The USA men's basketball team lost to Argentina in the semifinals at the Olympics. I blame this on Stephon Marbury. To be fair, I can't say for certain that it was his fault America lost, but if something goes wrong in basketball or even just in

The version of "Still Tippin'" that most know isn't the original version. The original was recorded in 2002. Both were built up from an old Slim Thug freestyle,[3] but they had different producers (Bigg Tyme produced the original; Salih Williams produced the famous one) and different lineups (Chamillionaire was on the original; Paul Wall replaced him on the famous one). The famous version ended up on a compilation tape in 2003 called *The Day Hell Broke Loose 2.* It was then plucked from there and used as the first single from Jones's *Who Is Mike Jones?* album in 2004 after Jones improbably proved to be a commodity.

♦

This is what Mike Jones did to jump-start his career, and it's really very smart and a fun thing to think about: At the beginning of his career—this was back around 2000—nobody in rap would pay attention to Jones. And nor should they have. Mike Jones is a talented marketer, and he is an opportunistic businessman, but he is not that great of a rapper. And being not that great of a rapper is not a very good thing if you want to be a famous rapper.[4] So he went to whom people in rap would pay attention to: strippers.

He started visiting the most popular strip clubs in Houston. He introduced himself to the dancers, talked to them about music, and then he started making personalized rap songs for them to dance to onstage. He'd put a girl's name in the song, describe her a little bit, talk her up. First it was one girl. He did it for free just to start. Then two girls. Then five girls. He started charging them for the songs. Demand grew and grew. Ten girls. Twenty girls. Eventually, all the girls in a particular club were dancing to his music. Then two clubs. Then five. He inundated the airspace with his adenoidal, unmistakable voice. What's more, on those songs (and in the songs that came afterward) he'd repeat his name over and over again, put his phone number in them, on T-shirts, on posters, on everything.[5] He seemed to exist only to promote his brand, and that's one way a not very good rapper becomes the most visible rapper in his city, then state, then country.

Sidebar: In *The Social Network*, Sean Parker (Justin Timberlake), the guy who invented Napster, sits down for a meeting with Mark Zuckerberg (Jesse Eisenberg) and Eduardo Saverin (Andrew Garfield). During the meeting, Parker asks Zuckerberg and Saverin about marketing strategy. Zuckerberg talks about how there was one instance where they wanted to get Facebook onto Baylor but Baylor already had its own independent social networking site. So what they did was target all the schools in a hundred-mile radius and get Facebook there. Soon enough, the kids at Baylor were transferring over to Facebook. That's basically exactly what Jones did, except instead of colleges he used strippers. All of a sudden, every stripper in the area had his music in their hands, and next thing Jones knew, it was in front of every tastemaker around.

In a 2014 mini-documentary that Complex.com did about the importance of "Still Tippin'," Michael Watts, one of the cofounders of Swishahouse, the record label in Houston that housed Slim Thug, Paul Wall, Chamillionaire, and later Mike Jones, said of pre-fame Jones: "He didn't come as just a rapper. He came with a plan. I was really impressed because I never had anybody that came to me with a plan that [hadn't], to that day that I know of, put out an album." That's the best summation.

Mike Jones eventually unraveled his own fame, setting fire to each rung of the ladder he used to climb toward stardom after each step. And so when his fall came, not too long after he'd watched *Who Is Mike Jones?* go double platinum, he plummeted toward the earth so fast and violently that when he struck it, he was atomized on impact. He's virtually invisible in music today. But his ascension remains a compelling story, and essential to the rise, and eventual market dominance, of southern rap.

♦

From 1992 to 2002, there were only two rappers from Houston who made albums that sold more than a million copies. Scarface did it in 1994 with *The Diary* and in 1997 with *The Untouchable*. And Lil' Troy, who caught magic with his single "Wanna Be a Baller," did it in 1999 with *Sittin' Fat Down South*. After "Still Tippin'" was released in November of 2004, it happened three times over eight months in 2005 (Jones, *Who Is Mike Jones?*; Paul Wall, *The Peoples Champ*; Chamillionaire, *The Sound of Revenge*). The exposure led to an influx of culture plumbing: the candy paint; the gold and diamond grills; the Styrofoam cups full of lean/drank, a mixture of promethazine, codeine,

---

1. There is a possibility this is not an accurate number.
2. Pharrell was seventy-five years old when he produced "Drop It Like It's Hot" for Snoop. Pharrell had come out of retirement to produce for Snoop. Pharrell Williams always lied about his age. He lied about his age all the time. When I was researching for this book I talked to Frank Sinatra. I said, "Frank, you hang out with Pharrell Williams. Just between me and you, how old is Pharrell Williams?" You know what Frank told me? He said, "Hey, Pharrell Williams is a hundred and thirty-seven years old." A hundred and thirty-seven years old!
3. It's from a song called "I'm a Ho (Whodini Freestyle)." In "Still Tippin'" Slim has a line where he mentions a Nintendo GameCube. In the freestyle, which came out years before, he mentions a Nintendo 64. I always thought that was very neat. Slim Thug likes his video-game references to be timely.
4. Though, being not that great of a rapper certainly does not exclude one from becoming a famous rapper. See: Cole, J.
5. In 2008, Jones released a straight-to-DVD-then-straight-to-the-Dumpster movie called *The American Dream* that was based on his life. There's a scene in it where his grandmother lays out what was to become his business model. She was the one who told him to do the phone number thing and the name repeat thing and the songs for strippers thing. Mike Jones's grandma.

and soda; and, most aggressively, the sound and style of DJ Screw, who pioneered the Chopped and Screwed subgenre of music, which was cutting up songs and playing them back over themselves while slowing everything down to an earthworm's inching pace.

In a 2010 email interview with the *Guardian*, Drake wrote, "Sometimes I feel guilty for how much I love Screw and the SUC. I feel like Houston must look at me as someone who is just latching on to a movement. But I just can't express how that shit makes me feel. That brand of music is just everything to me." That's the best summation.

◆

The worst Houston impression: In 2008, T-Pain, a large top hat with an R&B singer underneath it, released a song with Ludacris called "Chopped 'n' Skrewed" where he replaced the Screwed sound with his autotuned sound, then used the phrase "chopped and screwed" to mean that your advances have been disregarded by a female.

The best Houston impression: In 2011, A$AP Rocky, a rapper from Harlem, released a song called "Purple Swag." It was slow and sleepy but melodic and assertive. The video for the song, which went viral almost instantly, helped propel Rocky toward the $3 million record deal he ended up signing with RCA Records and Polo Grounds Music. There are two moments where a Mike Jones lift can be heard in the background: once at the 0:42 mark and once at the 2:00 mark. Each instance lasts less than a second. Still, even tucked away and hidden underneath the layered and loopy etherealness of the song, his voice is impossible to miss. Both times, it's Jones declaring, "I said!"

It's a micro-slice of him from "Still Tippin'," and it comes during a stanza at the end of his verse where he repeats the line "Back then, hoes didn't want me, now I'm hot, hoes all on me" four times in a row.

Mike Jones is eternal.

REBUTTAL: "KNUCK IF YOU BUCK" CRIME MOB, FEATURING LIL SCRAPPY

"Still Tippin'" isn't the most important song of 2004. Because while Swishahouse was just about to ascend to the peak of its mainstream prominence, crunk was already blowing the fuck up! And "Knuck If You Buck," the first single from Crime Mob's self-titled debut album, also featuring crunk prince Lil Scrappy, was the song of the moment. And really, it smacks just as hard today as it did back then, which is to say, with the impact of a speeding train; its super-essentialized beat and evergreen "I wish a bitch would" threats never go out of season. Like Mike Jones, Crime Mob didn't end up having a ton of longevity. But the legacy of "Knuck If You Buck" lives on in the trap music that's defined so much popular rap since 2010, and not just down south. And not only that, it was a watershed moment for female rappers not just holding their own on a track with men, but indisputably *owning* it—let's be real, when we talk about Crime Mob, we are talking about Diamond and Princess. What it really comes down to, though, is this: I went to prom in 2004, which was overall a pretty mediocre experience for me—but "Knuck If You Buck" blew the roof off that bitch.

—MEAGHAN GARVEY

AWWWREADY *adv.* **1** to express understanding. **2** to agree with something.

BALLIN' IN DA MIX *phrase.* an issuance of general well-being generally used in response to a salutation.

BIG BODY *n.* a large vehicle.

CANDY PAINT *n.* a custom paint job on a car that produces a look comparable to a piece of hard candy.

CHOPPED AND SCREWED *adj.* refers to a style of DJ mixing where a song is played back over itself over and over again while also being slowed down to a considerably smaller RPM rate.

CHOSE *adj.* to be selected by a member of the opposite sex, usually for intercourse, though not exclusively so.

COME DINE *phrase.* to arrive at a location in particularly impressive fashion, in regard to both appearance and overall attitude.

DINE *adv.* slang variation of the word "down."

GRIPPIN' GRAIN *phrase.* to be holding a steering wheel made of wood.

IT'S GOIN' DINE *phrase.* to say a thing is currently happening, or will happen at a later time, most often used in a positive tone.

LAY THE PIPE *phrase.* to have sex.

LEAN *n.* a mixture of soda (generally Sprite) and codeine-based prescription cough syrup.

MAYNE *n.* a variation of the word "man." can be used to expressed any number of sentiments.

NAHMTAHMBOUT *adv.* a portmanteau of the words "know what I'm talking about." used as an impromptu gauge of a listener's level of comprehension during conversation.

RIDIN' DIRTY *phrase.* to ride in an automobile with contraband.

RIDIN' FOREIGN *phrase.* to ride in a car manufactured outside of America.

SLAB *n.* **1** a large vehicle replete with many expensive accessories. **2** acronym for the phrase "slow, loud, and bangin.'"

SWANGIN' AND BANGIN' *phrase.* driving one's car in a snakelike pattern.

TALKIN' DINE *phrase.* saying negative things about a person, place, thing, or idea.

2005

GOLD DIGGER

Kanye West

featuring

Jamie Foxx

WHAT THIS SONG IS ABOUT

At first it's about a girl who's only interested in money, but then it's about a girl who isn't interested in money and gets ditched by her significant other when he gets some money.

....

WHY IT'S IMPORTANT

It's Kanye's proper induction into the Mainstream America canon, and it was a massive success. He only grew more powerful and more influential from there.

"'Gold Digger' is straight poetry. It uses profanity, and it's fucked-up and funny. It's so perfect and out of the park. I'd like to state this, and fuck whoever tells me I can't word it out loud: 'Gold Digger' is one of the biggest songs of our lifetime." —Kanye West, *Playboy*, 2006

"Gold Digger" is Kanye West's single most successful song. It was nominated for two Grammys (Record of the Year; Best Rap Solo Performance) and won one (Best Rap Solo Performance). *Billboard* loves lists, and the list that they made for their All-Time Top 100 Songs put "Gold Digger" at number fifty-eight. Also, the list they made for their Songs of the Decade for 2000–2010, it's number nine on that one. VH1 picked it as the twentieth-greatest rap song ever, and that seems a tad overzealous, though I suppose a great amount of zeal is needed to create a show around Flavor Flav in a hot tub with an older-aged white woman with an aggressive haircut, so that makes sense. "Gold Digger" was Kanye's first top ten single ever,[1] and it was number one on *Billboard*'s Hot 100 for ten weeks. Additionally, it jumped from number ninety-four up to number two on their Pop 100 chart and that was the biggest jump that'd ever occurred there. It also broke the record for most digital downloads in a week, as well as the fastest-selling digital download of all time.[2] Its weight is true: Measured against other songs, it was the ninth most successful U.S. single of the 2000s.

◆

Today we know Kanye to be a star. There is nothing odd about that, about his preening, about his fondness for his own self-fondness. But in the early aughts, after he'd produced four songs on Jay Z's *The Blueprint* album working as a house producer for Jay's Roc-A-Fella label, after he'd made clear his intent to ascend toward the sun, it was strange,

label had hoped it would.[4] When "Gold Digger" popped, when it spread like it did, it was the official affirmation: The Kanye West experiment was no longer an experiment, it was a business model. It helped to revitalize sampling soul music, it stitched together pop music with themes generally attributable to the easily ignorable "conscious rap" quadrant ("Gold Digger" is secretly a clever examination of the effects money has on relationships), and it created a precedent for the larger-scale gazing he'd go on to do. Rap followed along right behind him.

♦

Somehow, George W. Bush, the forty-third president of the United States of America, and Taylor Swift, a woman who one time sang about dressing ironically and eating pancakes at an inappropriate time of day, are tied together in history. It's a bizarre Six Degrees of Kevin Bacon branch, only it's not Kevin Bacon, it's Kanye West.

The connection is a feat only an ego as massive as Kanye's could orchestrate; a throbbing, pulsating ego so swollen and possessed of such gravitas that the time Kanye talked about one and the time he interrupted the other, events separated in real life by four years, are smudged together into one moment now, occupying the same pop time and pop space and pop infamy.

When Kanye talked about Bush, it was during a telethon for hurricane relief in 2005 in the wake of Hurricane Katrina, and it was part of a larger conversation he was having with himself on live TV, which is mostly either forgotten or ignored. He indicted himself on air first, saying he was guilty of turning the channel when the aftereffects of the catastrophe were shown on television, guilty of having gone shopping before considering giving a donation. Mike Myers, who was on camera with him, was mortified, but he wasn't entirely caught off guard—Kanye later told *Playboy* in an interview in 2006 that he hadn't planned what he was going to say that day, and you can definitely see that as the clip plays and

particularly when he said he wanted to move into rapping. He was a middle-class Chicagoan with then-upper-middle-class tastes who appeared to only be concerned with the existential crisis of his own existence. *How can that sell, how can that play, how can that stand where Tupac and Biggie stood, where Jay and Nas were standing, where 50 Cent was standing, how can that be rap* was the thought. Then his album *The College Dropout* came out. And that's what rap became. It sold more than 441,000 copies in its first week, and would go on to move four million worldwide. His second album, *Late Registration*, mimicked the sales and multiplied the acclaim. Its first single, "Diamonds from Sierra Leone," was compelling,[3] but it didn't move like the

Kanye stumbles along, but he did know that he was going to say something, and so he let Myers know before shooting[5] that he'd be going off script. Finally, after a bit of rambling, and after having steadied himself while Myers spoke his part, Kanye peeled away all layers of innuendo and implication and very plainly stated his thought: "George Bush doesn't care about black people."

When Kanye interrupted Taylor, it was during her award acceptance speech at MTV's Video Music Awards in 2009. He ran up there in protest, upset that she'd won for Best Female Video, more specifically that she'd won for Best Female Video over Beyoncé's "Single Ladies (Put a Ring on It),"[6] which Kanye described during his tiny tirade as "one of the best videos of all time."[7] If you strip the sting away from its application, Kanye's logic is actually very irrefutable: Beyoncé ended up winning the award for Video of the Year later that same evening. You can't very well have the best video of the year between all the men and women together and somehow not have the best video among only the women. Still, no matter, Kanye, a reputation for brashness and aggravation already long in place, became a pariah, became labeled a racist. Everything near him seemed to turn to ash, and even the new president, Barack Obama, was caught on camera calling him a jackass. Kanye made $25 million in 2009. In 2010, his earnings dropped to $12 million.[8] The biggest ramification: Three weeks after The Interruption, West ended up canceling a tour he'd had planned with Lady Gaga, and while he never said it was because of what had happened at the VMAs, everyone understood that this was the cause.

The Bush thing and the Taylor thing are connected obliquely, but also directly.

When the Bush thing happened, that was the first proper large-scale Kanye controversy. In other circumstances—say, if it'd come after his first album, which was a triumph itself but had less of an echo outside of rap—it might've been enough to

have disappeared him forever, to have had his fame swapped out for infamy. But it came in the same month that "Gold Digger" had consumed America. The song was so big and so clever and so much wider than "just rap" that it couldn't be discarded or denied or even disliked. It gave Kanye, at least in that moment, a tremendous amount of critical capital, and he leveraged all of it and then a tiny bit more. And so what happened was the "Gold Digger"–to–George Bush moment was the first instance of separation between Kanye West the musician and Kanye West the personality, which became a key component of his professional identity, and probably his personal one, too, if he's being truthful in the interviews he gives. When the Taylor thing happened, that was the widest the divide between the two sides was.

In Bush's 2010 book, *Decision Points*, he described West's public shaming of him as the lowest moment of his presidency, which certainly seems strange, given he (probably) fabricated a war motive and (probably) knew about the systemic torture of terrorism suspects that and (definitely) forgot how a door worked one time.

When Kanye was asked about Bush's evaluation of the event, he connected it back to the Taylor Swift thing: "Well, I definitely can understand the way he feels, to be accused of being a racist in any way, because . . . the same thing happened to me, you know, where I got accused of being a racist." It was the lowest moment of Kanye's career.

There's an easy joke to be made about Kanye taking a moment he created and reflecting it up against a separate moment he created. But sometimes that's just what it is. It's neat when things make a full circle like that.

◆

TWO STRAGGLER QUESTIONS

1. 50 Cent's gun-toting mayhem was the perfect antecedent to Kanye's endless critical self-evaluation. If one of those nine bullets that hit 50 in 2000 had proved fatal and he died and

---

1. Since it sampled "I Got a Woman" by Ray Charles, it was also the first time Ray Charles had a number-one song on *Billboard*'s Hot 100 as a songwriter.

2. Both records have since been broken.

3. It actually won a Grammy for Best Rap Song.

4. It topped out at number forty-three on *Billboard*'s Hot 100.

5. The term "shooting" here is meant as in "shooting the scene," but I suppose it could also be taken to mean "shooting a bazooka at George W. Bush's forehead," too.

6. "Single Ladies (Put a Ring on It)" was nominated for nine awards that night. It won three (Video of the Year; Best Editing; Best Choreography).

7. This was a completely inaccurate claim.

8. Poor guy.

never revitalized gangsta rap, would that've helped Kanye move forward quicker or would it have slowed him down (or would it have not affected him at all)? And what happens with Young Jeezy[9] and Rick Ross[10] in 2005/6?

2. Sometimes I think about a rapper named Shawnna, and I especially thought about her a lot this chapter, because when Kanye West made "Gold Digger" he'd intended for it to be used by her on her 2004 album, *Worth Tha Weight*. Shawnna, she was from Chicago, too, but she signed with Def Jam South. Her career was over before it started, really. She was on a song with Ludacris in 2000 that people seemed to like ("What's Your Fantasy") and she was on another song with Ludacris in 2003 that people seemed to like ("Stand Up"). But that's it. I wonder what would have happened had she taken the song,[11] and if Kanye not having "Gold Digger" would've somehow kept him from becoming the most influential rapper of the last ten years,[12] or at least slowed him down, or, worse still, prevented his marriage to Kim Kardashian?[13]

---

9. I'm guessing he'd have been okay. He was more an evolution of the Clipse than 50.
10. I'm guessing he flounders a bit.
11. Nothing. She was never really very good. Best possible outcome: It becomes her version of Mims's "This Is Why I'm Hot." Most likely outcome: It becomes her version of J-Kwon's "Tipsy."
12. Nope.
13. Not a chance.

REBUTTAL: "GO CRAZY" YOUNG JEEZY, FEATURING JAY Z

It's immensely audacious for a regionally semipopular rapper to open his first widely promoted single by crowing "Guess who's bizzack?" since most listeners probably hadn't even heard of him more than two seconds before. Maybe Young Jeezy's confidence came from knowing that "Go Crazy" would be the exact moment when the balance of power in hip-hop would shift from big-budget crossover stars like his guest Jay Z to wily, trap-haunted southern mixtape rappers like himself. But for all its historical signif-icance, "Go Crazy" remains the most important rap song of 2005 simply because it goes so hard—Jeezy tearing across a drum-rolling Impressions sample like an unstoppable swordsman from a samurai movie, filling every available millisecond with lines like "I'm emotional / I hug the block" that will be quotable until the end of time. Plus, "Gold Digger" never got any kids suspended from school for wearing T-shirts with a crudely drawn coke-dealing snowman on them. **—MILES RAYMER**

IS YOUR GIRL A GOLD DIGGER?

YES — NO

DOES SHE REFUSE TO ENGAGE IN A RELATIONSHIP, AMOROUS OR OTHERWISE, WITH BROKE NIGGAS?

DOES SHE HAVE A CHILD WHOSE FATHER IS POSSIBLY BUSTA RHYMES?

DOES SHE HAVE A PERSONAL HISTORY, AMOROUS OR OTHERWISE, WITH R&B SINGER USHER?

DOES SHE USE THE CHILD SUPPORT PAYMENTS SHE RECEIVES FOR COSMETIC SURGERY?

DOES SHE POSSESS A LEVEL OF MENACE WITHIN HER THAT WOULD ALLOW FOR HER TO LIE ABOUT WHO THE FATHER OF HER CHILD IS FOR NEARLY TWO DECADES?

GOLD DIGGER

NOT A GOLD DIGGER

2006

Hustlin'

Rick Ross

WHAT THIS SONG IS ABOUT

A good work ethic.

• •

WHY IT'S IMPORTANT

Rap has, nearly since its origination, celebrated itself, and it did so especially well in the late '90s up through the middle of the aughts. But it aspired to be planted in some sort of truth. "Hustlin'" marks the origination of rap that became more about imagination and the luxuriance of what was being said rather than the authenticity of it.

The following is a description of a Rick Ross music video that is not "Hustlin'." Though that would appear problematic, given that this is a chapter about "Hustlin'," I can assure you that it is the same philosophically.

Rick Ross is driving a very expensive car over a bridge in some part of Florida (probably Miami, were I to guess).

He is in the car with DJ Khaled, who is in the passenger seat, and two attractive women, both of whom are in the backseat and in good position to massage Ross's and Khaled's shoulders, so that's what they're doing. Ross gets pulled over. A cop, burly and wide but not offensively so, walks up to the side of the car and taps on the window. Ross lets the window down, smoke furling out from his nose; he very much looks like Waternoose from *Monsters, Inc.*, if not literally then at least metaphorically.

"What's the problem?" Ross asks. "Speeding," the officer replies back. DJ Khaled is exasperated. "Man, you must be new or something, man," he interjects. "We the best, man."

The "we the best" legal defense does not move the cop, as Khaled was hoping. "License and registration," the cop says.

Ross steps out of the car. He walks slowly toward the front of it, then, without warning, sprints—inasmuch as a three-hundred-plus-pound man can be said to sprint—toward the railing on the bridge and jumps over, falling the some twenty-five feet down to the water. This, to me, is an overreaction to the possibility of receiving a speeding ticket. I suppose it's not outside of reason that Ross had warrants, and so maybe he was trying to avoid getting locked up. But who knows? And who cares? Can Rick Ross even swim?

As his body splashes down into the bay (Biscayne Bay, were I to guess), the music starts. It's "Speedin'," an okay single from his okay second album, *Trilla*.

Now Rick Ross is in a speedboat with a handful of money and three new women, none of whom are massaging his shoulders, FYI. He is flanked by three other speedboats. One is driven by Fat Joe, one is driven by Puff Daddy, and the third by Gunplay, a lower-tiered rapper serving on Ross's Maybach Music Group record label, who I can only assume is in on this particular fantasy because somebody else who was supposed to show up to drive that boat in the video didn't make it. But again: Who knows? And who cares? Because reality doesn't matter. With Ross, it never has.

Rick Ross's reality is flexible, and the circumstances of it, and his abilities within it, are bound only by what he can think up to say.[1] One time he said that he moved a brick of cocaine per day. One time he said he kept rubber Uzis in his Jacuzzi. One time he said he owned a Mona Lisa painting that comes to life. One time he said Wale was a genius and Meek Mill was a superstar and I'm not sure which of the two is more offensive. Logic and reason and common sense and the truth are all just barely even visible to Ross, clouded by all the gold dust and diamond sparkles in the atmosphere around him. It's his whole aesthetic. That's how he became a superstar. That's how "Hustlin'," a song where Ross rhymes "Atlantic" with "Atlantic" and says the word "hustlin'" forty-six separate times, became the most important song of 2006.

Rick Ross makes sense if you suspend belief in everything else except for what he tells you and shows you. If you don't, then you're just watching a fat guy jump off a bridge for no real reason.

◆

Rick Ross spent August 2006 to July 2008 positioning himself as a drug-trafficking mega monster titan. He did so loudly and confidently and proudly, first with "Hustlin'," a gorgeously composed, unbeatably simple song, and then basically with everything that came after it.

I don't know that anyone actually believed him—he sampled the "Push it to the limit" line from *Scarface* on his second single, "Push It," which seemed especially ham-fisted, a lot like

taking a picture of yourself smoking weed on a beanbag chair in front of a Bob Marley poster and then captioning it "revolutionary"—but nobody was saying they didn't believe him, and so that was close enough for him to keep playing gangster uninterrupted, and he played gangster very well, so he just kept on doing it. But then, oh no:

Right around the boring part of the summer of 2008, photos of Rick Ross at what appeared to be the graduation ceremony for a class of correctional officers spread online. He was wearing a CO uniform and shaking hands with a white woman. He had hair and no beard, but it was very obviously him.

When he was asked about it, he said: "Online hackers [put] my face when I was a teenager in high school on other people's body. If this shit was real don't you think they would have more specifics, like dates and everything? Fake pictures are created by the fake, meant to entertain the fake."

It was the first time he'd told a lie to America that he didn't tell in good measure, or at least in a fun song, and so people wanted to unravel it, and so that's what happened. From then to October, more specific things, like dates and everything, were hunted down. His Social Security number was matched up with DOC records to establish his identity, then his salary,[2] then the time he worked there,[3] etc. When he was asked about it again, this time with enough supplemental incriminating evidence to box him in, he bowed. "Yes, it's me. I never tried to hide my past." He literally said, "I never tried to hide my past," and that was the moment he crystallized his superstar status as quite possibly the smoothest, not-batting-an-eye liar there ever was.

There was a tiny bit of pushback after his admission, but nothing major—at least not like the initial fervor the photos created, and certainly nothing close to what history had shown could come. 50 Cent, who took the nine bullets fired into his legs/arms/face and turned them into a true fortune, had taken it upon himself to end Ja Rule's career because Ja Rule was on a label called Murder, Inc., and he'd never actually murdered anyone.[4] Ross's misstep was way more egregious. The result? Nothing. It made his cartoonishness even more powerful.

That exorbitant lie-telling all began with "Hustlin'." It was a Trojan horse with a belly filled with fables.

◆

---

1. This maybe makes him like Neo in *The Matrix*, though I can't imagine Neo would ever do a record with Mario Winans and Ashanti.
2. His salary was $22,913.54.
3. December 1995 to June 1997.
4. This is a simplification of the events, though only marginally.

Ross, by either accident or design, began ex post facto legitimizing his illegitimacy at the same time he was building up his kingpin mythos. "Hustlin'," the first song most of America had heard from him,[5] established that early on. When he claimed he knew Pablo Escobar and Manuel Noriega, the real Noriega, that was his first YFR[6] moment. We've all only ever known Ross to be a liar.

After Ross admitted to being a CO, after he'd absorbed the nonresponse, his self-styled extravaganza floweredFloweredFLOWERED. On *Deeper Than Rap*, the album that followed the noncontroversy, he showed that he'd grown it into a science ("Vacation to Haiti, it nearly broke my heart / Seeing kids starve, I thought about my Audemar"). By *Teflon Don*, his fourth album, he'd turned it into performance art[7] (he chanted, "I think I'm Big Meech, Larry Hoover," and you yelled it, too, because it was so exciting and ridiculous, but also because you knew you were both telling the same amount of truth). By his fifth, *God Forgives, I Don't*, he was over the moon. (He fucking called the album *God Forgives, I Don't*.)

Ross's megalomania is the evolution of 50 Cent's true and real street tales. Ross is a copycat killer who'd never really killed. Rick Ross's megalomania is the countermeasure to Young Jeezy's existence, which was always doused with the sort of hinted regret that can only be fostered by actual experience. Ross is a copycat dealer who's (likely) never truly dealt.

Ross single-handedly adjusted the valuation of credibility in rap. He's hustled us since "Hustlin'." That's always going to be true.

◆

The irony: The moment it felt like the things that Rick Ross was saying were actually true (sometime between *Teflon Don* and *God Forgives, I Don't*), the moment where it felt like "Hey, I mean, he's worth about $35 million now, so he probably could be on a helicopter with thirty virgins headed to Monte Carlo," that's when people stopped caring about him.

◆

Rick Ross stole his name from "Freeway" Rick Ross, an illiterate drug dealer who was responsible for the movement of thousands and thousands of pounds of cocaine across the country[8] in the '80s. Freeway Rick spent 1996–2009 in prison behind drug-trafficking charges.

On May 1, 2012, I received a private message from whoever was running Freeway Rick's Facebook page (possibly him, but probably not). I'd been writing a lot for *LA Weekly* around that time, and Freeway Rick wanted me to post some video of Rap Rick Ross talking about where he got his name. In the weeks that followed, I received several more messages from him, each one a link to something Freeway Rick Ross was saying about Rap Rick Ross. I'm under no illusion that I was the only writer being sent the stuff that was being sent. Still, after I started ignoring his messages, I felt semibad about it.

◆

The difference between Rick Ross and 50 Cent, discussed only via threats against the women in your life.

Rick Ross has a song called "Walkin' on Air." In it, he shouts, "Pull up to your trap, strapped in my armored truck / Your mami house next, tell that bitch to duck." Even when he's pretending that he's going to shoot at your girlfriend's house, he wants you to know that it's coming so that you can warn her to get down because he doesn't really want to hurt her.

50 Cent has a song called "Heat." On it, he grits, "If you was smart, you'd be shook of me / 'Cause I'd get tired of looking for ya, spray ya mama crib / And let ya ass look for me." Hot, hot hate in 50's heart turns the atrocious and deplorable act of shooting at your mother's house into an ancillary activity, a vehicle meant only to drive you from hiding, so he can shoot you, too.

---

5. Some might remember his guest verse on Erick Sermon's "Ain't Shhh to Discuss" from 2000, though Ross was calling himself Teflon Da Don back then.

6. Yeah fucking right.

7. Lots of people for sure tried to replicate what Ross was doing. The best impression: Kanye West and Jay Z on *Watch the Throne*. The worst impression: Ace Hood on everything that wasn't "Bugatti." The best variation of it: Riff Raff's bizarro brags. He called himself the white Eddie Murphy in a song once, and I don't know how or why that line isn't engraved into the side of the Statue of Liberty yet.

8. *Esquire* wrote this big story on him in 2013 that said Freeway Rick sold more than nine hundred million dollars' worth of cocaine in 1980 alone.

9. This is the only chapter with two Rebuttals. These two are together because Sean and Rob, both incredible writers, are guys whom I've basically accidentally linked in my brain just through regular association. Reading one of them always seems to make me want to read the other, and I'm not sure why but it's just that way. It seemed natural to connect them here.

HUSTLIN'

"WHO THE FUCK YOU THINK YOU FUCKING WITH, I'M THE FUCKING BOSS" (0:48)

"WHEN THEY SNATCHED BLACK I CRIED FOR A HUNDRED NIGHTS" (1:31)

"WHITE ON WHITE, THAT'S FUCKING ROSS" (0:53)

"WHIP IT REAL HARD, WHIP IT WHIP IT, REAL HARD" (1:51)

"I KNOW PABLO, NORIEGA, THE REAL NORIEGA, HE OWE ME A HUNDRED FAVORS" (1:10)

"JOSÉ CANSECO JUST SNITCHIN' BECAUSE HE'S FINISHED" (2:14)

"SEE MOST OF MY NIGGAS STILL REALLY DEAL COCAINE" (1:19)

"MO' CARS, MO' HOES, MO' CLOTHES, MO' BLOWS" (2:34)

 CONFRONTATIONAL BOASTFUL DESCRIPTIVE COOL ON PURPOSE SELF-REFLECTIVE INSIGHTFUL HISTORICAL REFERENCE

REBUTTAL: "WHAT YOU KNOW" T.I.⁹

This feels small, a tiny monarch presiding over a kingdom in ruins. But ten years ago, T.I. was the one with heft, with presence, with girth. Rick Ross was merely an interloper, a harrumphing flab who rhymed "Atlantic" with "Atlantic." T.I. wasn't clever, either, but he commanded, with a lolling flow that gurgled and soared in equal measure. And there was no one who made songs soar to great heights and swing low to scrape the earth like DJ Toomp. It was with T.I. that Toomp—who cut his teeth in rap with southern mold breakers MC Shy-D, Raheem the Dream, and 2 Live Crew—realized his sense of scope and glimmering grandeur. Never better or bigger than on "What You Know," a statement of fact and of purpose. Like all great anthems, it's not what it's about, but what it makes you see—a man scaling a mountain, a statue blocking out the sun, a diminutive but cocksure man rapping right into your face: "See, all that attitude's unnecessary, dude / You never carry tools, not even square, he cube / You got these people fooled, who see you on the tube / Whatever, try the crew, they'll see you on the news." T.I. wins, film at eleven. —SEAN FENNESSEY

REBUTTAL: "THROW SOME D'S" RICH BOY, FEATURING POLOW DA DON

Yeah. Couple things here. First, Polow Da Don coproduced this jam with a guy named Butta, and it's like the sun rising and setting every ten seconds. (With Rich Boy jabbering in your ear the whole time, but he grows on you.) Second, PDD also raps the second verse, which includes the line "Every freak should have a picture of my dick on they wall," which is incredible, which is the Eleventh Commandment, which is like God himself texting you all the emojis at once. It was also the best moment of 2007, and the best moment of 2008 was Obama getting elected, if you get what I'm saying. I'm not arguing with you about this. Thank you for your time. —ROB HARVILLA

2007

INTERNATIONAL PLAYERS ANTHEM

—

UGK

FEATURING

OUTKAST

WHAT THIS SONG IS ABOUT

Getting married, or at least choosing one woman, for marriage or for other things.

• •

WHY IT'S IMPORTANT

It represented the death knell for the condescension that had been aimed at southern rap since southern rap became a thing.

"International Players Anthem" was a southern rap legend event song. It was a UGK record, and UGK is the greatest Texas rap group of all time.[1] It had guest verses from Outkast, and Outkast is the greatest Atlanta rap group of all time. And it was produced by Three 6 Mafia, the greatest Tennessee rap group of all time. It was not specifically a celebration of the South, but it certainly felt like that, and still feels like that. It still feels like the moment when the South began to shake free of the caricature it'd been portrayed as.

Let's make two arguments here, and maybe they're wrong, but they're probably not. Before we get there, though, here is some information that will be helpful:

1. For the rest of this passage, I'm going to use the phrase "the South" to mean "rappers and people in the rap industry who are from southern states." It's almost always a bad idea to write roundly like that. And the characters who constitute "the South" certainly don't operate as a singularity. But this particular instance calls for that kind of grouping. Otherwise, the chapter would be sixty-five thousand words, and that's about sixty-three thousand words over the limit, which is a lot to be over, FYI.

2. Bane is a bad-guy character from *Batman*. He's been in the comics and in a video game and even cartoons, too, but when he's mentioned here it's in reference to when Tom Hardy played him in *The Dark Knight Rises* in 2012.

Now we can start:

For its first two decades, rap in the South existed as its own entity. The focus on the genre bounced from coast to coast and back again as it settled into itself, just out of reach

of Texas, Georgia, Louisiana, and the other states in between. The South was trying to participate, but it wasn't being engaged by anyone from outside its borders, and a lot of times it was actively being ignored, or pickled. Picture kids playing Monkey in the Middle. It was like that, except instead of a ball it was rap, and instead of kids playing it was rappers, and instead of *a game* it was *the game*, and instead of *being it* you *weren't it* and that was the problem, and so maybe not like Monkey in the Middle after all. But, you get it.

   This was happening, and the South could see that it was happening, so it did what it was forced to do: adapt. There were few-to-no major label record deals to be had, so rappers in the South created their own record labels and gave themselves their own deals. They booked their own smaller tours throughout the area and learned to generate a fan base out of nothingness. They brokered relationships with small distributors and basically sold their tapes one by one wherever they could. They figured out how to brand themselves (style of dress, of talking, of production), even if they weren't aware all the time that that's what they were doing. All of that was happening in the South all the time, and so it grew into its own kind of self-sustaining biosphere, containing its own regional stars and regional millionaires. UGK, Three 6 Mafia, Outkast, Master P and the No Limit label, the Cash Money family, etc.— their popularity didn't instantly stretch across the United States on the back of MTV like how the New Yorkers' popularity and the Californians' popularity had, but it didn't have to. Their importance was slow-cooked, but unquestioned, and that's just as impactful. Think on it like this: Each of Ja Rule's first four albums went platinum. JEFFREY ATKINS HAS FOUR PLATINUM ALBUMS. Do you know how many platinum albums UGK has? Zero. But nobody's cared about Ja since 50 Cent shoved him into a burial plot in 2003. Bun B remains a hero, and Pimp C, who died in 2007, remains a hero, too.

   That's a Photoshopped version of the story, but it's a version of the story nonetheless. So here are the two arguments, and they're both about how the South was able to slide into dominance:

1. When the Internet began to flex its grip on the music industry, when the guaranteed platinum and gold plaques weren't so guaranteed anymore, when album sales began to crater after 2004, it had a minimal effect on the southern rappers (or, at the very least, it had less of an effect). The South had (literally) operated out of the trunk of a Cadillac for so long that it felt natural to have to do it when that (metaphorically) became the way it had to be done. The southern rappers had accidentally prepared for that exact scenario. There's a scene in *The Dark Knight Rises* where Bane and Batman are fighting in the sewer and Batman is getting housed so he cuts the lights off to try to gain an advantage. But Bane is unfazed. He'd been raised in a lightless prison pit, he tells Batman. "You think darkness is your ally?" he asks. "You merely adopted the dark. I was born into it." Then he grabs Batman by the neck and pummels him some more. That's not an exact metaphor for this situation, but it's pretty close.

2. The best iteration of rap is the self-aware one (or the self-reflective one). That's why gangsta rap was crucial early on (it drew from the crack plague), and G-Funk (it drew from the tempering and normalization of inner-city strife), and big-money music (it drew from rap's own success), etc. So when sales turned downward, the way rap music sounded, and the way it was going to sound, changed direction as well. It aimed more toward locality, toward music identities that could be extended outward without being homogenized. The Internet fragmented rap's landscape. It made it easier for a sound specific to an area—like drill music in Chicago, or Chopped and Screwed music in Houston, or club music in Baltimore—to not just be confined to that area. Subgenres of subgenres became nourished and vetted. There was still success to be found sounding like someone else had sounded, but there was iconography to be had sounding like something that'd not been heard en masse yet. The South had accidentally prepared for that exact scenario, too.

◆

Beyond the cultural implications and relevancy, "International Players Anthem" is just an amazingly constructed song. There were eleven songs that came before it that also sampled Willie Hutch's "I Choose You" but none as effectively. Andre 3000's verse, the way it lies in the grass at the beginning of the song,

---

1. There's an argument to be made for the Geto Boys claiming that title. But UGK buzzer-beats them out because they pioneered the country rap sound, because their lineup never changed, because their best album (*Ridin' Dirty*) is slightly more cohesive and slightly more perfect than the Geto Boys' best album (*We Can't Be Stopped*), because Scarface is a better rapper than Bun B and Pimp C, but Bun B and Pimp C are better rappers than Bushwick Bill and Willie D, because Pimp C said, "Top notch hoes get the most, not the lesser," and also, "I eat so many shrimp I got iodine poisoning."

we have to get the original copy of Leonardo da Vinci's *The Last Supper*, rip it out of the frame, then replace it with his verse, because it's real and true art. The two snare snaps that happen right before Pimp C's verse, we have to take those two snare snaps and vote them president of the United States. The claps that happen during Bun B's verse, we have to teach all the children that because that's the new currency. Big Boi's rubbery coo, put it in a time capsule and bury it for a billion years because we're not ready for anything that buttery and soothing.

And then there's the video that came with it.[2]

Pimp C's fur coat and hat . . . Andre's kilt . . . the premarriage mini roast . . . Bishop Don Magic Juan kissing a white woman . . .

♦

The Source today isn't what *The Source* was in 1995. In 1995, it was operating as a premier publication. It was top notch, a true tastemaker magazine that could semi-seriously be referred to as the hip-hop bible, a nickname they gave themselves. So when they held their awards show in New York that year, it was a very large event and (almost[3]) all of the very important people were there.

Outkast, who'd released the trenchant *Southernplayalisticadillacmuzik* the year before, won the award for Best New Artist, as well they should have. And that maybe doesn't sound strange or eventful right now because we are far enough removed from that time period, but consider this: The Source Awards gave out sixteen awards that night. Fourteen of them went to someone who was from either New York or California. The fifteenth was an award for Soundtrack of the Year, so a single person couldn't win that. But even there, the winner was the soundtrack for *Above the Rim*, a movie that had been filmed in New York. And if the subtext wasn't clear enough, what followed was.

As Big Boi and Andre 3000 walked up onstage, they were booed loudly. It was rough and unfair and representative of the way the South had been treated by rap up until (and then well beyond) that point. But it provided an opportunity. And Andre's response was indicative of the way the South would respond from that moment forward.

Big Boi offered the setup. "So what's up, Dre?" he asked. Andre, twenty years old and suddenly standing in front of an arena filled with rap stars, slid in front of the mic, his dashiki looking very much like a war flag, and, after a moment to gather himself, swaggered: "The South got somethin' to say, that's all I got to say," and then he stomped away. It was so beautiful, and his defiance was a place marker. "It finally gave—clear-cut—an incision from New York wannabe-ism," said Killer Mike, another respected Atlanta rapper. "It was a great thing that they were handled in that way because it finally cut the umbilical cord, saying, 'We don't have to impress you. We don't have to be influenced by you in the same creative way. We're gonna show you.'"

♦

"International Players Anthem" came fifteen years after UGK's first album, *Too Hard to Swallow* (1992), thirteen years after Outkast's first album in 1994, and twelve years after Three 6 Mafia's *Mystic Stylez* came out in 1995. It was nominated for a Grammy, picked the tenth-best song of the year by *Rolling Stone*, and one of the 500 best songs of the decade by *Pitchfork*. These are the rap artists who had albums that topped *Billboard*'s R&B/Hip-Hop Albums chart the same years these groups made their debuts:

1992: Kris Kross (*Totally Krossed Out*), Das EFX (*Dead Serious*), Ice Cube (*The Predator*). Only Ice Cube was still a force in 2007.

1994: Snoop Dogg (*Doggystyle*), Heavy D (*Nuttin' But Love*), Warren G (*Regulate . . . G Funk Era*), Da Brat (*Funkdafied*), MC Eiht (*We Come Strapped*), Method Man (*Tical*), Redman (*Dare Iz A Darkside*). Only Snoop maintained his level of stardom.

1995: Too Short (*Cocktails*), DJ Quik (*Safe + Sound*), Tupac (*Me Against the World*), Naughty By Nature (*Poverty's Paradise*), Luniz (*Operation Stackola*), Bone Thugs-N-Harmony (*E. 1999 Eternal*), Kool G Rap (*4, 5, 6*), AZ (*Doe or Die*), Tha Dogg Pound (*Dogg Food*). Tupac was Tupac, and Too Short is a folk hero, but that's it from this list.

Fifteen years after their debut, UGK proved that they—and ipso facto southern music—were as relevant as they had ever been, if not more so, and probably more so.

---

2. Teeny, tiny sidebar here: Bryan Barber directed the video. He's who Andre 3000 wanted. Andre said if Bryan wasn't directing the video, then he wasn't going to be in it.

3. Tupac was in jail. But Biggie, Puff, Nas, Suge, the Wu-Tang Clan, Ice Cube, Snoop, Dr. Dre, etc.—they were all there. Tupac had attended the inaugural Source Awards the year before and had run up onstage during A Tribe Called Quest's set. I can't even imagine the way he'd have magnified the mayhem of the 1995 awards.

AN INTERNATIONAL PLAYERS QUIZ

Big Boi typed a text to a girl he used to see. (T) (F)

Spaceships do not come with rearview mirrors. (T) (F)

Money is located on the dresser. (T) (F)

Trash likes to fuck with $50 in the club. (T) (F)

Smashed the gray one, got a blue one. (T) (F)

There are seven wonders of the world. (T) (F)

Million-dollar macks require million-dollar bitches. (T) (F)

Impregnating a woman is akin to making it rain every month. (T) (F)

Child support can reach up to $30K a month. (T) (F)

The gut is the appropriate place to dump. (T) (F)

REBUTTAL: "GOOD LIFE" KANYE WEST, FEATURING T-PAIN

Kanye West is a pop-culture wonder of the sort whose grand gestures kick up grand gestures of their own. See: *The College Dropout*'s sharp-dressed-everyman revolution or the still-cresting wave of sad singers post *808s & Heartbreak*. 2007's less heralded *Graduation* is increasingly important as a fulcrum between rap phenomenon Kanye and the present world-beating polymath Kanye. If you listen closely, you can hear the birth of the latter on "Good Life" as Ye sneers, "50 told me 'Go 'head, switch the style up / And if they hate, then let 'em hate, and watch the money pile up.'" "Good Life" encapsulates all the tired-of-being-humble grandstanding, post-regional, kitchen-sink maximalism, auto-tune appreciation, and MJ idolization of the next decade of Kanye West in miniature. Ye has revisited all these elements frequently since but rarely with the sated champagne splendor he and T-Pain splash over DJ Toomp's blown-out keys here.

—CRAIG JENKINS

2008

A MILLI

Lil Wayne

A famous story about Lil Wayne is that he accidentally shot himself in the chest when he was twelve years old. He has changed how it happened a few times,[1] but the crux of the story has always stayed the same: He was home alone with a gun and then a little bit later he was home alone with a gun and also a hole in his body.

He told VH1 during a *Behind the Music* special in 2009 that the doctors said he missed his heart by less than an inch and that fragments of the bullet were still in there and they could never be removed because it was too unsafe, and that was pretty scary. Then he said it was okay because they weren't going to move—unless, for some reason, he traveled through some sort of very large magnetic field, and when he said that he stretched his eyeballs for dramatic effect and also jutted his teeth forward for dramatic effect, too, and that was pretty goofy and weird.

And that's Lil Wayne, given we can surmise the entirety of a person's professional identity in a two-paragraph extrapolation.

He's an intimidatingly talented technical rapper, and he showed that off early on as a rifle-mouthed marksman in a group called the Hot Boys; particularly on his first solo album, 1999's *Tha Block Is Hot*; and especially on "Respect Us," where the stutter step of his cadence was matched impeccably by the complexity of the structure of his verses. And he's a rapper who allows himself to *be* goofy and weird, which he showed off beginning in the second stanza of his career, particularly on 2007's *The Drought Is Over 2: The Carter 3 Sessions*, and especially on "I Feel Like Dying," which sounds like he's scuba diving around in the folds of his own brain.

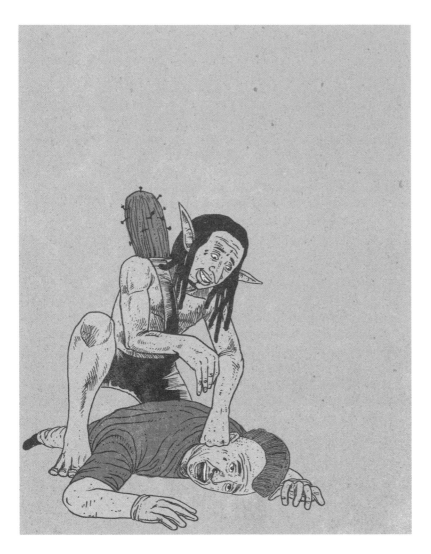

Wayne had sold well in the past—*Tha Block Is Hot* went platinum, and *Tha Carter II* (2005) went platinum as well. But the success of *Tha Block Is Hot* was, to a degree, fated and blind, an ancillary effect of the country's sudden infatuation with Cash Money Records, an independent label in New Orleans that had signed a distribution deal with Universal Music Group and presented a new brand of rap.[3] And *Tha Carter II*, while well received structurally, arrived in the shadow of Kanye West's wonderful *Late Registration*, and so when it came it was fine, but it also felt a bit like maybe rap had already moved on. That was the skepticism.

The excitement was because of the music Wayne had been creating away from his label during the break between *Tha Carter II* and *Tha Carter III*.

Prior to recording *Tha Carter* in 2004, Wayne purged himself of all of the unused lyrics he had written down. He carried a notebook into a recording studio, clicked record, then rapped everything in the book until there was nothing left. He put it all on one thirty-five-minute song called "10,000 Bars." That's a slight simplification of the process, though only barely. But that's not important. What's important is what it led to.

With no prepared lyrics, and with an idea not to write anything down anymore, Wayne changed everything. He still had the technical ability to rap, but in the absence of material to reference it became augmented: less burdened, more organic, weirder, more fun. He piled words and phrases up on top of each other, mushed together similes. He spent four mixtapes and twenty-five-thousand guest features practicing it. It was great, and unexpected, and enthralling. The only question was: Can he—can ANYONE—do anything like this on a proper album?

And then "A Milli" popped. And it was perfect.

The beat was magical and feverish and instantly intimidating. Wayne's lyrical sprint, his utter disregard for structure or linear compatibility, was intoxicating. Together, they were mas-

When he began to balance out those traits against one another at just the right pitch, he walked toward becoming a superhero, unstoppable, unbeatable.[2] And when he figured out how to turn it all into something consumable beyond mixtape fodder, like he did during 2008's *Tha Carter III*, where we find "A Milli," where he perfected the mixture, he proved to be irreversibly influential.

◆

There was skepticism before *Tha Carter III* was released, as there should have been, and there was a tremendous amount of excitement before *Tha Carter III* was released, as there should have been.

sive. 50 Cent was the first guy who showed that a big mixtape buzz could be swapped out for a major record deal. Wayne took that idea and advanced it. He showed it could do that, but that maybe that wasn't the end goal anymore, because rap was heading in that direction now, heading toward a weirdo bonanza and mixtape-as-a-model sound, because that's where he was taking it, and that's where it's been ever since. Perfect examples of what Lil Wayne set in motion are Gucci Mane's "Lemonade" (2009) and Waka Flocka Flame's "Hard in the Paint" (2010).

Kelefa Sanneh wrote this about Lil Wayne for the *New York Times* after watching him in concert in February of 2008, about a week before "A Milli" was released as a single: "Lil Wayne is at the strange, magical point in his career when popular acclaim seems like total freedom, when hyperjudgmental fans suspend judgment, willing to follow their hero wherever he goes, whatever he does."

The goofy single "Lollipop" was *Tha Carter III*'s biggest commercial hit, but it had zero gravity. "A Milli" had the density of a neutron star; it pulled everything toward it, and then into it. Wayne had gone pop without losing any of his eccentricities, so he carried them right TF into the room.

◆

When the sales numbers for *Tha Carter III* were released, Wayne and his team were in Los Angeles. A celebration was ordered. Wayne never showed up. He spent the evening in the tiny recording studio on one of the buses they were traveling in. By the time the party was over, by the time the others had returned to the bus, he'd recorded three new songs. This is my second favorite Lil Wayne anecdote. My first is that Wayne wandered into a nightclub one evening not knowing he'd walked into a Stevie Wonder party and Stevie Wonder yelled at him for making too much noise. Stevie Wonder is the greatest.

◆

"Maybe you are the next Lil Wayne, but probably not, in which case you need to stay in school."

That was Barack Obama, talking to a bunch of children at a campaign event in 2008. That's how famous Lil Wayne was in 2008. He was so famous that the man who would eventually become the president of the United States, a country where we're sold that anything is possible, was running around telling children that they should not dream to be Lil Wayne because it was too impossible.

Let us pretend that you and I have the ability to snatch up mini time periods of pop culture and claim them as our own, time periods that were enjoyable and impressive and that would be pretty great to experience absent of all of the work and hurt it (probably) took to create them. You and I, we will not take all of them, because you and I are not selfish. But we will have some of them, because you and I deserve them because we are good people and have never intentionally murdered anyone.[4] May I please have:

Give me Omar Epps, 1992–1995: He had four movies during that time. There was *Juice*, which is as incredible and transcendent and still important and relevant right now. There was *The Program*, a fun and faux-serious movie about football that most people remember because there was a scene in it where the main players on the team lie down in the middle of a busy road just because. There was *Major League II*, the somehow not terrible sequel to *Major League*. Epps took over Wesley Snipes's role for *MLII*, and he was the only person who even had a chance. And there was *Higher Learning*, an ambitious movie about race relations in America in the 1990s. He was a different kind of cool in each of them (Youthful Cool then Funny Sporty Cool then Quiet Sporty Cool then Angry Cool). I can't even be one kind of cool. ☹

Give me Jennifer Aniston, 1997–1999: This was the season four to season six stretch of *Friends* where the show had truly become something special, and if not "special" then at

---

1. The most fun version of the story is that he was pretending to be Robert De Niro in *Taxi Driver*. I suppose if you're going to shoot yourself pretending to be a Robert De Niro character, Travis Bickle would be the one to go with. You certainly don't want to shoot yourself being the *Little Fockers* Robert De Niro.
2. The inverse here is true as well: When he is too silly or trying to be too weird, when he decided to pretend to understand the guitar and accidentally recorded and released the emo rock album *Rebirth*, he is a mess and, worse, ignored creatively.
3. In the context of this chapter, Cash Money Records sounds somewhat small and somewhat unimportant. They were not. That's where Juvenile and Birdman came from, and also the parent label that eventually delivered Drake and Nicki Minaj, too.
4. If you actually happen to be reading this book in prison under the weight of a murder charge, then I would like to extend the invitation to you to continue reading. I would also like to encourage you to strap this book to your body as armor in the event of a prison riot. It is hearty and thick and will serve as good protection. Good luck.

least "unstoppable." Aniston as Rachel was the best member of the cast. Ross was fun but too annoying and goofy to want his spot.[5] Chandler was too frustrating. Joey was too dumb. Phoebe was too aloof and long-necked. Monica was too anal and shriek-ish. But Rachel, she was perfect. She could do all the things the other members were best at, except she was just one person doing it. Maybe more important: Aniston's hair was first class. She might've had the best head of hair for a decade straight. Do you even know how much easier your life is when you have nice hair?

Give me Manu Ginobili, 2003–2005:[6] He won two NBA titles (2003, 2005), and those two titles made him a star in the league and a superhero in San Antonio, where he was the only Latino player on the only professional franchise in a city filled with Latinos. He won a gold medal at the 2004 Summer Olympic Games, and that made him a legend in Argentina, where he is from. He won back-to-back Olimpia de Oro awards.[7] And he got married. Do you know what I did from 2003 to 2005? I played a lot of Halo 2 and I tried to learn how to become a street magician.

But before I have any of those, may I please have Lil Wayne's 2008?

5. David Schwimmer, who played Ross, directed a movie called *Trust* that was released in 2010. It was about a fourteen-year-old who gets sexu-ally assaulted by a man she met on the Internet who'd pretended to be a boy her age. I rented it blind when I saw that he'd directed it—he'd headed two movies prior that were lighthearted. I didn't even read the description for it. I figured *Trust* was going to be fun and funny or at least one of those things. But it was not. It was super not.

6. I would just close my eyes very tightly for 2004, when Derek Fisher tore the Spurs' heart from their chest with his so-fucking-terrible 0.4 shot in Game 5 of the playoffs.

7. It's a sports award given out annually in Argentina and it is an important thing.

REBUTTAL: "SWAGGA LIKE US" JAY Z AND T.I., FEATURING LIL WAYNE AND KANYE WEST

In no way should "Swagga Like Us" crack any top-twenty-songs list for T.I., Lil Wayne, Jay Z, or Kanye. But as a moment—the *Voltron*-ness of it all—its existence (and success) makes it the most important rap song of 2008. It's a Kanye West production that samples an M.I.A. song ("Pa-per Planes") that samples a song by the Clash ("Straight to Hell") that went on to be T.I.'s fifth *Paper Trail* single (of eight total), one that eventually climbed its way to a Grammy performance (and a Grammy win) in which the four rap-pers exchanged their typical baggy fare for a tuxedoed Rat Pack look, all while a very pregnant M.I.A. bopped around stage in a polka-dotted bumblebee swimsuit. If you want to know what rap music and hip-hop culture were like in 2008, as well as where they were headed, it's all there, inside "Swagga Like Us."

—REMBERT BROWNE

"I'm a Young Money millionaire, tougher than Nigerian hair" (0:24)

"'Cause my seconds, minutes, hours go to the almighty dollar" (0:38)

"Got the Maserati dancing on the bridge, pussy popping" (0:48)

"Okay, you're a goon but what's a goon to a goblin" (1:25)

"I go by them goon rules, if you can't beat 'em then you pop 'em" (0:55)

"Never answer when it's private" (1:37)

"Sicilian bitch with long hair, with coke in her derriere" (1:13)

"It ain't trickin' if you got it (1:07)

"They say I'm rapping like Big, Jay and Tupac" (2:21)

"I don't O U like two vowels" (2:39)

"Don't play in her garden and don't smell her flower" (2:59)

"Bitch, I could turn a crack rock into a mountain" (3:19)

"They don't see me but they hear me" (3:27)

BOASTFUL   PSYCHOLOGICAL   HOPEFUL   INSIGHTFUL   THRILLING   GET MONEY   DESCRIPTIVE

Best
I Ever
Had

———

WHAT THIS SONG IS ABOUT

It's about a guy who likes a (lot of) girl(s), and a lot of time is spent reasserting his assessment of them.

● ●

WHY IT'S IMPORTANT

It was the insta-start of Drake's career, and Drake went on to widen rap's purview by making it undeniably okay to rap about your feelings, and by actualizing the Internet to propel him to fame, when everyone before him had failed to pull this feat off.

It's easy to make fun of Drake, and so a lot of people do that. Sometimes, even when you aren't trying to do that, you still do that. The art for this chapter, it's Drake doing pottery. It wasn't meant as an insult, and it's not an insult.

I told the illustrator, "Do something cool and something that Drake would do but that's not rapping or rap-related," and a few days later that picture was in my inbox. And when I saw it I said, "Well, that's pretty perfect." Drake probably doesn't do pottery, but Drake might do pottery. Drake might do anything. It doesn't matter what you say after "Drake doing . . ." There's a possibility he'd do it, or has already done it, and that's half the reason it's funny, and the other half is because he's Drake.

Drake riding a ten-speed bicycle.

Drake opening a ketchup bottle.

Drake shopping for a fern.

Drake making a Where the Red Fern Grows *joke while shopping for that fern.*

None of those things are insults, but they kind of are, but they're definitely not. So Drake might do pottery. And if he doesn't do it sincerely, he'll (almost certainly) do it ironically. Because he's funny and charming and transcendent, and sometimes only two of those things, and sometimes all three. When he was on Ellen DeGeneres's show there was a segment where he read the side effects for an antidepressant drug in a sexy voice (funny). When he hosted the Juno Awards[1] he did a thing where he hung out with old

first proper single, "Best I Ever Had," was an instant success that verified his creative existence before he'd fully developed it.

Drake's funny on "Best I Ever Had" on purpose, like when he says, "When my album drop, bitches'll buy it for the picture / And niggas'll buy it, too, and claim they got it for their sister." And he's funny on it by accident, like when he says, "I be hittin' all the spots that you ain't even know was there," as though he's discovered a new area of the vagina, as though he is the Ferdinand Magellan of vaginas.

Drake accidentally making a Ferdinand Magellan of vaginas joke.

♦

Quick stats: "Best I Ever Had" was nominated for two Grammys, and that's crazy because it was basically from a mixtape,[4] and so this is a really good example of how Lil Wayne turned rap inside out with his mixtape run from 2006 up through 2008. "Best I Ever Had" rose to number one on *Billboard*'s Hot R&B/Hip-Hop Songs chart and also their Hot Rap Songs chart, which are two different things. It's been downloaded from iTunes more than two million times, a feat more impressive than the (already impressive) number would suggest, given that it was easily available for free on the Internet.

♦

people and formed Old Money, a takeoff of the Young Money record label he's signed to (funny and charming). When he hosted the ESPYs[2] he blew into the ear of a basketball player named Lance Stephenson because Lance had done it to LeBron James a few months earlier in a play-off game (funny and charming and transcendent). Could you ever even picture one single other rap superstar blowing into Lance Stephenson's ear, or that of any player from the Charlotte Hornets[3] for that matter? No, you cannot. Only Drake.

Drake is a force. Drake is a force created by the Internet. Drake is a force created by the Internet and Kanye West's *808s & Heartbreak* album and also some Andre 3000 verses. His

In the "Best I Ever Had" video, Drake is the coach of a female basketball team full of large-breasted women who are very bad at basketball and never ever wear bras. His team plays a game against what would appear to be a team of Amazons. And they get pummeled. With two minutes left in the fourth quarter and his team down 42–4,[5] Drake calls a time-out. He brings his girls close, gives them a motivational speech, then sends them back out to finish the game in what is to be the most stirring comeback of all time. Except it never materializes. We see a shot of a girl on his team trying a jumper and getting it blocked, then the next shot shows thirty seconds left on the clock and now his team is down 91–14, and then the game is over. Four things:

1. Drake is not that great at rah-rah speeches. That's surprising.

2. I don't think I understand the rules of the Music Video Basketball Association, and I say that because as the aforementioned girl was preparing to take the aforementioned shot, she looked especially hopeful, a hopefulness that was matched only by dejection in Drake when he saw it get blocked. Nobody looks that irritated when a shot gets blocked unless that shot carries with it the potential to win a game. So I figure maybe she was shooting a 78-pointer, like from a special spot on the floor or something? That would have given her team a one-point lead. I guess it's like MTV's Rock N' Jock basketball game, only except without Dan Cortese.

3. The Amazons scored forty-nine points in ninety seconds at the end of the game. That's astounding. That's the most dominant stretch of basketball that's ever been played. The 2012 U.S. men's Olympic basketball team beat Nigeria by eighty-three points, and that's the largest margin of victory in the history of Olympic and professional basketball, but even there their points-per-possession rating is way subpar to the Amazons. You can blame Drake for the defeat if you like, but that hardly seems fair. He was up against an unprecedented mismatch.

4. The song is all about the best girl(s) Drake has ever had. That's the whole point. He's so happy and excited about it. But then in the video it ends with him sad and alone in his coach's office. The dichotomy would seem to serve as an indicator for the manner in which Drake navigates relationships, in that even when they are very good, they are also historically bad and unsettling. Which circles to:

Kanye West directed the "Best I Ever Had" video, and I'm happy about that because it allows for an easy transition to talk about *808s & Heartbreak*, the album that West made in 2008 that was the template for Drake's professional angst, and also the (unintentional) permission for him to be able to pursue it, and not just to pursue but to be successful at it.

To be short: *808s* was an album where Kanye, already a star, emoted for fifty-two straight minutes about the spiritual consequences of love, sometimes literally (there's a song called "Heartless," there's a song called "Welcome to Heartbreak," things like that) and sometimes aesthetically—the last three minutes and fifteen seconds of "Say You Will," for example, there aren't any words, just a couple of cold and lonely drums, two robo-tinks, and lots of chilled gray air to walk around in and explore your feelings. *808s* wasn't panned, but it wasn't revered like West's prior three albums had been.[6] The quickest, best summation came when Jon Caramanica wrote "Drake took Mr. West's self-examination and stripped it of all its agitation, preserving only the emotional turmoil" in the *New York Times* in September 2013.

There are parts of this book where conclusions and connections are made, where insight is developed or deduced based on evidence of observations. The Drake to Kanye (and Andre) thing, though, that's not one of them. I mean, it's an easy observation to make. But in this instance, there were no parts to snap together. Drake just said it:

"I think Kanye deserves a lot of credit and Andre 3000 deserves a lot of credit for the shift in what you have to be to be a rapper, and what your music has to sound like," he told the *Daily Beast* in 2011. "Those guys made it OK for melody to be introduced. They made it OK to not necessarily be the most street dude." It was a long interview. He clarified: "For me, I started to believe more in myself when I saw those two guys. I thought, 'I'm good at rapping, so if they just respect the talent

---

1. The Juno Awards are "Canada's Music Awards." You have to have lived in Canada for at least the last six months of the eligibility process to receive one.

2. The ESPYs are sports awards handed out by ESPN. (You can live wherever you want.)

3. Lance Stephenson played for the Indiana Pacers when Drake did the ear-blow thing. He plays for the Charlotte Hornets as I write this. Fingers crossed he stays there a bit so that this tiny section is accurate. I had not anticipated being emotionally invested in where a toothsome shooting guard works when I started writing a book, but that's just the way the universe works sometimes.

4. So Far Gone, which Drake ultimately rebundled and rereleased as a seven-song EP for sale. It was somehow the ninth-best-selling rap album of 2009, despite having only two new songs on it and despite having been released in September.

5. I don't know if you follow basketball a lot or not, but 42–4 is not that great of a score.

6. 808s & Heartbreak is a mammoth album, and its influence has been just as big as any other album he's made. It's his third-best solo album. It goes: My Beautiful Dark Twisted Fantasy, Graduation, 808s, Late Registration, Yeezus, The College Dropout.

and don't crucify you for what your past is or who you are, then I should be OK.'"

◆

Drake shifted rap in observable ways, the most important being that he commoditized the investigation of heartache better than any rapper ever had, and that made it an acceptable business model, and so now there are one hundred thousand rappers rapping about their ninth-grade girlfriend, and you can go either way with that. But there's also his relationship with the Internet.

His music had traveled from Canada to Houston via the Internet, and then from there to Lil Wayne,[7] so there's an actual functional aspect there. But he was the first (and thus far only) rap giant that the Internet actualized, and from there it was fine if the Internet was part of your origin story. The Internet tried to push Wale up into the clouds in 2008, but Wale was always too goofy and never interesting enough for the throne. It tried to shove Kid Cudi up there after that, too, but Cudi was always too weird and too untrustworthy to be given the crown. There were others, and there will certainly be others to come,[8] but those were the first true ones. And they failed. Drake was the one.

I remember watching Drake in concert early on in his career—this was right around the time *Thank Me Later* had crystallized his arrival; it shipped more than a million copies, he'd been nominated for five Grammys, all that.

Near the end of the show, he stopped the music and asked for the lights to be turned up. Then he started pointing out peo- ple in the crowd, making jokes, engaging them. He did it with the same ease that Dave Chappelle does stand-up,[9] the same ease that Jay Z interacts with interviewers. It's always been easy to see that Drake was a king.

---

7. Jas Prince, son of J. Prince, founder of Houston's Rap-A-Lot Records, is credited with having put Drake's tape in front of Lil Wayne.
8. Compton's twitchy Kendrick Lamar will hopefully get there next.
9. Before he went nuts, obvs.

REBUTTAL: "LEMONADE" GUCCI MANE

Gucci Mane was in prison when 2009 started, and he was back in when it ended. He still found a way to own the year completely. In the eight or so months Gucci was free, he rapped on hundreds of songs, cranked out mixtapes at a baffling rate, and had more fun talking shit than anyone else. Gucci made it possible to be the hardest rapper out there while playing nursery-rhyme language games, wheezing like a grandma, and making entire (great) songs about how he was "wonderful" or "gorgeous." "Lemonade" was Peak Gucci. It banged hard enough to start club riots, despite being a goofy meditation on the color yellow with a maddening kids'-choir sample. Its stupidity transcends: "Lemonade my townhouse in Miami, I want yellow carpet / Woke up in the morning, fuck it, bought a yellow Aston Martin." Gucci's mania, the thing that made him great, derailed his career soon enough. But we'll always have his 2009.

—TOM BREIHAN

DRAKE'S MOOD

SO FAR GONE, 2009

THANK ME LATER, 2010

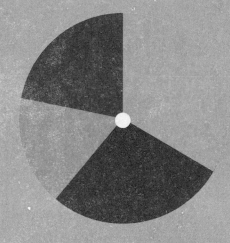

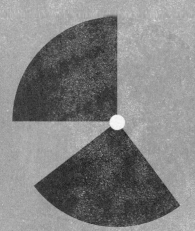

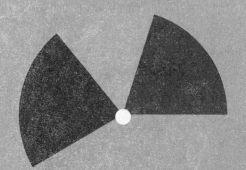

TAKE CARE, 2011

NOTHING WAS THE SAME, 2013

HAPPY   ANGRY   **SAD**   **INDIFFERENT**

[METHODOLOGY: LISTENED TO DRAKE'S FIRST FOUR TAPES. TRACKED EACH INSTANCE DRAKE SAID SOMETHING THAT COULD BE CONSIDERED EVIDENCE HE WAS FEELING HAPPY, ANGRY, SAD, OR INDIFFERENT. TURNED INFO INTO PIE CHARTS.]

2010

MONSTER

Kanye West

FEATURING

Rick Ross, Jay Z, Bon Iver, AND Nicki Minaj

WHAT THIS SONG IS ABOUT

It's about things that are associated with literal monsters and also things that are associated with figurative monsters.

. . . .

WHY IT'S IMPORTANT

It loudly marks the exact point Nicki Minaj became undeniable and also quietly marks the moment Kanye West began making radio singles that weren't structured like traditional radio singles.

There's this clip of Nicki Minaj from back before she was very famous, and it's part of a mixtape DVD series called *The Come Up*[1] (basically just videos of rappers rapping in the street stitched together). In the clip, she looks not at all like what she looks like today, which is to say alternating between a box of highlighters and a vampire very interested in sex. She's wearing a silly brown zip-up hoodie with writing all over it, and she's also wearing very ordinary jeans and a silly black patrol cap with buttons on it. Her hair is all the way black and straight, and it looks nice enough to not look like an afterthought, but it also doesn't look premeditated and central to her creative existence like it has since 2010.

When the video opens up, Minaj is rapping about things (Chinatown, Big Pun's weight, a car the color of bubble gum, etc.), then there's a small break, then Minaj begins an a cappella rap, then she stops and begins talking about how she only became a rapper because she happened to be so naturally good and devastating at it, which doesn't sound like a lie. Then she says, "*That's* why I act the way I act. [But] don't get it twisted. If you see me, holler at me. I'm never too ill to say 'what up.' Like, it's not that serious. Trust me, I know that."

In November 2010, Nicki Minaj was scheduled to make an appearance at an unattractive nightclub off a major freeway in Houston, Texas. I was working for the alt-weekly in Houston at the time, so I was supposed to be there to cover it. And I was excited, inasmuch as someone can be excited about standing in a nightclub for a couple of hours. This was about a week before her first album, *Pink Friday*, came out, but still, she had no small amount of buzz around her, owing to an impressive couple of mixtapes and guest-feature runs, as well as the backing of Lil Wayne, who had helped turn Drake into a megastar the year before behind nearly an identical set of circumstances. She was scheduled to be there from nine P.M. to two A.M., though nobody honestly expected her to get there until midnight, and it was $35 to get into the club that evening, so that meant we were all paying $17.50 per hour to stand in the same building as her.

Just prior to her arriving, a short man wearing a lot of cologne who was working as one of the event's promoters went around and told all of the members of the media[2] that nobody was allowed to take any pictures of her while she was there. He said something close to, "Her management said she'd leave if she saw one single camera," or something equally dramatic. I didn't understand why, because what's the point of making a scheduled appearance if not to be photographed appearing? But the tone was set, and the instructions were firm: Any cameras and she'd leave. He was very serious. She was very serious.

She played at cocky on the DVD but felt the need to explain it away immediately afterward. She played at silly as she began method-acting her way toward stardom, but felt the need to have a handler explain her seriousness. It was an inversion.

And in between both of those moments is her verse on "Monster," which changed her everything immediately.

♦

"Monster" has a bunch of pieces. Let's go in reverse order, from least to most impactful.

BON IVER, BUT REALLY JUSTIN VERNON

Bon Iver is a group, not a person, first of all. They're a folk band, to be slightly more accurate, and Justin Vernon is their main singer and songwriter. He sings the intro to the song. He told *New York* magazine's Vulture.com that Kanye had heard Bon Iver's album *For Emma, Forever Ago* and appreciated the way he stretched and contorted his auto-tuned singing, and so that's why Kanye called him and how Vernon ended up on "Monster," stretching and contorting his auto-tuned singing at the very beginning of the song. Kanye recorded all of *My Beautiful Dark Twisted Fantasy* in Hawaii. He flew the people who were contributing to the album out there to work on it with him. Vernon also told Vulture.com that he and Kanye would start each day by playing basketball. Kanye West shooting a lay-up is my all-time favorite thing to think about.[3]

HI, RICK ROSS

Rick Ross comes in immediately after Vernon, and he raps a bit, but it's such a short bit that it's more fair to say it's a bridge between Vernon and the rest of the song than a verse itself. Ross was never actually supposed to be on "Monster"; that's why his verse is so short. He was in Hawaii working with Kanye on a different thing[4] and happened into hearing the song, and that led to him being on it. Ross was still floating from the release of *Teflon Don*, which had come out earlier that year and was (correctly) being called the most lush, most impressive album of his career, and so Kanye siphoned some of Ross's energy from him for it. Kanye's a very real master at that sort of thing. More than that: He's a very true master at extracting only the most essential parts of a person's creativity. Ross sounds like a hero on "Monster."

JAY Z: A ZOMBIE WITH A CONSCIENCE

All of the parts of a rap career are represented on "Monster," and I can't imagine that's by accident. There's Nicki, who was about to become huge but ultimately had not done anything of true note yet. There's Ross, who was certified and also as influential as anyone in rap that year.[5] There's Kanye, who was an unquestioned star who suddenly became questioned following the blowback from the Taylor Swift debacle.[6] And then there's Jay Z, who checks off the Legend box. There's one part of the song where he raps, "Sasquatch, Godzilla, King Kong, Lochness / Goblin, ghoul, a zombie with no conscience," and that's an easy way to tell that he was eighty-seven years old when this song came out, because only a very old person would answer "Name a monster" with "King Kong."

KANYE, THE GENIUS

First, there's the artistry of the song, which was dark and sophisticated and foreboding and helped pull rap in that direction, too, because of the surprising gravity of its beauty.[7]

---

1. It looks like 2007 or 2008, though I can't say for certain.
2. I say "all." There were three of us there.
3. There's actually a line in "Monster" where he says, "Triple-double, no assists," and that's a very Kanye way to get a triple-double, if you ask me. I assume it was points, rebounds, and steals. I just don't see Kanye getting ten blocks.
4. Kanye produced and guest-featured on a song called "Live Fast, Die Young" from Ross's album *Teflon Don*.
5. Drake being the one clear exception.
6. It's bizarre to think about it now, but "Will Kanye recover from this?" was a very real conversation happening at the time. Andre 3000 even told him he had to move out of America.
7. It's easy to draw a line from "Monster" to gothic Internet rap, which became popular afterward.

Then there's the construction of the song, which was atypical, especially for a radio single from an album. It's choppy and unhurried (more than six minutes long) but still energetic and overwhelming, and it seems okay to say that Kanye perfected the traditional radio single with "Gold Digger" in 2005 and then ripped it to shreds for this new version of it five years later.

Then there's the overarching theme of the song (this villainous, ugly thing trying to become beautiful and lavish by association), which was really an overarching theme of his life.

Then there's the backstory: how *My Beautiful Dark Twisted Fantasy* was the (gorgeous) result of his having his flesh peeled from his bones after his drunken and swollen attempt at valor at the 2009 VMAs;[8] how it was a pitch-perfect coalescence of his creative existence (which was, and is, mostly adored) and his personal existence (which was, and is, mostly loathed); and how "Monster" was the most obvious signal of his awareness of the conundrum on the album and of his career.

Also, he rhymed "sarcophagus" with "esophagus," and that's (probably) the first time that had ever happened.

NICKI MINAJ, AND THE VERSE THAT CHANGED HER CAREER, AND RAP, TOO

Writing about Nicki Minaj's verse on "Monster" is like writing about the solar system or Steph Curry's jump shot, in that words can be used to describe it, but none ever hold all of what it is or does. Picture an atomic bomb going off inside of a bank vault, or picture someone pumping your head full of air until it bursts, kind of like the guy from *Big Trouble in Little China* but not exactly like that. That's her verse. It twists and bends and she alternates between her characters to have a conversation with herself, and it sounds so perfectly placed and crushing in front of what Kanye created. Complex.com said it was the best rap verse over a five-year period (from 2008 to 2013). The *New York Times* called it "legendary." *Pitchfork* called it "masterfully manic." On and on and on and on. Picture a submarine filled with neon paint crashing into the sun at light-speed. Picture a hundred thousand parrots dive-bombing right TF into a Mardi Gras parade. It was gargantuan. It was, to be clever, monstrous. That's what her verse was.

Prior to the release of *Pink Friday*, there was a modicum of doubt about Nicki Minaj's potential, specifically after the release of "Massive Attack," which was supposed to have been the album's first single. It was a clear departure from her rap-heavy mixtape songs, but not nearly clever enough to survive as a pop single, and so it tanked, and it tanked so badly that it was eventually removed from *Pink Friday* altogether.

And yet, there she stood, a month away from the release of her first album, anchoring a song that celebrated the bigness of Rick Ross, the mythic Jay Z, and the transcendent return of Kanye West.

"Monster" was built to culminate with Nicki Minaj's verse, and that Kanye West would do that is indicative of the way she was already being seen by rappers, despite having not even put out an album yet. But "Monster" was really the culmination of her arrival as rap's next great figure.

---

8. The Taylor Swift thing (see page 171).

REBUTTAL: "HARD IN DA PAINT" WAKA FLOCKA FLAME

"Hard in the Paint," the most important rap song of 2010, is the ultimate inclusive anthem, that song for anyone who has ever been persecuted, has ever triumphed, or has simply felt passionate about something. You could do the *shit* out of your taxes to this song. ("I'ma die for this, shorty, man, I swear to God.") Lex Luger's simple, minor-key synth line resembles a horror movie score, but the effect is that *you* are the movie's protagonist, and the guy with the knife isn't going to win, *you* are. It's not a song about moving silently or putting one over on someone or getting away with something, it's about doing whatever you want, as loudly as you'd like, in front of whomever ("Broad day, in the air, like this shit is legal"). And it's perfectly fine if the things you like to do *actually* are legal; Waka just wants you to get excited. Since his 2010 breakthrough, he's an increasingly mainstream, inclusive presence, epitomized by his embrace of electronic dance music. He's doing him. As for you? He'd encourage you to do that, too. —**BEN WESTHOFF**

MONSTER

"The best living or dead hands down, huh" (0:54)

"Do the rap and the track, triple double no assists" (1:07)

 "Bitch, I'm a monster, no-good bloodsucker" (0:24)

"I still hear fiends scream in my dreams" (2:44)

"Bought the chain that always give me back pain" (1:17)

"Love, I don't get enough of it" (2:57)

 "Goblin, ghoul, a zombie with no conscience" (2:29)

"Fucking up my money so, yeah, I had to act sane" (1:20)

"All I see is these niggas I made millionaires, milling about, spilling their feelings in the air" (3:07)

 "Have you ever had sex with a pharaoh?" (1:51)

"Just killed another career, it's a mild day" (4:38)

"Pink wig, thick ass, give 'em whiplash" (4:46)

"50K for a verse, no album out" (4:12)

"I'm a motherfucking monster" (4:55)

 "Okay, first things first I'll eat your brains" (3:48)

   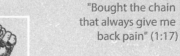

DECLARATIVE   **DEADLY**   **THRILLING**   **AGGRESSIVE**   **CONSIDERATE**   **BOASTFUL**   **POWERFUL**

2011

Niggas

in

Paris

—

Jay Z

and Kanye West

WHAT THIS SONG IS ABOUT

It's about celebrating being able to attain wealth while being black, which is hard. It's about celebrating being black while wealthy, which is also hard.

WHY IT'S IMPORTANT

It was the apotheosis of luxury rap, which turned out to be just as biting and trenchant as gangsta rap. (Gangsta rap reported the street-level overt carnage that came with being an underprivileged black male in a society that seemed better equipped to destroy black men than raise them up. Jay Z and Kanye's luxury rap reported the mental lashing that came with being a wealthy black male in a high society that was better equipped at ignoring wealthy black men than understanding them.)

On Kanye West's first album, *The College Dropout*, there's a song called "All Falls Down." It's about being self-conscious, but really it's about being insecure. In the second verse, West, rapping about shopping above his base-bottom level of consumerism, says, "I can't even pronounce nothing; pass that Ver-say-see." It's a half-joke, but really it's no joke at all, and this is the point from which we need to stand to see the entirety of the scope of "Niggas in Paris," because it is a big, big, expansive song, with big, big, expansive ideas.

◆

When Kanye produced five beats for Jay Z's album *The Blueprint*, including "H to the IZZO," which fire-started Kanye's career, Jay was already a superstar, and so their relationship since has always carried a big brother–little brother tone.[1] But by the time *Watch the Throne* came, the album they collaborated on in 2011, they were on (mostly) equal celebrity footing, albeit for different reasons, and for reasons that would influence the album (Jay = unflappable, sophisticated, affable; Kanye = flamboyant, emotional, impassioned).

A quick story about Kanye West from early in his career:

Kanye's first major placement came when he sold a beat to Jermaine Dupri, who was somehow famous at the time. That led to a meeting with Michael Mauldin, an executive with Columbia Records. Now, this was before Kanye was *Kanye*, in that he wasn't super-duper famous yet, but he was still very much Kanye, in that he was full of himself. Here's Rhymefest, who cowrote Kanye's "Jesus Walks," talking to VH1 for the Driven documentary series in 2005: "He went in there acting like, 'I'ma be better than Jermaine Dupri, I'ma sell more records than he would ever sell,' and they wasn't ready for that." What Kanye didn't know, and what he would come to find out, was that Mauldin was Jermaine Dupri's father. Kanye has always been a bit of a loudmouth, it seems.

A quick story about Jay Z from early in his career:
Jay Z's first album, *Reasonable Doubt*, a true and real classic project, has a song called "Regrets" on it. In the first line, Jay says, "I sold it all, from crack to opium," only he pronounces it "oh-pee-um," kind of slow and tilted, because he wanted it to rhyme perfectly with the lines that followed ("I don't wanna see 'em . . . / With my peoples how to 'G' 'em / From a remote location in the BM"). He practiced saying "opium" over and over again for "at least an hour, maybe two"[2] so he'd get it just right. Jay Z has always been a bit of a machine, it seems.

Without that juxtaposition, loudmouth and machine, this song could never have worked.

♦

"Niggas in Paris" is very fun. That's why it was successful.[3] It's this exciting and impressive elegy about obsessive-compulsive materialism, and an A1 version of luxury rap,[4] a term Kanye came up with on a song called "Otis," which was also on *Watch the Throne*, which was a very luxuriant album. Its front two-thirds are fast-paced and brakeless, the production whipping around the curves without much care for consequences. And then the last third is this crunchy, dominating, copycat take on dubstep, a subgenre of electronic dance music that had gained popularity through 2011 but was still mostly a thing rap tended to avoid borrowing from. The whole thing just felt pricey and imposing and cool and exciting. When Jay and Kanye performed it during their *Watch the Throne* tour, even that was an exercise in overabundance. They'd play it three, four, five, eight, ten times. When they did the show in real-life Paris, they performed the song twelve times in a row, and that's a thing that had never happened before.

But "Niggas in Paris" is also very smart. Without that it couldn't be nearly as important.

There are two viewpoints expressed on "Niggas in Paris," and they work together to form a single thesis statement. There's Jay Z's viewpoint, which, if you look at all of it at once, is about overpowering and overtaking all of rap, because that's always what Jay Z has been about for the length of his career.

Example: He talks about being fined by the NBA[5] ("I ball so hard motherfuckers wanna fine me"), and how inconsequential it was ("What's fifty grand to a motherfucker like me? / Can you please remind me?"), and now seems like a good time to point out that Jay Z famously left the waitresses at the *Watch the Throne* release party a $50,000 tip on a $250,000 bill. He raps, "Psycho; I'm liable to go Michael / Take your pick / Jackson, Tyson, Jordan, Game Six," and the implication is clear: "I am as important to rap as each of these Michaels were to their field," and he is not lying. Every last bit of the verse is very confrontational, but in the most dismissive way achievable, and it's a justifiable condescension because Jay Z is one of the eight most influential rappers of all.

And then there's Kanye's viewpoint, which, if you look at all of it at once, is about overthrowing rap, because that's always what Kanye has been about for the length of his career, and one example would be the way he starts, "You are now watching the throne," to say that they're the tastemakers, but the most straightforward example of Kanye's sway is his turning the word "cray" into an acceptable way to describe something.

But the most important line in the song, the one fattest with historical inferences (and ramifications, too, really), is also the most startling.

After talking about having too many watches to keep up with, Jay Z, in a tone that suggests befuddlement, then awe, then hubris, glows, "I'm shocked, too / I'm supposed to be locked up, too / If you escaped what I escaped, you'd be in Paris getting fucked up, too," and, truly, this kind of writing (and thinking) is a first-class example of how Jay has managed to stay relevant—but more than that: beloved—in rap since 1996's *Reasonable Doubt*.

He does three separate things here.

1. With "I'm shocked, too," he perpetuates the us-against-them, rich vs. poor arm of his mythos. In a 2011 *GQ* story, Alex Pappademas wrote, "No hip-hop artist who owes his credibility to the street has moved farther beyond it and into the rarefied air of twenty-first-century high society than Jay has," and

---

1. This is a far less clever observation than it appears to be, if it even appears to be that. Kanye literally had a song called "Big Brother" on his *Graduation* album.
2. This is a quote from a story Reggie Ossé (Combat Jack), who was an entertainment lawyer and worked with Jay Z at the time, told Complex.com in 2010.
3. It won a Grammy for Best Rap Song and a Grammy for Best Rap Performance, went 4x platinum, and made it onto *Billboard*'s Hot Digital Songs chart before it was even released, if you can even believe that.
4. Rapping about very expensive things, basically.
5. Jay Z visited the Kentucky Wildcats locker room after they'd won a place in the Final Four in the 2011 NCAA basketball tournament. He was a minority owner of the Nets at the time, and that sort of thing is prohibited by the NBA, so the Nets fined him $50K.

the way he's done that without losing his credibility (the way, say, 50 Cent did) is he has always presented all of his winnings less as business ventures and more as the spoils of war conquerings. He lives in a different world than the regular non-wealthy humans do, but he is in that other world as an outsider looking to annihilate rather than assimilate;[6] he's a Trojan horse in black sunglasses and a Yankees cap. And he does it without undercutting his own accomplishments, and that's just as necessary to the story.

Here's David Samuels, writing about Jay Z for *The Atlantic* in an article titled "What Obama Can Learn from Jay-Z": "[Jay Z's] ability to stand before his audience without pretending to be any less skilled or less wealthy than he actually is, and to present his wealth and privilege as having been fully earned, while also identifying with the streets he grew up on, makes him the most important popular artist in America today."

2. With "I'm supposed to be locked up, too," he (once again) addresses the impropriety with which the American justice system incarcerates black males. In 2014, a report by the Brookings Institution's Hamilton Project showed that black males born between 1975 and 1979 who dropped out of high school had a 70 percent chance of spending time in prison by their mid-thirties. Compare that with a 10 percent chance for white males who fall into the same set of circumstances. Jay Z does not have a high school degree. He has about half a billion dollars but no degree.

3. With "If you escaped what I escaped, you'd be in Paris getting fucked up, too," he introduces the story of black Americans escaping to Paris for a more hospitable territory to rap. It's no accident that this song is called "Niggas in Paris" and not "Niggas in Germany" or "Niggas in China." There's a long history of blacks migrating to Paris in search of a more accommodating (i.e., welcoming) living environment, from the post–World War I soldiers to black culture renaissance figures like Josephine Baker and Richard Wright and Nina Simone and James Baldwin. Andrew Hoberek, an English pro-

fessor at the University of Missouri who lectures a class devoted to examining the careers of Kanye West and Jay Z, takes this a step further, explaining in an interview with Forbes.com in 2014 that they've ideologically aligned themselves with some of literature's most imposing figures. "I think both artists are fully aware of this element of their work. Jay's song 'D.O.A. (Death of Auto-Tune),' for instance, begins with Jay—who is no singer —performing an intentionally out-of-tune version of the band Steam's 1969 song 'Na Na Hey Hey Kiss Him Goodbye.' To my ears this sounds a lot like the way modernist writers such as T. S. Eliot, James Joyce, and Virginia Woolf produced intentionally difficult poems and fiction to counter writing that they thought had become (like auto-tuned pop vocals) too smooth and pretty. And the video shows Jay performing the song with a small jazz band, harkening back to similar experiments by bebop musicians in the mid-twentieth century." Jay and Kanye recorded "Niggas in Paris" in Paris. That wasn't an accident, either.

♦

There was a reactionary pushback to the extravagance of *Watch the Throne* when it began rolling—this was all happening near the same time as the Occupy Wall Street[7] stuff was going on, so it was very timely to call out the album's opulence. But the criticism faded as it became more and more clear that it (the album, but also "Niggas in Paris") possessed the same sort of social critique that more lauded rap songs before it contained, and that, if anything, it had its finger on the pulse of these same anti-capitalist ideologies. It was just being delivered from a place no rappers had ventured into before. It made smarter the artistry of this particular discussion and did it with a beat that you couldn't get out of your head.

Really, "Niggas in Paris" echoed the fundamental premise of W. E. B. Du Bois's *The Souls of Black Folk*.[8] It was just the new version of that. That's what it was about. That's the whole point of "Niggas in Paris." I guess that viewpoint was kind of surprising. But it shouldn't have been.

---

6. I can't say for certain that these are his true intentions—there certainly are moments where it feels like he only wants to belong with the top 1 percent—but that's how he tells that story, and he tells it more convincingly than anyone ever has.

7. Occupy Wall Street was an anti-consumerist movement that was meant to act as a rally against "social and economic inequality worldwide." Best I could tell, it was mostly just a bunch of people holding poorly made signage.

8. "After the Egyptian and Indian, the Greek and Roman, the Teuton and Mongolian, the Negro is a sort of seventh son, born with a veil, and gifted with second-sight in this American world,—a world which yields him no true self-consciousness, but only lets him see himself through the revelation of the other world. It is a peculiar sensation, this double-consciousness, this sense of always looking at one's self through the eyes of others, of measuring one's soul by the tape of a world that looks on in amused contempt and pity. One ever feels his two-ness,—an American, a Negro; two souls, two thoughts, two unreconciled strivings; two warring ideals in one dark body, whose dogged strength alone keeps it from being torn asunder."

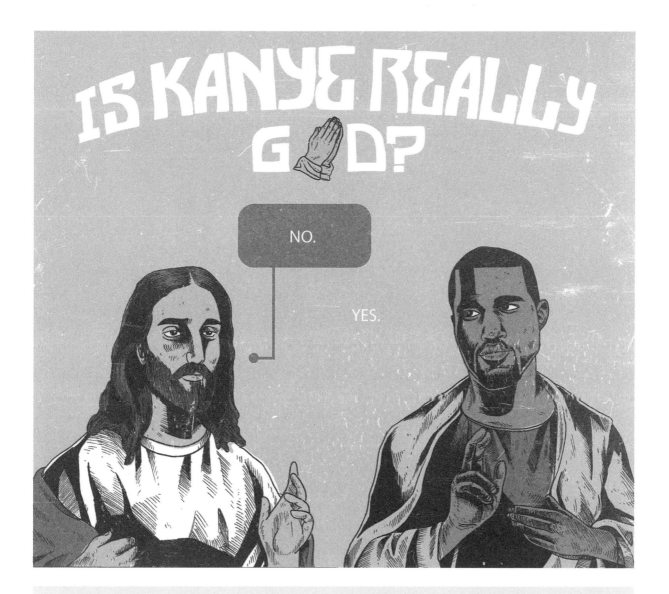

REBUTTAL: "OTIS" JAY Z AND KANYE WEST

It's rare that something that's hyped actually lives up to it. So, in 2011, when the first leak off of Jay Z and Kanye's collaborative *Watch the Throne* album was "H.A.M.," Yeezy fans lost their shit at hearing the two dovetail their verses over a recycled, lackluster Lex Luger beat. Months later came "Otis," with the Otis Redding "Try a Little Tenderness" sampling that loops underneath their verses reminding everyone that fans expected the actual sample itself to trade off verse for verse (a humblebrag of how much time they spent crafting this album). "Otis" had a close-to-perfect Kanye chop of the beat, pairing it with soulful screams to those classic Memphis horns, organ, and drums. But perhaps what's most important to its legacy is that, for three minutes, Jay and Ye just stunt—it's just bar after bar of luxury, which led to its winning Best Rap Performance at the 2012 Grammys. **—LAUREN NOSTRO**

2012

SAME
LOVE

MACKLEMORE
& RYAN LEWIS

WHAT THIS SONG IS ABOUT

Gay and lesbian rights, mostly as
they relate to marriage.

· ·

WHY IT'S IMPORTANT

It was the first rap song about gay
and lesbian marriage to make it
into the Top 40.

This is an easy pick to make, but it's also a difficult pick to make. And to that point, it should be explicitly stated that the "difficulty" part of that statement has zero percent to do with the song's general premise, which is civic egalitarianism, which should never, ever be a problem. There is a lot to unpack here.

Let's go "easy" first:

WHY IS "SAME LOVE" AN EASY SONG TO PICK AS THE MOST IMPORTANT SONG OF 2012?

Because of what it is. "Same Love" wasn't the first rap song advocating for gays. There's an entire subgenre made up of queer rappers that began gaining popularity outside of itself near 2010 (homo-hop), and well before that there was sissy bounce, which is an offshoot of New Orleans's bounce music, which was regionally popularized in the early '90s, and it's not explicitly a gay rap subgenre but it's certainly gay friendly.

"Same Love" isn't even the first song by a straight guy advocating for gay rights. Murs, a decidedly less popular rapper, released a song in 2011 called "Animal Style" that was about a turbulent high school relationship between two guys.[1]

But what "Same Love" *is* is the first rap song about gay rights to receive significant radio airplay, or any kind of radio airplay, really. It was the fourth single from Macklemore & Ryan Lewis's *The Heist*, and it piggybacked off (a) the gigantic success of "Thrift Shop," which had turned Macklemore into a star, (b) the momentum the gay rights movement had gained when President Obama officially endorsed same-sex marriage in May 2012, (c) the emotional response elicited by R&B singer Frank Ocean in July 2012 when he wrote to a letter posted on his Tumblr how he'd fallen in love with a man once, and (d) what appeared to be a noticeable shift in the tolerance of homosexuality in rap, and I mean this literally[2] and metaphorically, with artists like Lil Wayne and Drake and Andre 3000 blurring the edges of what masculinity in the genre meant.

"Same Love" was perfectly timed and gorgeously executed. It had weight and consequence.

IS "SAME LOVE" DIFFICULT BECAUSE MACKLEMORE IS CORNY?

No. If Macklemore is corny, it's a by-product of being overly sincere or eager, and that's a by-product of being perpetually concerned he might be intruding on rap. He has a song called "White Privilege," where he talks about that exact thing, saying things like, "Hip-hop started off on a block I've never been to / To counteract a struggle I've never even been through." Enough of that can be annoying, I suppose, but with Macklemore it's always more tone-deaf than malicious.

The easiest example: His post-Grammys debacle. After he'd won four awards on seven nominations in 2014,[3] he felt it necessary to apologize. One of the awards he'd received was for Best Rap Album. Kendrick Lamar was the popular choice for that award, and with good reason: His album *good kid, m.A.A.d. city* was a triumph, and a truly enjoyable piece of art. *The Heist* was fun enough, but it stood only waist-high to *GKMC*. Still, it won, and so the day after the show Macklemore sent Kendrick a text apologizing, saying Kendrick had deserved to win that award, that he felt weird about having "robbed" him of it. And that was an okay thing to do. A better thing to do would've been nothing, but sending the text wasn't terrible. But then Macklemore took a screenshot of the text and posted it to his Instagram. That was not an okay thing to do. That was terrible. That was corny. It was mawkish, and (probably) self-serving, and felt a lot like a grasp at absolution, even if it wasn't meant to. But "Same Love" doesn't have that same hue. There is no hedge in it.

"Same Love" isn't an adoption of values or culture; it's a reflective, anecdotal song based on his own ideas and experiences.[4]

IS "SAME LOVE" DIFFICULT BECAUSE IT'S A CORNY SONG?

A little bit. This is a criticism that gets tossed at a fair number of Macklemore songs, and sometimes it's accurate to describe a small amount of his music that way, and there *are* a handful of threadbare aphorisms that push "Same Love" in that direction ("Live on! Be yourself!"; "No law's gonna change us / We have

to change us"; "No freedom 'til we're equal / Damn right I support it"). But it's not all the way corny. It's also thoughtful and it's also well intentioned, and it's slicker than it would appear to have you believe, too. Especially, to paraphrase a conceit from a paper written by Dr. R. J. Snell, the relationship between images and lyrics in the video, which traces the life from birth to death of a gay male born into an unwelcoming home:

When Macklemore talks about how "right-wing conservatives" think being gay is a decision, he raps, "And you can be cured with some treatment and religion," and we're shown video clips of children exiting a Catholic church in the '60s, and the implication is that gay by choice and not design is an outdated and impractical idea. He reinforces his position with the line "Man-made rewiring of a predisposition," and we're shown clips of a Bible and a cross. When he raps the phrase "Playing God," we see the video's protagonist sitting with his mother in a church pew. The first time we see him crying is the first time we hear Mary Lambert singing, "And I can't change, even if I tried." We see him and his mom arguing after that as Lambert completes her thought, singing she couldn't change "even if I wanted to." And when she sings the couplet for a second time, we see the protagonist texting a boy and then meeting up with him and appearing very happy. The line "A culture founded from oppression" is paired with clips from the civil rights movement. "Gender to skin color" is matched with a little black girl holding a WE BELIEVE IN THE SUPREME COURT sign. When Macklemore talks about people who've had their rights stolen, we see a clip of Martin Luther King Jr. speaking, and then right after that he says, "I might not be the same, but that's not important," and we see a gay rights parade.

It's all very smart. Smart is rarely corny.

IS "SAME LOVE" DIFFICULT BECAUSE MACKLEMORE IS WHITE?

No.

IS "SAME LOVE" DIFFICULT BECAUSE MACKLEMORE IS WHITE AND IS RAPPING?

That's probably closer to the point, but still not completely accurate, and certainly not completely troublesome. Being a

---

1. This one was super-dark. It ended with one of the boys shooting and killing his boyfriend before shooting and killing himself.
2. By this point, Jay Z, Kanye, 50 Cent, Eminem, Nicki Minaj, and more, and more, and more had openly expressed positive viewpoints regarding homosexuality.
3. FYI: Mos Def, Snoop, Tupac, and Biggie all have zero Grammys.
4. Macklemore was raised in a liberal part of Seattle and is close to several gay family members. In fact, the uncles he mentions in the song—they're the ones who are on the single's cover art.

white rapper isn't necessarily *a thing*, at least not like it maybe once was. White people rap. And Macklemore has always shown himself to be aware of the privileges afforded to him for being a white rapper. When he interviewed with New York's Hot 97 in 2014 following the string of high-profile, racially charged murders that occurred, he spoke openly and intelligently about his position. "For me, as a white dude, as a white rapper, I'm like, 'How do I participate in this conversation?' How do I participate, how do I get involved on a level where I'm not co-opting the movement or I'm not making it about me, but also realizing the platform that I have and the reach that I have and doing it in an authentic, genuine way, because race is uncomfortable to talk about, and white people, we can just turn off the TV when we're sick of talking about race." He's always nervous about messing up, like how a guy who's caught the attention of a girl who's too pretty for him behaves.

IS "SAME LOVE" DIFFICULT BECAUSE MACKLEMORE IS WHITE AND IS RAPPING AND SEEMS TO IMPLY THAT RAP, A GENRE THAT WAS FOUNDED BY BLACKS AND IS STILL MOSTLY BLACK, IS MORE HOMOPHOBIC THAN ANY OTHER SECTION OF MUSIC, AND SO HERE HE IS, THE GREAT WHITE SAVIOR, ENLIGHTENING EVERYONE?

No. I suppose a very cynical person could see it that way if he or she squinted enough. But Macklemore is a rapper, and has always identified himself as a rapper, and has only ever been careful when talking about, or even hinting at, anything that has to deal with race. Also, penalizing him for not being a thing would appear to be the exact opposite of the song, or of life, really.

IS "SAME LOVE" DIFFICULT BECAUSE MACKLEMORE IS NOT GAY?

This is a central criticism of "Same Love," and the thought is: How can Macklemore be the voice of gay struggle if he is not gay? And the answer is simple: I don't imagine he intended to become that, and he's for sure never presented it that way in any interview or quote. He largely avoids even being shown in the video for the song, his only appearance coming as a cameo during a wedding scene.

◆

When Macklemore performed "Same Love" at the Grammys, there was a break near the end of the performance where the music still played but the rapping had stopped. Queen Latifah walked out, and Madonna was there, too, and there was an aisle full of couples, gay and straight, whom Queen Latifah was marrying. It was kind of amazing to see, but it was also kind of silly to see, because who gets married at the Grammys, and who gets married by Queen Latifah, and where did Madonna even come from? Then the camera zoomed and panned across the faces of the couples who were being wed, and several of them had very big, very wet, very happy eyes, and it continued being amazing but stopped being silly.

In hip-hop, at that point, about this issue, no one had ever had that effect before.

REBUTTAL: "BANDZ A MAKE HER DANCE" JUICY J

I believe in miracles. Not the kind with bippities, boppities, or boops; none of that fairy dust and garbanzo bean bullshit. Water isn't walked on and doesn't get turned into wine; there's barely enough of it to fuel this dying marble. And it's weird, because I like to think I have a pretty firm grasp on reality. It's just that there's certain things that simply . . . happen; that—no matter how you turn it—make no sense without cosmic interference. Maybe science can explain away the gift of life or the taste of Nutella, but there's just no way a white lab coat can define how—for a time—the clouds parted and our national catchphrase became "You say no to ratchet pussy, Juicy J can't." Or how Juicy J, an over-the-hill thirty-seven-year-old rapper at the time, became the patron saint of frat basements across the country; how "twerking" entered the conversation of mothers and local news correspondents everywhere. How Lil Wayne finally put out a good verse. How 2 Chainz 2 Chainz'd it. Miracles on top of miracles. Mike Will made a miracle sandwich for all of us to eat.

But, hey, if you think Macklemore put out the most important song of the year, that's fine. That's on you and your god. Because science can't explain that, either.

—JEFF ROSENTHAL

SAME Love

"When I was in the third grade, I thought that I was gay" ("0:43)

"America the brave still fears what we don't know" (1:20)

"The right-wing conservatives think it's a decision" (1:08)

"If I was gay I would think hip-hop hates me" (2:04)

"And 'God loves all his children' is somehow forgotten" (1:25)

"'Gay' is synonymous with the lesser" (2:24)

"It's the same hate that's caused wars from religion" (2:29)

"If you preach hate at the service, those words aren't anointed" (2:46)

"It's human rights for everybody, there is no difference" (2:36)

"Progress, march on" (3:38)

"A world so hateful some would rather die than be who they are" (3:50)

"About time that we raised up" (4:07)

POWERFUL

HOPEFUL

AUTOBIOGRAPHICAL

INSIGHTFUL

HISTORICAL REFERENCE

INTROSPECTIVE

EXAMINING

CONTROL

BIG SEAN

featuring

KENDRICK LAMAR

and

JAY ELECTRONICA

WHAT THIS SONG IS ABOUT

Big Sean talks about champagne (and some other things), Kendrick Lamar talks about how he'd like to murder everyone (and some other things), and nobody knows what TF Jay Electronica is ever talking about, so who knows.

• •

WHY IT'S IMPORTANT

Because it was the best kind of cage-rattling, and because it turned Kendrick Lamar's assumed, almost predetermined, stardom into an inarguable stardom.

"It's funny how one verse can fuck up the game." —Jay Z, "Imaginary Player," 1997

"Control" is a song by Big Sean, except it's not a song, and it doesn't belong to Big Sean.

It for sure arrived as a Big Sean song. He teased it on Twitter a few hours before *Hall of Fame*, the album he was promoting, became available for preorder. He said he was going to post it himself because it was a toss-away that he wasn't able to include on the album due to sample-clearance issues.[1] He said it was "straight rap" shit, that it was grimy, that it was seven minutes long, that "IT IS NOT no radio shit," and he capitalized "IT IS NOT" just like that. He was energetic. But I don't know that anyone else was really as excited about it as his caps-locked letters were.

He'd already released three singles from the album and none of them was very interesting (or successful).[2] There was "Guap," which was about money, and he also talked about having sex with seventeen girls at once on it, and that seems excessive, but I guess that's why they call him Big Sean and not Normal Sean. There was "Switch Up," featuring Common, and that was probably the first time anyone had ever talked about R. Kelly and Charlie Brown in the same verse of a song. And there was "Beware," featuring Lil Wayne and Jhené Aiko, and nobody had invented a time machine by then, which means it was 2013 Lil Wayne and not 2008 Lil Wayne, so you can imagine how well that went. Those songs, they were okay, but they were also very forgettable. And so again: I don't know that anyone else was really as excited about "Control" as Big Sean himself seemed to be. But then he released it, and then people heard it, and then, all at once, it felt like it was all anybody could talk about. And it had nothing to do with Big Sean.

Let me be clear when I say this, because this is a thing that should be clear: "Control" is Big Sean's song, but only in the strictest legal sense, in that it's his because he technically owns it, in that it is his property. But it's not really a *Big Sean song*.

And let me also be clear when I say this, because this is also a thing that should be clear: "Control" *is* a song, but only in the literal sense, in that it's presented as a song, in that it has production and some verses and some bridges. But it's not a *song*. What "Control" is, at least what it's known for now and will be known as forever, is a verse. And that verse belongs to Kendrick Lamar.[3]

♦

This is a short, personal anecdote, and I've (unsuccessfully) tried to avoid telling them for most of this book, because who really cares, but this one at least ties in to the chapter:

In December 2012, I was at a Kendrick Lamar concert in Houston. This was after his album *good kid, m.A.A.d city* had been released but before it had gone platinum, so he was already climbing toward true stardom[4] (*good kid* received near-unanimous praise, and sold a completely unexpected 262,000 copies its first week), but not 100 percent there yet. I was there for work, covering the show and also interviewing some people. I was backstage before the show started, trying to hurry up because being backstage at a concert is the worst place to be. And as I'm standing there, this kid, who couldn't have been more than fourteen years old, came rushing past me. He jostled me just enough so that I noticed him, but not enough to where I'd be like, "Okay, looks like I'm fighting a teenager at a rap concert tonight." But when he went past, I was watching, and he cruised right on up the stairs, stopped at the curtain, motioned at the DJ, took off his hoodie, grabbed a microphone, then ran out onstage. Turned out, it was Kendrick who'd rushed past. I'm only about five-foot-seven, and he was a good two feet shorter than me. I was happy about that.[5] The music came on, the lights were flashing, the whole place went fucking yo-yo. He didn't seem that tiny anymore. I was happy about that, too.

By December 2013, Kendrick had ascended, and "Control" had helped shove him way up high. It had its own stats—Complex.com had it as their tenth-best song of the year, saying it would "go down in history as a milestone in hip-hop"; RollingStone.com had it as the third-best rap song of the year, and didn't even bother to mention Big Sean or Jay Electronica; the *XXL* website had it as a top-five song of the year; Pitchfork.com had it on their list; the *NME* website had it on theirs; on and on—and it paired perfectly with Kendrick's album, and the two together created this mysterious, smart, all-of-a-sudden devastating rapper.

While being interviewed by *GQ* for their Rapper of the Year slot (which, FYI, came after MTV had picked him as the "Hottest MC in the Game," because that's the kind of year he was

having), Kendrick was asked about having seen the ghost of Tupac, which he'd mentioned in a song. He said a fair amount about it, but eventually he explained the situation like this: "I remember being tired, tripping from the studio, lying down, and falling into a deep sleep and seeing a vision of Pac talking to me. Weirdest shit ever. I'm not huge on superstition and all that shit. That's what made it so crazy. It can make you go nuts. Hearing somebody that you looked up to for years saying, 'Don't let the music die.' Hearing it clear as day. Clear as day. Like he's right there. Just a silhouette."

I can't say for certain that this is true, but I also can't say for certain that it's not.

◆

Kendrick's verse on "Control" lasts just over three minutes. It's 550-plus words, and they're all packed together extra tight, braided together into the density of steel, or a black hole, or a black hole made of steel, if that's even a thing.[6]

Here is a very small example:

"Bitch, I've been jumped before you put a gun on me / Bitch, I put one on yours, I'm Sean Connery / James Bonding with none of you niggas."

His tone here, as it is throughout the song, is aggressive. The phrase "James Bonding," smart in itself, is a clever way to say he's not interested in making any new friends. Earlier in the year, Drake, a more powerful figure but less of a tactician, made a similar announcement on DJ Khaled's "No New Friends," except he presented it as a straight line rather than a squiggle, singing, "No new friends, no new friends, no new friends no, no new." It was nakedly enjoyable, as most Drake moments tend to be, but Kendrick's execution of the idea was, to be sure, at a level higher, as his raps tend to be.[7]

And we can unpack its levels even more: Consider that Kendrick prefaced the James Bonding line with "I'm Sean Connery," who defined the James Bond character,[8] and so he's

---

1. It samples two songs (Jay Z's "Where I'm From" and Quilapayún and Sergio Ortega's "*El Pueblo Unido Jamás Será Vencido*") and interpolates a third (Terrace Martin's "Get Bizy"), but he's never said which one was the problem.

2. As it were, *Hall of Fame* does not belong in the Rap Hall of Fame.

3. The only people who seem to feel otherwise are Big Sean and Jay Electronica.

4. Only four rappers who had not already had a platinum-selling album before 2006 have had one go platinum since then: Drake, Nicki Minaj, Kendrick Lamar, and Macklemore.

5. I automatically like anybody who makes me feel taller.

6. It's not. I checked.

7. Kendrick exists as a duality. He is equally good at framing rap as a fun thing and an artistic thing, and that's a trick only the very best rappers on the planet are capable of doing. (The easiest comparison to make is to Andre 3000.)

8. Six different people have been James Bond in a Bond movie. Connery was the best. Daniel Craig was second. Pierce Brosnan was last. Get him and his invisible car all the way TF outta here.

low-key aligning himself with greatness, and so that's two levels higher than the forthrightness of what Drake did.

And his opening bit, the thing about having a gun pulled on him, that's a metaphor, so now we're three levels higher. But it's also a reference to the story of early Hollywood gangster Johnny Stompanato busting onto a movie set in 1957 and pulling a gun on Sean Connery because he thought Connery was sleeping with his girlfriend, and that puts us four levels higher. (That's Sean Connery = Kendrick, Johnny Stomp = hating ass rappers, the gun = hate, and the girlfriend = rap.)

Connery responded by grabbing Stompanato by the hand + gun, torquing it back until Stomp let go, then coldcocking him, and that's the implied extension of the metaphor. We're at five levels higher than normal.

So the three lines from the song quoted above are twenty-seven words in length, and the two paragraphs it took to explain them took 355 words. That's how his whole verse on "Control" is compressed. And, really, that's impressive enough, but it was what followed the James Bonding that was so apocalyptic.

Kendrick uncorked all of his fury, and he presented it with zero camouflage, calling out the names of just short of a dozen of the most talked about new rappers. There's a whole chunk of destruction, but here's the heart of it:

I'm usually homeboys with the same niggas I'm rhymin' with
But this is hip-hop, and them niggas should know what time it is

And that goes for Jermaine Cole, Big K.R.I.T., Wale
Pusha T, Meek Mill, A$AP Rocky, Drake
Big Sean, Jay Electron',[9] Tyler, Mac Miller
I got love for you all but I'm tryna murder you niggas
Tryna make sure your core fans never heard of you niggas
They don't wanna hear not one more noun or verb from you niggas[10]

Almost instantly, it absorbed all of rap. Everyone knew it was a moment. 50 Cent had done something similar with "How to Rob," but that was more than two years before he'd released his album and become a champion. Kendrick did it AFTER, and so there was no misconstruing the message he was sending. To state it plainly: Fuck you, dudes.

Saying names is a thing top-tier guys just don't do. War takes time. It's supposed to build. Jay Z and Nas danced around each other for six years before Jay finally fired a direct shot at Nas's forehead, saying his name in a song (see page 142). Kendrick had no interest in that. He found the crowd of rappers who were waiting, all standing around chatting and glad-handing each other, then fired a bazooka gun into it.

---

9. How real do you have to be to get invited to be on a song and then go on that song and dump all over the other two dudes on the song with you? Kendrick was on some true Charles Darwin shit.

10. Mac Miller, Pittsburgh's endlessly likable goofball rapper, had the best response of all to Kendrick, tweeting out, "If I can't do no more nouns or verbs ima start comin with the wildest adjective bars that anyone has ever heard."

REBUTTAL: "NEW SLAVES" KANYE WEST

"Control" is a pretty good song. But it's not a particularly great song. It does, however, have some very great bars, the greatest of which are from Kendrick Lamar and about being greater than other rappers. It got Twitter-hyped for like seventy-two hours or whatever, which is well and good, but the most important song of 2013 is clearly, easily, "New Slaves" from Kanye West. Unlike "Control," people still actually play "New Slaves"—in the club, in their car, in their headphones. Unlike "Control," "New Slaves" is talking about real, actual issues—racism, the prison-industrial complex, income inequality, the media. Kendrick is talking about rap music. Kanye is talking about American history. And at the end of the day, only one of these two songs still has people moshing on the dance floor. Isn't that what it's all about?

—GREG HOWARD

ALTERNATE realities

WHAT IF A DIFFERENT SONG WAS THE MOST IMPORTANT SONG OF 2013?

CHANCE THE RAPPER, "CHAIN SMOKER"

MORE PEOPLE START WEARING OVERALLS

NASA ANNOUNCES ITS ROVER *CURIOSITY* FOUND LIFE ON MARS

CHANCE BECOMES FIRST PERSON TO RECORD A SONG WITH AN ALIEN

KANYE WEST, "BLACK SKINHEAD"

IT BECOMES THE POLITICAL ANTHEM HE INTENDED

KANYE ANNOUNCES HIS PLANS TO RUN FOR PRESIDENT IN 2016

KENDRICK LAMAR'S *TO PIMP A BUTTERFLY* SOUNDS WAY DIFFERENT

MIGOS, FEAT. DRAKE "VERSACE (REMIX)"

PRINCE WILLIAM AND KATE MIDDLETON NAME THEIR BABY "VERSACE VERSACE"

GIANNI VERSACE IS RESURRECTED

QUAVO PREVENTS THOSE TORNADOES FROM HITTING OKLAHOMA

2014

Lifestyle

Rich Gang

featuring **Young Thug**

and **Rich Homie Quan**

WHAT THIS SONG IS ABOUT

It's about two sirs who are excited about not being poor anymore, which is for sure a thing to celebrate.

• •

WHY IT'S IMPORTANT

Young Thug's bizarreness had already been proved a creative commodity. "Lifestyle" showed it could be a commercial one, too, and that legitimized it, which offered it up for appropriation for rappers to come.

I. "Lifestyle" is a song by Rich Gang, which maybe you figured out because the title of this chapter says exactly that.

II. Rich Gang is a supergroup, and that's just a more political way to say there are more members than in a usual group and things are often disorganized. One is a rapper named Young Thug and another is a rapper named Rich Homie Quan, which maybe you also figured out because the art in this chapter is of their faces, though that seems less likely because Young Thug and Rich Homie Quan are not famous in the way a sizable portion of the rappers in this book are famous, which is to say very famous, or recognizably famous.

III. While Rich Homie Quan is talented and fun and very likely a more technically proficient rapper, Young Thug is uniquely mesmerizing, and it feels easy to say that, between the two of them, he already has been, and will remain, more important to rap. Of course, all of that is to say: Most of this chapter is about Young Thug. Thank you.

♦

Let us not pretend that you or I really know anything about Young Thug, and maybe that's the entire point of Young Thug, and if it's not then it's definitely (at least a very small) part of the reason he's interesting.

Through the last quarter of 2013, Young Thug existed mostly as a product unknown to everyone who either wasn't from Atlanta, which is where he's from, or who wasn't actively involved in the upkeep of a website devoted to rap music. Then, right at the beginning of 2014, separate from each other by about two weeks, a clip of Drake enthusiastically rapping along to a Young Thug song[1] in a nightclub in Miami and

a clip of Kanye West doing the same thing at a nightclub in Paris began pinging around the Internet, and it's just that easy. There's this tool on Google that allows you to identify trends based on the number of times something is searched on the Internet. It displays the results as a line graph. Until October 2013, which marked the official release of "Stoner," Young Thug's first song to wiggle its way into prominence, the quantified search return for "Young Thug" was basically zero, and it should be made clear that Young Thug had been releasing mixtapes since 2011. From October 2013 to January 2014, there was a rise, and then, when Drake and Kanye high-fived him, there was a sharp, definite incline, and it's semiweird to be able to see the recalibration of rap aggregated into a line graph, but that's exactly what it is, and I guess it all makes sense because everything about Young Thug has always been weird, or at least presented that way.

◆

These are the reasons Young Thug is important: Because of the way he dresses, because of the way he talks, and because of the way he raps. None of them are intentional challenges to what came before him, but they all have become that. Let's go in reverse order of their gravity:

3. THE WAY HE TALKS, SPECIFICALLY THE WAY HE TALKS TO MEN

He calls them "lover" and "hubby" and "bae." He's explained several times that he's not gay, simply that he is not uncomfortable making other people uncomfortable, and that sounds right. I asked Tom Breihan about Young Thug once. Breihan is a music writer who I know to be eager and intelligent and concise. His response included the sentiment that Thug was inadvertently challenging homophobia in rap just by existing. That sounds right, too. More on that:

2. THE WAY HE DRESSES, BECAUSE HIS CLOTHES ARE OFTEN VERY TIGHT AND OCCASIONALLY A DRESS

(1) The tight clothes: Young Thug did not pioneer wearing tight clothes, but he certainly embraced them as enthusiastically as any rapper had (or has). His shirts grab his arms firmly and his pants grab his legs just as firmly. When he stands straight up, he looks like a flamingo in black Levi's. He wears a flimsy white

button-down shirt in the "Lifestyle" video and his arms look like straws in unopened paper sleeves. It should be ridiculous, but it's not, like when Jared Leto wore that fanny pack, or when Shia LaBeouf wears anything. (2) The dress: Young Thug posted a picture of himself wearing a dress at a photo shoot on Instagram. During an interview with *Complex*, the interviewer tried to give him an out ("Now, was that a shirt or was that . . . a dress?"). Young Thug smiled and explained that it was a dress for a "seven- or eight-year-old" girl, because Young Thug doesn't need an out.[2] Young Thug is a beautiful evolution.

1. BECAUSE OF THE WAY HE RAPS, WHICH IS TRANSCENDENT

On "Lifestyle," the most moving moment is when he wobbles out the line, "I've done did a lot of shit just to live this here lifestyle," because he says it with the exultation of a person who's gone from a very poor lifestyle to a very rich lifestyle very quickly, because that's what happened to him. It's meaningful for another reason, too, and one that is way heavier.

"I've done did a lot of shit just to live this here lifestyle" is not an altogether original proclamation, and that's fine, because Young Thug is not altogether interested in original proclamations. His focus slants in the reverse direction; he's interested in proclaiming things originally. He yelps and mumbles and takes words and strips them of all their meaning until they're just sounds and then splashes them on the floor. Imagine if you could hug your own happiness. Imagine if you took both of your feet and stuck them in a bucket full of warm mud and wiggled your toes around, except that mud isn't mud, it's your soul. That's how Young Thug raps. He's maybe the first post-text rapper, in that he doesn't even really need words.

The most obvious comparison to make to Young Thug is the loopy, ephemeral, post-drugs-phase Lil Wayne, who turned stupor-rambling into true prose. That's where Young Thug's center is. He took that, then advanced it, adding the humdrum brilliance of Gucci Mane; the electricity of Waka Flocka; the spazzy, auto-tuned gargling of Rich Homie Quan; and the rubble of all the rest of the new wave Atlanta rap satellite scenes and mushed them together into a glob of ectoplasm. He's like a human coagulation. The result became a powerful and new style that also felt warm and familiar.

---

1. "Danny Glover."
2. Other rappers who have worn dresses (or skirts): A$AP Rocky, Puff Daddy, Pusha T (he wore a leather skirt after he started hanging out with Kanye West, and that's just beautiful), Wiz Khalifa, Mos Def, Andre 3000 (in the "International Players Anthem" video), Kid Cudi (of course), Snoop, CeeLo Green (he wore a wedding dress), and, of course, Kanye West.

LIFESTYLE

"Hundred bands still look like the fuckin' Titans" (0:48)

"I've done a lot shit just to live this here lifestyle" (0:23)

"Even though I ain't gon' hit it, I'ma still make sure that she gushy" (0:56)

"Hop up in my bed full of forty bitches and yawnin'" (1:09)

"I got a moms, bitch, she got a moms, bitch" (1:20)

"I do this shit for my daughters and all my sons, bitch" (1:15)

"I ain't got AIDS but I swear to God I would bleed 'til I D.I.E." (2:14)

"And I'ma die for my nigga, aye" (1:55)

"Pee on top of these bitches" (2:20)

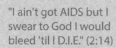

"They wanna know how I got M's and I didn't finish college" (2:30)

"God told me they can never stop me so they ain't gon' stop me" (2:23)

"Money on money, I got commas in every bank" (3:03)

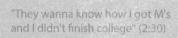

"I'm skatin' like that nigga Lupe" (3:28)

"Aye, I'm in her mouth just like toothpaste" (3:35)

COMPARATIVE   AUTOBIOGRAPHICAL   GET MONEY   INSIGHTFUL   CONSIDERATE   BOASTFUL   PSYCHOLOGICAL

Young Thug is the crossing of all the parts of rap that matter that aren't specifically rap-based—persona, style, rebellion. "Lifestyle" is a celebration of that.

♦

When I started working on this book, I was way too nervous about writing the first few chapters and way too nervous about writing the last few (2014 especially), though for wholly separate reasons.

The first few, I figured, had happened before I was even paying any attention to rap (I was negative two years old in 1979). How was I supposed to put together all of the pieces surrounding the genesis of the most impactful, most influential genre of music of the last thirty-five years? Because to write about why a song is important is superdifferent than just writing about, say, why it's good, or fun. You have to consider the external variables that were bending and shaping and forcing the music forward, and then consider the gravity of those changes and all of the orbits of everything after a particular song was released. This, it turned out, was not that hard, because a lot of very smart people had already gone about the work of chronicling the history of rap, so basically all I was doing was reading history books and listening to music, trying to maybe make a handful of connections nobody'd considered before.

It was the opposite with the last few chapters. The songs for the recent years had literally just occurred, and so sussing out their impact was going to be trickier, or at least more of a gamble, I thought. It was easy to peek back to 1987 and identify that that's when Rakim perfected rap as an art, because I could look at the years that came after it and see how it eventually all spiraled back to him, and that's very helpful. *Without that benefit, how was that going to play?* I worried, and I worried about it a fair amount until I realized there was no need to. The concern was unfounded, for 2014 especially. Because Young Thug is superobvious—what he came from, who he became, what he will become, and what will come, eventually, from what he created.

Hip-hop generally celebrates personal power; this devastating tag team is about watching it get crushed. Over churning dystopian synths, Killer Mike draws a scene that might've stepped out of Michelle Alexander's *The New Jim Crow*: A cop shakes down an unarmed man "just tryin' to smoke and chill" in his neighborhood, who begs, "Please don't lock me up in front of my kids, and in front of my wife," and adds, with no trace of sarcasm, "I respect the badge and the gun." No matter: He's cuffed and carted off like chattel.

El-P's verse bears witness, with details that suggest an atrocity, while Boots's pained falsetto hook leaves the title an open question. Too early for what? To wake up to another day of Sisyphean grinding? For a boy to see the subjugation of his father? For a young man to be branded a criminal? To be murdered by a police state?

In the year of Ferguson, Eric Garner, and worldwide #BlackLivesMatter protests, this would have resonated deeply even if it wasn't featured on what plenty of heads and bean counters considered the year's best rap LP. And spitting at a nation of millions on Letterman, the pair took it to another level, with a full band plus backing vocalists in Day of the Dead makeup. Up front: a white man—El-P, arms raised in Hands Up Don't Shoot solidarity—and a black man, Killer Mike, who pulls up his hood after ending his tale on the declaration "My life changed with that sound." Your life might, too.

—WILL HERMES

Acknowledgments

There are so many people I need to thank. It's a gross amount, really. I'm going to break it into Professional and Personal sections, even though those two categories blend together quite a bit.

Professional: First, I need to thank my book editor, Samantha Weiner, because without her there is no book, and I don't mean that to be a stylistic statement, I mean that as a fact. The premise of this book was actually her idea. It just happened to be that she picked me to write it. So thank you for that, Samantha. And thank you for all the phone calls and the emails and the encouragement and really for just dragging my lifeless corpse all the way to the seventy-two-thousand-plus words it ended up being. Sorry I was such a chore sometimes. I hope you like the way it turned out. And I hope we do more books together. And even if we don't, I hope you are very successful still. You deserve it. You deserve great things. (My secret is that this isn't true. I'm just being polite. If we don't do more books together, then I hope all the rest of your authors are human headaches.)

Thank you to Arturo Torres for illustrating this book. You did great work. It's so crazy to think about how I found your artwork on an obscure flyer online and now here we are with a book together, connected for life.

Thank you to Ice-T for writing the foreword. I still really can't even believe that it happened. It means a tremendous amount, and I want you to know that I purposely didn't answer the phone the first time you called me because I wanted to have an Ice-T voicemail. It's a top five thing of my whole life. Thank you. (And for sure thank you to Jorge Hinojosa for arranging for Ice-T to do the foreword. Thank you, Jorge. Genuinely.)

Thank you to Sebit Min and Sally Knapp from Abrams, and Rob Sternitzky, for designing and editing and copyediting all of my everything and turning it into this beautiful and airtight book. I hope a thousand great things happen to you and then I hope a thousand more great things happen to you after that.

Thank you to the amazing and smart and talented writers and editors who were nice enough to contribute blurbs to this book. That includes Sean Fennessey, Rob Harvilla, Chris Ryan, Jon Caramanica, Jessica Hopper, Chris Weingarten, Rembert Browne, Molly Lambert, Claire Lobenfeld, Randall Roberts, Bomani Jones, Will Hermes, Greg Howard, Lauren Nostro, Tom Breihan, Brandon Soderberg, Devon Maloney, eskay, Wesley Morris, Jeff Rosenthal, Nathaniel Friedman, Chuck Eddy, Paul Cantor, Rob Markman, Meaghan Garvey, Jonah Bromwich, Miles Raymer, Ben Westhoff, Jozen Cummings, Emma Carmichael, Mike Ayers, Dave Bry, Craig Jenkins, Benjamin Meadows-Ingram, Jayson Greene, Amos Barshad, and Ryan Dombal. Just typing out all of your names is legit overwhelming. You're for real some of the best music writers in the country, and I'm so proud that I get to have my name on something that also has yours. I'm terrified that I forgot to list someone in there. I really hope I didn't.

A thank-you goes to Reggie Ossé (Combat Jack) for helping vet the list of songs chosen for this book early on, and a thank-you goes to Chris Weingarten for the same thing. And since we're here, an extra thank-you goes to Chuck Eddy, too, for helping me form the chapters for 1979–1985 and also 1987. Your insight was extremely helpful. That same extra thank-you also goes to Brandon Soderberg, who helped with the chapters for '81, '84, '85, '87, '90, '96, '02, '05–08, '10, and 2011, and who I think has a V8 engine for a brain.

Let me also say more thank-yous to Sean Fennessey and Chris Ryan and include Mark Lisanti in here, too. They've been my editors at Grant-land since I started working there in July 2014 (and freelancing for about a year before that), and writing for them is a thing that I recommend everyone do, because they are sincerely smart and have a monumental ability to turn even the goofiest idea or halfway thought you present to them into something challenging and interesting.

I also need to include Dan Fierman and Bill Simmons in this section, too. They have only ever given me good counsel and for real changed my life when they asked me to come work for them. Thank you both for everything. I will never be able to say thank you enough but I will never stop trying. And I will 100 percent fight anyone you tell me to fight, on sight.

Thank you to Zein Nour, Evan Auerbach, and Nick Lucchesi for helping with the research that you two helped with. You guys are neat and I hope when we finally meet in person I don't hate you and you don't hate me.

Thank you to anyone else who helped with the book either directly or indirectly, including but not limited to Bill Barnwell, Jason Concepcion, Henry Abbott, UGK, Young Jeezy, Juvenile and the rest of the Hot Boys, Amin Elhassan, Twitter, the 2014 San Antonio Spurs, Jodeci, Berry Gordy's *The Last Dragon*, *carne guisada*, the collected works of Chuck Klosterman, and any person who's ever been on MSNBC's *Lockup*.

Thank you to Chris Gray and Margaret Downing, two people I will always owe very much to.

Personal: Thank you to my three younger sisters: Yasminda, Nastasja, and Marie. I hope you dudes know that I love you very much and that you can always ask me for anything and talk to me about anything. I should probably call you more. I'm definitely going to call you more.

Thank you to my mom and my dad. I am glad that you two let me listen to rap music when I was younger and I'm even more glad that you taught me that the only things I should ever really cherish or care about are my family and good on-the-ball defense in basketball. Sorry if I wrote anything in this book that was embarrassing.

Thank you to my grandma. I think about you a lot and I wish you'd have been able to see this. I'd love to know what you would've said.

Thank you to my three sons: Braxton, Caleb, and Parky. I'm so proud watching you nerds grow up. I can't believe I had any part in making anything as perfect as you all are. I want you to know that I'm always very happy any time you talk to me or even pay any sort of attention to me, and I want you to know that I will explode all of the planets in the galaxy to protect you if I have to. I also want you to know you should never root for the Rockets.

And, of course, thank you to my wife, Larami, who is smarter than me and more caring than me and more attractive than me and just better than me in basically every way. Thank you for the boys you've given me, the life you've made for me, the way you're always deeply thoughtful and endlessly charming, the way you have supported and stood by me through all of my terrible decisions and half-baked ideas. Remember when I was going to be a professional skateboarder? Remember when I dyed the tips of my hair blond? Remember when I watched that David Blaine special and started practicing street magic? Fucking street magic. And you didn't miss a step. You were like, "That sounds like a really good idea. I can film you." Oh, man. I love you so much. You are fascinating and perfect. I love you so much.

Works Cited

FOREWORD

4 Schoolly D. "P.S.K. (What Does It Mean)." *Schoolly-D*. Schoolly-D Records SD-114, album, 1985.

4 *Colors*. Directed by Dennis Hopper. Orion Pictures, 1988.

5 Public Enemy. "Fight the Power" video. Directed by Spike Lee, 1989.

1979

10 The Sugarhill Gang. "Rapper's Delight." Sugar Hill Records SH-542-A, single, 1979.

12 David Menconi. "The Riff That Lifted Rap." (Includes Chip Shearin quoting Sylvia Robinson.) Originally published in *News & Observer*, March 14, 2010. Reprinted on PopMatters.com, April 10, 2010. http://www.popmatters.com/article/123756-chip-shearin-and-the-bass-riff-that-lifted-rap.

12 *Dancing in the Street: Planet Rock*. (Includes Fab Five Freddy interview.) BBC TV documentary series, season 1, episode 10. Directed by Don Letts. Originally aired in 1996.

13 *Dancing in the Street: Planet Rock*. (Includes Melle Mel interview.)

15 Paulette and Tanya Winley. "Rhymin' and Rappin'." Paul Winley Records 12X45-5A, single, 1979.

1980

16 Kurtis Blow. "The Breaks." Mercury MDS-4010, single, 1980.

18 Russell Simmons. *Life and Def: Sex, Drugs, Money, and God* (New York: Crown Publishers, 2001; New York: Three Rivers Press, 2002), 59. Citation refers to the Three Rivers Press edition.

20 Kool Moe Dee. *There's a God on the Mic: The True 50 Greatest MCs* (New York: Thunder's Mouth Press, 2003), 117–18.

20 Afrika Bambaataa and Cosmic Force. "Zulu Nation Throwdown." Paul Winley Records 12X33-8A, single, 1980.

20 Afrika Bambaataa and Soul Sonic Force. "Zulu Nation Throwdown," Volume #2. Paul Winley Records 12X33-9A, single, 1982.

20 David Toop. *Rap Attack: African Rap to Global Hip Hop*, third ed. (Boston: South End Press, 1985; London: Serpent's Tail, 2000), 99, 115. Citations refer to the Serpent's Tail edition.

1981

22 Afrika Bambaataa and the Jazzy Five. "Jazzy Sensation (Bronx Version)." Tommy Boy Records 8122-74777-1A, single, 1981.

22 Afrika Bambaataa and the Jazzy Five. "Jazzy Sensation (Manhattan Version)." Tommy Boy Records 8122-74777-1B, single, 1981.

26 Nelson George. *Hip Hop America* (New York: Viking, 1998; New York: Penguin, 2005), 18. Citation refers to the Penguin edition.

27 Funky 4 + 1. "That's the Joint." Sugar Hill Records SH-554-A, single, 1980.

27 "Deborah Harry Invited the Funky 4 + 1 on to *SNL* for the First Televised Rap Performance." (Includes Chris Stein interview.) *Wax Poetics*, January 6, 2015. http://www.waxpoetics.com/music/videos/deborah-harry-invited-funky-4-1-snl-first-televised-rap-performance.

1982

28 Grandmaster Flash and the Furious Five. "The Message." *The Message*. Sugar Hill Records SH 268, album, 1982.

29 John Leland. "Armageddon in Effect." *Spin* 4, no. 6 (September 1988): 48.

30 Brother D and the Collective Effort. "How We Gonna Make the Black Nation Rise?" Clappers CL-12-0001-A, single, 1980.

33 Melle Mel. Interviewed by the 21st Century, backstage at Capone's Production's "The Legends of Hip Hop." Paradise Theater, Bronx, New York, May 14, 2011. SnS Productions. Video uploaded on YouTube by MainsWorld365.com, June 15, 2011. https://www.youtube.com/watch?v=ISByDZiXCdo.

33 Busy Bee. "Making Cash Money." Sugar Hill Records SH 591 A, single, 1982.

1983

34 Run-DMC. "Sucker M.C.'s. (Krush-Groove 1)." Profile 7019A, single, 1983.

38 Grandmaster Flash and Melle Mel. "White Lines (Don't Don't Do It)." Sugar Hill Records SHPX 130, single, 1983.

1984

40 Whodini. "Friends." Jive 1-9227, extended play, 1984.

41 Harry Weinger. "Whodini Makes 'Friends' at Radio, Retail." *Billboard* 95, no. 46 (December 1, 1984): 61.

42 Weinger. "Whodini Makes 'Friends' at Radio, Retail." *Billboard*, 60.

42 *Beat Street*. Directed by Stan Lathan. Orion Pictures, 1984.

42 Jean-Claude Van Damme. *Breakin'*. Directed by Joel Silberg. MGM, 1984.

43 *Breakin' 2: Electric Boogaloo*. Directed by Sam Firstenberg. TriStar Pictures, 1984.

43 Tupac, featuring Danny Boy. "I Ain't Mad at Cha." Death Row Records DRW 5-A, single, 1996.

43 Biz Markie. "Just a Friend." Warner Bros. Records 7-22784-A, single, 1989.

43 *Sharknado*. Directed by Anthony C. Ferrante. Southward Films, 2013.

43 *Sharknado 2: The Second One*. Directed by Anthony C. Ferrante. The Asylum, 2014.

43 Master P, featuring Pimp C and Silkk the Shocker. "I Miss My Homies." No Limit Records PVL 53290, single, 1997.

43 Young Jeezy. "Talk to 'Em." *Let's Get It: Thug Motivation 101*. Def Jam Recordings B0004421-02, album, 2005.

44 DMX, featuring Magic and Val. "A'Yo Kato." *Grand Champ*. Def Jam Recordings Def 15920-1, album, 2003.

44 50 Cent and Olivia. "Best Friend." *Music from and Inspired by* Get Rich or Die Tryin' *The Motion Picture*. G Unit/Interscope Records 0602498866030, album, 2005.

44 U.T.F.O. "Roxanne, Roxanne." Select Records FMS 62254, single, 1984.

44 Roxanne Shanté. "Roxanne's Revenge." Pop Art Records PA-1406, single, 1984.

44 Ralph Rolle. "Roxanne's a Man (The Untold Story)." Streetwise Records SW-2239A, single, 1985.

1985

46 Doug E. Fresh and M.C. Ricky D [Slick Rick]. "La Di Da Di." Reality Records D-242, single, 1985.

50 Run-DMC. "King of Rock." Profile Records Pro 764-A, single, 1985.

1986

52 Ice-T. "6 in the Mornin'." *Rhyme Pays*. Techno Hop Records THR-13, album, 1986.

53 Robert Duvall and Sean Penn. *Colors*. Directed by Dennis Hopper. Screenplay by Michael Schiffer. Orion Pictures, 1986.

53 Ice-T and Douglas Century. *Ice: A Memoir of Gangster Life and Redemption—from South Central to Hollywood* (New York: One World Books, 2012), 90.

54 Ice-T and Douglas Century. *Ice*, 104.

55 Ice-T on the Congressional Black Caucus. *The Arsenio Hall Show*, episode 172. Originally aired June 14, 1990.

55 Ice-T interview. Behind the Music: Ice-T, season 4, episode 4. VH-1, originally aired August 27, 2000.

56 Ice-T. The Arsenio Hall Show, 1990.

56 Run-DMC. "Walk This Way." Profile Records PRO-7112A, single, 1986.

1987

58 Eric B. and Rakim. "Paid in Full." *Paid in Full*. 4th & B'way BWAY-4005, album, 1987.

60 Donald Glover. "Best Time to Be Alive." *Weirdo*. Comedy Central TV special. Directed by Shannon Hartman. Originally aired November 19, 2011.

61 Chairman Mao. "The Microphone God." *Vibe* 5, no. 10 (December 1997/January 1998): 134.

61 "Five-Percent Nation." *Wikipedia*. Last modified May 2, 2015. http://en.wikipedia.org/wiki/Five-Percent_Nation.

62 Eric B. and Rakim. "My Melody." *Paid in Full*, 1987.

62 Mao. "The Microphone God." *Vibe*, 135.

62 Boogie Down Productions. "9mm Goes Bang." *Criminal Minded*. B Boy Records BB 4787 JBM, album, 1987.

1988

64 N.W.A. "Straight Outta Compton." *Straight Outta Compton*. Ruthless Records SL-57102, album, 1988.

65 "Hip-Hop's Greatest Year: Fifteen Albums That Made Rap Explode." *Rolling Stone*, February 12, 2008. http://www.rollingstone.com/music/news/hip-hops-greatest-year-fifteen-albums-that-made-rap-explode-20080212.

67 Ice-T on *The Oprah Winfrey Show*. Originally aired March 17, 1990.

68 Slick Rick. "Children's Story." Def Jam Recordings 44 68223, single, 1988.

1989

70 Public Enemy. "Fight the Power." Motown MOT-1972, single, 1989.

72 "Up from the Underground." *The History of Rock 'n' Roll*, vol. 10. (Includes Chuck D interview.) Time-Life Videos/Warner Bros. Entertainment B0002234XQ, 5-DVD box set, 2006. Originally released on VHS, March 21, 1995.

72 Samuel G. Freedman. "New York Race Tension Is Rising Despite Gains." *New York Times*, March 20, 1987. http://www.nytimes.com/1987/03/29/nyregion/new-york-race-tension-is-rising-despite-gains.html?page-wanted=1.

75 Chuck Klosterman. *I Wear the Black Hat*. (Includes Ice Cube quote.) (2013; New York: Scribner, 2014), 105. Citation refers to the 2014 edition.

75 Tone Loc. "Wild Thing." *Lōc-ed After Dark*. Delicious Vinyl DV3000, album, 1989.

1990

76 A Tribe Called Quest. "Bonita Applebum." *People's Instinctive Travels and the Paths of Rhythm*. Jive ZL74548, album, 1990.

81 *Beats, Rhymes & Life: The Travels of A Tribe Called Quest*. Directed by Michael Rapaport. Rival Pictures, 2011.

81 LL Cool J. "Around the Way Girl." Def Jam Recordings 44 73610, single, 1990.

1991

82 Geto Boys. "Mind Playing Tricks on Me." *We Can't Be Stopped*. Rap-A-Lot Records SL 57161, album, 1991.

83 Jon Pareles. "Distributor Withdraws Rap Album Over Lyrics." (Includes Bryn Bridenthal interview.) *New York Times*, August 28, 1990. http://www.nytimes.com/1990/08/28/arts/distributor-with-draws-rap-album-over-lyrics.html.

85 Isaac Hayes. *Three Tough Guys*. Directed by Duccio Tessari. Paramount, 1974.

86 Bushwick Bill. Interviewed by Billy Jam. *Put the Needle on the Record*. KUSF, San Francisco, 1991. Uploaded on YouTube, October 26, 2012. https://www.youtube.com/watch?v=7LaX9ijjRKY.

86 Bushwick Bill interview. *The Howard Stern Radio Show*. Originally aired April 24, 1999.

86 Kmurphy. "Full Clip: Scarface Breaks Down Geto Boys & Solo Catalogue." *Vibe*, August 6, 2010. http://www.vibe.com/2010/08/full-clip-scarface-pg-2.

86 A Tribe Called Quest. "Check the Rhime." *The Low End Theory*. Jive 1418-2-J, album, 1991.

1992

88 Dr. Dre, featuring Snoop Dogg. "Nuthin' but a 'G' Thang." *The Chronic*. Death Row Records/Interscope PI 57128, album, 1992.

90 *Rhyme & Reason*. (Includes Dr. Dre interview.) Directed by Peter Spirer. Asian Productions/City Block Productions, 1997.91 Beastie Boys. "So What'cha Want." *Check Your Head*. Grand Royal/Capitol CDP 7 98938-2, album, 1992.

92 Beastie Boys. "So What'cha Want." *Check Your Head*. Grand Royal/Capitol CDP 7 98938-2, album, 1992.

1993

94 Wu-Tang Clan. "C.R.E.A.M." *Enter the Wu-Tang Clan (36 Chambers)*. Loud Records/RCA 07863 66336-1, album, 1993.

95 Brandon Perkins. "Wu-Tang: Widdling Down Infinity." *URB* magazine (July/August 2007). Reprinted in *Best Music Writing 2008*, ed. Nelson George, Daphne Carr (Boston: Da Capo Press, 2008), 62–63.

98 The RZA and Chris Norris. *The Wu-Tang Manual* (New York: Riverhead Freestyle, 2005), 76.

98 "Ol' Dirty Bastard Gets Paid." MTV, originally aired March 30, 1995. Text quoted in Kathy Gilsinan, "Wu-Tang Forever: Ol' Dirty Bastard's Role in American Welfare Reform," with video post. *Atlantic*, November 13, 2014. http://www.theatlantic.com/politics/archive/2014/11/wu-tang-forever-ol-dirty-bastards-role-in-american-welfare-reform/382679.

98 "Ol' Dirty Bastard Gets Paid," MTV. Video posted in Gilsinan.

99 The Pharcyde. "Passin' Me By." *Bizarre Ride II the Pharcyde*. Delicious Vinyl 14221-1, album, 1992.

1994

100 The Notorious B.I.G. "Juicy." *Ready to Die*. Bad Boy Entertainment/Arista Records 78612-73000-2, album, 1994.

105 Bone Thugs-N-Harmony. "Thuggish Ruggish Bone." Ruthless Records 88561-5527-1, single, 1994.

1995

106 Tupac. "Dear Mama." *Me Against the World*. Interscope Records IND 92339, album, 1995.

107 *Juice*. Directed by Ernest R. Dickerson. Island World, 1992.

108 Billy Garland interview. "True Blood: Billy Garland, Tupac's Father, Speaks [Feature from the Sept. 2011 Issue]." *XXL*, September 10, 2012. http://www.xxlmag.com/news/2012/09/true-blood-billy-garland-tupacs-father-speaks-excerpt-from-the-sept-2011-issue.

108 Michael Eric Dyson. *Holler If You Hear Me: Searching for Tupac Shakur* (orig: 2001; New York: Basic Civitas Books, 2006), 41.

108 Tupac interview. Bill Bellamy. MTV, 1996. As uploaded on YouTube, "MTV Interview 1996: Tupac Shakur & Dr. Dre," April 30, 2012. https://www.youtube.com/watch?v=qmnZfBtf-G8.

110 *Tupac: Resurrection*. Directed by Lauren Lazin. Amiru Entertainment/MTV Films, 2003.

110 Mobb Deep. "Shook Ones Pt. II." *The Infamous*. Loud Records/RCA 07863 66480-1, album, 1995.

1996

112 Tupac, featuring Dr. Dre and Roger Troutman. "California Love." All Eyez on

Me. Death Row Records/Interscope 314-524 204-2 (524 205-2), album, 1996.

115 Tim Sanchez. "The Story of How Tupac Appeared on 'California Love.'" (Includes Chris Taylor interview.) *LA Weekly*, August 22, 2014. http://www.laweekly.com/music/ the-story-of-how-tupac-appeared-on -california-love-4996082.

115 "Music News: Suge Knight on the Origins of Tupac's 'California Love.'" BET.com, video, season 2014 (April 17, 2014). http://www.bet.com/video/musicnews/ 2014/suge-knight-on-the-origins-of-tupac-s -california-love.html.

116 Bone Thugs-N-Harmony. "Tha Cross-roads." Ruthless Records 663195 2, single, 1996.

1997

118 Puff Daddy, featuring Mase. "Can't Nobody Hold Me Down." Bad Boy Enter-tainment BBDP-9081, single, 1996.

123 Missy Elliott, featuring Timbaland. "The Rain (Supa Dupa Fly)." *Supa Dupa Fly*. East West Records 62062-1, album, 1997.

1998

124 DMX. "Ruff Ryders' Anthem." *It's Dark and Hell Is Hot*. Def Jam Recordings Def 224-1, album, 1998.

124 Ralph Basui Watkins. *Hip Hop Redemption: Finding God in the Rhythm and the Rhyme*, Engaging Culture series (Grand Rapids, MI: Baker Academic, 2011), 84.

126 DMX and Smokey D. Fontaine. *E.A.R.L.: The Autobiography of DMX* (2002; New York: HarperEntertainment, 2003), 56. Citations refer to the 2003 edition.

127 *Behind the Music: DMX*. (Includes Lyor Cohen interview.) VH-1. Originally aired June 7, 2010.

127 DMX interview on MTV Diary, 1999. Uploaded on YouTube, December 21, 2012. https://www.youtube.com/ watch?v=XyKXX8ptjTM.

127 *Behind the Music: DMX*. (Includes DMX interview.)

129 Juvenile. "Ha." Cash Money Records/Uni-versal Records U8P 1326, single, 1998.

1999

130 Eminem. "My Name Is." *The Slim Shady LP*. Aftermath Entertainment/Interscope Records D128121/INTD-90287, album, 1999.

131 Ice-T. *The Oprah Winfrey Show*, 1990.

133: *Real Stories: Eminem*. (Includes Carson Daly interview.) Channel 4 music documen-tary, series 3, episode 1. Hosted by Dave Berry. Originally aired in December 2011.

133 Bobbito Garcia. "Bobbito's Sound Check: Bobbito Garcia Plays the Tracks; Q-Tip

States the Facts." *Vibe 2*, no. 6 (August 1994), 122.

133 Labi Siffre. "I Got the (Blues)." Originally released 1975. Reissued on *Shaolin Soul, Episode 2*. Delabel/Hostile Records 7243 8488172 6, France, album, 2001.

134 JT Money. "Who Dat." Priority Records PVL 53472, single, 1999.

2000

136 Jay Z, featuring UGK. "Big Pimpin'." Roc-A-Fella Records DEFR 15069-1, single, 2000.

137 Jay Z. *Decoded* (2010; New York: Spiegel & Grau, 2011), 112, 113. Citations regard the 2011 edition.

137 Jay Z. *Decoded*, 113.

140 Roni Sarig. *Third Coast: OutKast, Timbal-and, & How Hip-Hop Became a Southern Thing*. (Includes Pimp C interview.) (Boston: Da Capo Press, 2007), 58.

140 Jake Rohn. "Bun B: Doing 'Big Pimpin'' Was the Best Decision We Ever Made." BET.com, October 1, 2014. http://www.bet .com/news/music/2014/10/01/bun-b-doing -big-pimpin-was-the-best-decision-we-ever -made.html.

140 Outkast. "So Fresh, So Clean." LaFace Records LFDP 4543, single, 2000.

2001

141 Jay Z. "Takeover." *The Blueprint*. Roc-A-Fella Records 314 586 396-2, album, 2001.

142 Nas. "Ether." *Stillmatic*. Columbia C2 85736, album, 2001.

145 Nas. "We Will Survive." *I Am . . .* Colum-bia C2 68773, album, 1999.

146 Memphis Bleek, featuring Jay Z. "My Mind Right (Remix)." *The Understanding*. Roc-A-Fella Records 314 542 587-2, album, 2000.

146 DJ Clue, featuring Nas. "Eye 4 an Eye (Freestyle)." Recorded 2000. Featured on *Best of Clue: The Freestyles Part Two*. BQE Recordings, digital album, 2009.

146 Nas. "Stillmatic (Freestyle)." No label (ZZ series) ZZ-031, single, 2001.

148 Jay Z, featuring Eminem. "Renegade." *The Blueprint*, 2001.

2002

150 The Clipse. "Grindin'." Arista 07822-15078-1, single, 2002.

151 *The Wire*, TV show. Created by David Simon. HBO, aired June 2, 2002–March 9, 2008.

151 Omar Little quote. "Lessons." *The Wire*, season 1, episode 8. Directed by Gloria Muzio. Teleplay by David Simon. HBO, originally aired July 28, 2002.

152 Stringer Bell quote. "Time After Time." *The Wire*, season 3, episode 1. Directed by

Ed Bianchi. Teleplay by David Simon. HBO, originally aired September 19, 2004.

152 Avon Barksdale quote. "Homecoming." *The Wire*, season 3, episode 6. Directed by Leslie Libman. Teleplay by Rafael Alvarez. HBO, originally aired October 31, 2004.

152 Cutty quote. "Hamsterdam." *The Wire*, season 3, episode 4. Directed by Ernest Dickerson. Teleplay by George Pelecanos. HBO, originally aired October 10, 2004.

155 Bubs quote. "Old Cases." *The Wire*, season 1, episode 4. Directed by Clement Virgo. Teleplay by David Simon. HBO, originally aired June 23, 2002.

155 Slim Charles quote. "Mission Accom-plished." *The Wire*, season 3, episode 12. Directed by Ernest Dickerson. Teleplay by David Simon. HBO, originally aired December 19, 2004.

155 Ta-Nehisi Coates. "Keepin' It Unreal: Sell-ing the Myth of Black Male Violence, Long Past Its Expiration Date." *Village Voice*, June 3, 2003. http://www.villagevoice .com/2003-06-03/news/keepin-it-unreal/3.

155 Missy Elliott. "Work It." Elektra 67340-0, single, 2002.

2003

156 50 Cent. "In Da Club." *Get Rich or Die Tryin'*. Shady Records 0694935442, album, 2003.

157 Toure. "Is This Rap's Logical Conclu-sion?" (Includes 50 Cent interview.) *The Guardian*, March 27, 2003. http://www .theguardian.com/music/2003/mar/28/ artsfeatures

157 Beth Altschull. "The Ludacris Life." (Includes Ludacris interview.) *GQ*, June 2006. http://www.gq.com/entertainment/ music/200604/ludacris-actor-rapper-al-bum-crash.

157 Oprah as interviewed by Ed Lover. *The Ed Lover Morning Show*. WWPR (Power 105), New York. November 4, 2008. (This interview has been removed from the radio station's website.)

159 Andrew Goldman. "Cent and Sensibility." (Includes 50 Cent interview.) *Elle*, Decem-ber 26, 2006. http://www.elle.com/culture/ celebrities/a9198/50-cent-interview.

160 Shaheem Reid. "50 Cent: Money to Burn." MTV.com, February 12, 2003. http://www .mtv.com/bands/123/50_Cent/news_ feature_021203.

161 Nas. "Made You Look" (Apache Remix). No Identity ID006, UK single, 2002.

2004

162 Mike Jones, featuring Slim Thug and Paul Wall. "Still Tippin'." Asylum PR 301620, single, 2004.

166 Jesse Serwer. "DJ Screw: From Cough Syrup to Full-Blown Fever." (Includes Drake email interview.) *The Guardian*, November 11, 2010. http://www.theguardian.com/music/2010/nov/11/dj-screw-drake-fever-ray.

166 Crime Mob, featuring Lil Scrappy. "Knuck if You Buck." Warner Bros. Records 0-42736, single, 2004.

2005

168 Kanye West, featuring Jamie Foxx. "Gold Digger." Roc-A-Fella Records B0005118-11, single, 2005.

169 Rob Tannenbaum. "*Playboy* Interview: Kanye West." *Playboy* (March 2006), 49.

172 Young Jeezy, featuring Jay Z. "Go Crazy." Def Jam Recordings B0005456-11, single, 2005.

2006

174 Rick Ross. "Hustlin'." Def Jam Recordings B0006463-11, single, 2006.

177 "Screw Rick Ross: Despite Denials, Records Show Rap Star Worked as Corrections Officer." *Smoking Gun*, July 21, 2008. http://www.thesmokinggun.com/documents/crime/screw-rick-ross.

179 T.I. "What You Know." Grand Hustle/Atlantic Records 0-94251, single, 2006.

179 Rich Boy, featuring Polow Da Don. "Throw Some D's." *Rich Boy*. Zone 4/Interscope Records B0008556-01, album, 2007.

2007

180 UGK, featuring Outkast. "Int'l Players Anthem (I Choose You)." Jive 88697-11063-1, single, 2007.

181 Tom Hardy as Bane. *The Dark Knight Rises*. Directed by Christopher Nolan. Legendary Pictures/DC Entertainment, 2012.

185 Kanye West, featuring T-Pain. "Good Life." *Graduation*. Roc-A-Fella Records B0009541-02, album, 2007.

2008

186 Lil Wayne. "A Milli." *Tha Carter III*. Cash Money Records B0011033-02, album, 2008.

190 Jay Z and T.I., featuring Lil Wayne and Kanye West. "Swagga Like Us." Roc-A-Fella Records B0012284-11, single, 2008.

2009

192 Drake. "Best I Ever Had." Cash Money Records DBESTCDP1, single, 2009.

195 Jon Caramanica. "A Sensitive Rap Star Toughens Up." *New York Times*, September 18, 2013. http://www.nytimes.com/2013/09/22/arts/music/drake-finds-his-tougher-side-on-nothing-was-the-same.html.

195 Marlow Stern. "Drake on 'Take Care,'

Rihanna, Chris Brown 'Fight,' Acting, and More." *Daily Beast*, November 15, 2011. http://www.thedailybeast.com/articles/2011/11/15/drake-on-take-care-rihanna-chris-brown-fight-acting-and-more.html.

196 Gucci Mane. "Lemonade." *The State vs. Radric Davis*. Warner Bros. Records 520540-2, album, 2009.

2010

198 Kanye West, featuring Rick Ross, Jay Z, Bon Iver, and Nicki Minaj. "Monster." *My Beautiful Dark Twisted Fantasy*. Roc-A-Fella Records B0014695-02, album, 2010.

199 Nicki Minaj. "Yeah Yeah Yeah" freestyle. *The Come Up: Spittin' TOUGH*. DVD. Uploaded on YouTube, February 20, 2012. https://www.youtube.com/watch?v=7pRDoaeow7Y.

202 Lauren Nostro et al. "The 25 Best Rap Verses of the Last 5 Years." *Complex*, May 29, 2013. http://www.complex.com/music/2013/05/best-rap-verses-of-the-last-5-years.

202 Brent Staples. "Nicki Minaj Crashes Hip-Hop's Boys' Club." *New York Times* Sunday Review, July 7, 2012. http://www.nytimes.com/2012/07/08/opinion/sunday/nicki-minaj-crashes-hip-hops-boys-club.html.

202 Tom Breihan. "Monster" review. *Pitchfork*, "Best New Track," September 7, 2010. http://pitchfork.com/reviews/tracks/11970-monster-ft-justin-vernon-rick-ross-jay-z-and-nicki-minaj.

202 Waka Flocka Flame. "Hard in Da Paint." *Flockaveli*. 1017 Brick Squad Records 523481-2, album, 2010.

2011

204 Jay Z and Kanye West. "Niggas in Paris." *Watch the Throne*. Roc-A-Fella Records B0015958-02, album, 2011.

207 Alex Pappademas. "King: Jay-Z." *GQ* Men of the Year 2011. Accessed April 29, 2015. http://www.gq.com/moty/2011/jay-z-gq-men-of-the-year-issue?currentPage=2.

208 David Samuels. "What Obama Can Learn from Jay-Z." *Atlantic*, November 7, 2012. http://www.theatlantic.com/entertainment/archive/2012/11/what-obama-can-learn-from-jay-z/264933.

208 Melissa S. Kearney and Benjamin H. Harris. "Ten Economic Facts About Crime and Incarceration in the United States." Brookings Institute, The Hamilton Project, chapter 2, fact 7/figure 7, May 1, 2014. http://www.brookings.edu/research/reports/2014/05/10-crime-facts.

208 Rahim Kanani. "An English Class Devoted to Jay-Z and Kanye West at the University of Missouri." (Includes Andrew Hoberek

interview.) Forbes.com, February 10, 2014. http://www.forbes.com/sites/rahim-kanani/2014/02/10/an-english-class-devoted-to-jay-z-and-kanye-west-at-the-university-of-missouri.

208 W. E. B. Du Bois. *The Souls of Black Folk* (Chicago: A. C. McClurg and Co., 1903; Mineola, NY: Dover, 1994), 2. Citation refers to the Dover edition.

209 Jay Z and Kanye West. "Otis." *Watch the Throne*, 2011.

2012

210 Macklemore and Ryan Lewis. "Same Love." *The Heist*. Macklemore & Ryan Lewis LLC (self-released album), 2012.

213 R. J. Snell. "How Songs Like Macklemore's 'Same Love' Change the Marriage Debate." FirstThings.com, June 25, 2013. http://www.firstthings.com/web-exclusives/2013/06/how-songs-like-macklemores-ldquosame-loverdquo-change-the-marriage-debate.

214 "Macklemore Joins the Great Race Debate on *Ebro in the Morning*." Hot97.com video, December 29, 2014. http://www.hot97.com/news/new-hot97/macklemore-joins-great-race-debate-ebro-morning-video.

214 Juicy J, featuring Lil Wayne and 2 Chainz. "Bandz a Make Her Dance." Columbia, digital single, 2012.

2013

216 Big Sean, featuring Kendrick Lamar and Jay Electronica. "Control." Self-released digital single, 2013.

219 "Rapper of the Year: Freestyling with Kendrick Lamar." 2013 *GQ* Men of the Year photo shoot. *GQ* video, November 12, 2013. http://video.gq.com/watch/gq-rapper-of-the-year-freestyling-with-kendrick-lamar.

220 Kanye West. "New Slaves." *Yeezus*. Def Jam Recordings B0018653-02, album, 2013.

2014

222 Rich Gang, featuring Young Thug and Rich Homie Quan. "Lifestyle." Cash Money Records, digital single, 2014.

227 Run the Jewels, featuring Boots. "Early." *Run the Jewels 2*. Mass Appeal MSAP0005, album, 2014.

227 Michelle Alexander. *The New Jim Crow: Mass Incarceration in the Age of Colorblindness* (New York: The New Press, 2010).

Index

Editor: Samantha Weiner
Designer: Sebit Min
Production Manager: Kathleen Gaffney

Library of Congress Control Number: 2014959337

ISBN: 978-1-4197-1818-2

Printed and bound in the United States
10 9

Abrams Image books are available at special discounts when
purchased in quantity for premiums and promotions as well
as fundraising or educational use. Special editions can also
be created to specification. For details, contact specialsales@
abramsbooks.com or the address below.

ABRAMS The Art of Books
115 West 18th Street, New York, NY 10011
abramsbooks.com